Seeds of Mobilization

EMERGING DEMOCRACIES

Series Editor
Dan Slater is James Orin Murfin Professor of Political Science
and Director, Center for Emerging Democracies
University of Michigan

---

*Struggles for Political Change in the Arab World: Regimes, Oppositions,
and External Actors after the Spring*
Lisa Blaydes, Amr Hamzawy, and Hesham Sallam, Editors

Seeds of Mobilization: The Authoritarian Roots of South Korea's Democracy
Joan E. Cho

None of the Above: Protest Voting in Latin American Democracies
Mollie J. Cohen

The Development of Political Institutions: Power, Legitimacy, Democracy
Federico Ferrara

Lobbying the Autocrat: The Dynamics of Policy Advocacy in Nondemocracies
Max Grömping and Jessica C. Teets, Editors

Ghosts in the Neighborhood: Why Japan Is Haunted by Its Past and Germany Is Not
Walter F. Hatch

*The Dictator's Dilemma at the Ballot Box: Electoral Manipulation,
Economic Maneuvering, and Political Order in Autocracies*
Masaaki Higashijima

*State Institutions, Civic Associations, and Identity Demands:
Regional Movements in Greater Southeast Asia*
Amy H. Liu and Joel Sawat Selway, Editors

Opposing Power: Building Opposition Alliances in Electoral Autocracies
Elvin Ong

*Aid Imperium: United States Foreign Policy and Human Rights in Post–Cold War
Southeast Asia*
Salvador Santino F. Regilme Jr

SEEDS OF MOBILIZATION

The Authoritarian Roots of South Korea's Democracy

Joan E. Cho

University of Michigan Press
Ann Arbor

Copyright © 2024 by Joan E. Cho
Some rights reserved

This work is licensed under a Creative Commons Attribution-NonCommercial 4.0 International License. *Note to users:* A Creative Commons license is only valid when it is applied by the person or entity that holds rights to the licensed work. Works may contain components (e.g., photographs, illustrations, or quotations) to which the rightsholder in the work cannot apply the license. It is ultimately your responsibility to independently evaluate the copyright status of any work or component part of a work you use, in light of your intended use. To view a copy of this license, visit http://creativecommons.org/licenses/by-nc/4.0/

For questions or permissions, please contact um.press.perms@umich.edu

Published in the United States of America by the
University of Michigan Press
Printed and bound by CPI Group (UK) Ltd, Croydon, CR0 4YY

First published February 2024

A CIP catalog record for this book is available from the British Library.

Library of Congress Cataloging-in-Publication Data

Names: Cho, Joan E., author. | Michigan Publishing (University of Michigan), publisher.
Title: Seeds of mobilization : the authoritarian roots of South Korea's democracy / Joan E. Cho.
Other titles: Authoritarian roots of South Korea's democracy | Weiser Center for Emerging Democracies series.
Description: Ann Arbor, Michigan : University of Michigan Press, 2024. | Series: Weiser center for emerging democracies | Includes bibliographical references and index.
Identifiers: LCCN 2023033219 (print) | LCCN 2023033220 (ebook) | ISBN 9780472076604 (hardcover) | ISBN 9780472056606 (paperback) | ISBN 9780472904037 (ebook other)
Subjects: LCSH: Democracy—Korea (South) | Authoritarianism—Korea (South) | Korea (South)—Politics and government—1960–1988. | Korea (South)—Politics and government—1988–2002. | Korea (South)—Politics and government—2002–
Classification: LCC DS922.35 .C47143 2024 (print) | LCC DS922.35 (ebook) | DDC 320.53095195—dc23/eng/20230826
LC record available at https://lccn.loc.gov/2023033219
LC ebook record available at https://lccn.loc.gov/2023033220

DOI: https://doi.org/10.3998/mpub.12738649

The University of Michigan Press's open access publishing program is made possible thanks to additional funding from the University of Michigan Office of the Provost and the generous support of contributing libraries.

Cover illustration by John Cho.

To my family

Contents

List of Figures	ix
List of Tables	xi
Abbreviations	xiii
A Note on Romanization	xv
Acknowledgments	xvii

ONE Introduction: Reexamining South Korea's Democratization — 1

TWO Industrialization as a (De)stabilizing Force — 26

THREE Manufacturing Protests: Ecology of Industrial Complexes
and the Labor Movement — 55

FOUR Learning to Dissent: Education and Authoritarian Resilience — 89

FIVE From College Campuses to Ballot Boxes:
Mobilizing for Democratic Reforms — 120

SIX Beyond the Democratic Transition: Democratization and
Generational Divides — 146

SEVEN Conclusion: Development, Democracy,
and Authoritarian Legacy — 175

viii   *Contents*

Appendix: Datasets and Data Sources   191

Notes   197

Bibliography   215

Index   241

Digital materials related to this title can be found on
the Fulcrum platform via the following citable URL:
https://doi.org/10.3998/mpub.12738649

Figures

1.1	Development vs. Democracy in South Korea, 1955–2010	5
1.2	Graphical Representation of the Relationship between Modernization and Authoritarian Resilience: Classical Modernization Theory vs. My Argument	9
1.3	Graphical Representation of the Relationship between Modernization and Authoritarian Resilience: Scope Conditions	21
2.1	Number of Labor Disputes and Labor Unions, 1963–91	42
2.2	Number of Labor Protests during the 1987 Great Workers' Struggle and the Location of Industrial Complexes	44
2.3	Average Controlled Direct Effect of Industrial Complexes as a Function of the Fixed Level of Manufacturing Firms	49
2.4	Coefficients on Presence of IC Compared	52
2.5	Concentration of Workers, 1966–85	53
3.1	Beehive Houses in Karibong-dong in Kuro District, Seoul	63
3.2	Floor Plan of the Ground Floor of a Beehive House in Karibong-dong	64
3.3	Diffusion of Protests during the Great Workers' Struggle: The Number of New Protests in Pusan and Kyŏngnam vs. the Rest of South Korea	76
3.4	Layout of the Kuro Industrial Complex	80
3.5	Sit-in Strike Organized by Daewoo Apparel Workers on June 24, 1985	81
4.1	Number of Schools and Levels of Student Enrollment by School Type, 1962–87	98

x   *Figures*

4.2 Organizational Chart of the National Federation of Student
     Associations   112
4.3 Number of Student Protests in Seoul vs. Outside of Seoul,
     1980–87   114
4.4 Number of Colleges/Universities and Students in Seoul vs.
     Non-Seoul Areas, 1970–87   116
5.1 Protest Sites during the 1987 June Democratic Uprising
     and the NKDP Vote Share in 1985   134
5.2 Number of Mass Events during the 1987 June
     Democratic Uprising   138
5.3 The Relationship between NKDP Vote Share and
     Protest Intensity at Different Levels of Proportion of College
     Students, with 95% Confidence Intervals   140
6.1 Voter Participation. Baseline: 386 Generation   159
6.2 Political Ideology. Baseline: 386 Generation   160
6.3 Voter Turnout by Generation Group, 2003–12   161
6.4 Political Ideology by Generation Group, 2003–12   162
6.5 Attitude toward North Korea. Baseline: 386 Generation   163
6.6 Attitude toward North Korea by Generation Group, 2003–12   164
6.7 Attitude toward the U.S. by Generation Group, 2003–12   165
6.8 Preference for Economic Development vs. Democracy
     by Political Generation, 2003–2015   171
7.1 Development vs. Democracy in Taiwan, 1955–2010   179

Tables

2.1	Number and Size of Industrial Complexes by Administrative Region, 1963–1987	33
2.2	The Great Workers' Struggle Protests and Electoral Support for the Opposition Candidates in the 1987 Presidential Election	45
2.3	Summary Statistics	46
2.4	Effects of Industrial Complexes	48
2.5	Additional Effects from the Variation in the Duration of Industrial Complexes	50
3.1	Size and Number of Firms and Employees of Industrial Complexes	59
4.1	Educational Development and Economic Development in South Korea	93
4.2	Location of Joint On-Campus Protests in the 1980s	115
5.1	Number of Districts and Events (per 100,000 People) for Each Province during the 1987 June Democratic Uprising	135
5.2	1985 NKDP Vote Share and Combined Vote Shares of the Opposition Candidates in the 1987 Presidential Election	135
5.3	Predictors of Protest Intensity during the 1987 June Democratic Uprising	138
6.1	South Korea's Political Generations	149
6.2	Attitudes toward the United States, Japan, North Korea, China, and Russia by Generation Group	163
6.3	Odds Ratios for Logistic Regression Analysis of the Generational Differences in Civic Engagement in 2004 and 2009	167

Abbreviations

ACDE	average controlled direct effect
ATE	average treatment effect
DJP	Democratic Justice Party
ED	Emergency Decree
FKTU	Federation of Korean Trade Unions
FYED	five-year economic development
GWS	Great Workers' Struggle
GQP	Graduation Quota Program
HCI	heavy and chemical industry
HHI	Herfindahl-Hirschman Index
IC	industrial complex
IMF	International Monetary Fund
IRR	incidence rate ratio
ISI	import-substitution industrialization
JOC	Young Catholic Workers (Jeunesse Ouvrière Chrétienne)
KDF	Korea Democracy Foundation
KGSS	Korean General Social Survey
KIC	Kuro Industrial Complex
KMT	Nationalist Party (Kuomintang; in Taiwan)
NFSA	National Federation of Student Associations
NKDP	New Korea Democratic Party
NMHDC	National Movement Headquarters for Democratic Constitution

xiv *Abbreviations*

PMCDR People's Movement Coalition for Democracy and
Reunification
SNU Seoul National University
UIM Urban Industrial Mission
YCDM Youth Coalition for Democracy Movement

A Note on Romanization

Korean names and words were Romanized using the McCune-Reischauer system. Following the Korean convention, surnames precede given names (e.g., Yi Ch'ŏl). Exceptions were made for authors who have published in English, and for names, places, and organizations with standard or official English spellings that are more widely known and accepted (e.g., Syngman Rhee, Park Chung Hee, Sim Sang-jung, Seoul, and Kyungpook National University). Names of institutions, organizations, and laws and regulations are translated into English. The fully translated names are used in their first appearance in the text, followed by their abbreviations. Abbreviations are used thereafter.

Acknowledgments

I have come full circle by authoring this book on South Korean politics. It is still difficult to articulate why this was the case, but I initially wanted to study something other than Korean politics. Perhaps my paternal grandfather's personal connection to Kim Dae Jung, my maternal grandfather's service and death as a policeman during Park Chung Hee's time, my father's involvement in Heungsadan (Young Korean Academy) and the Korean student movement, and my mother's witnessing of the 1980 Kwangju Massacre were all too personal to me.

As an undergraduate student at the University of Rochester, I wrote my senior honors thesis on globalization and support for radical right parties in Western Europe. (My thanks to Richard Niemi for being the first to encourage me to pursue a doctorate degree in political science, Bonnie Meguid for her mentorship as my undergraduate and thesis advisor, and Mark Kayser and Bingham Powell for their teaching and advice.) But, as a graduate student, the more I tried to avoid studying Korea, the more I struggled to commit to a dissertation topic that genuinely excited me.

It was my advisors at Harvard—Daniel Ziblatt and Steve Levitsky—who told me that I light up when I talk about Korean politics and suggested that I consider writing my dissertation on Korea. Daniel's historical and subnational approaches to analyzing state-building and democratization in Europe inspired me to study South Korea's democratization historically in a data-intensive fashion. Steve's research on competitive authoritarianism helped me better understand the changes in the nature of authoritarian rule in South Korea. They both exemplified what it entails to be a comparativist by challenging me to develop generalizable theories and to situate Korea in a broader theoretical framework. This book, I hope, showcases their imprints on how I study Korea as a comparativist.

Paul Chang joined the Sociology Department during my dissertation writing stage and reassured my pivot toward Korean political studies. Growing up, I never received a formal education on Korea's *modern* history. (Even the formal education I received in Korea was limited to the history of premodern Korea.) Paul provided the guidance I needed to ensure I "did justice" to Korea's political history. He introduced me to the Korean studies network and helped me to grow as a scholar of political science *and* Korean studies. His first book on South Korea's democracy movement in the 1970s served as a model for this book.

At Harvard, I was also very fortunate to be surrounded by many other faculty members, graduate students, and visiting scholars who provided me with insightful conversations and feedback on various aspects of my earlier research and writings that served as the backbone of this book. Cosette Creamer and Mai Hassan provided helpful comments and suggestions on numerous versions of this project. Matthew Blackwell, Patrick Lam, and Anton Strezhnev taught and helped me with the statistical components of my research. I also benefitted from the advice and feedback I received from Aditya Dasgupta, Amy Catalinac, Emily Clough, Iza Ding, Carter Eckert, Grzegorz Ekiert, Sheena Greitens, Peter Hall, Kyle Jaros, Iain Johnston, Jeehye Kim, Pattie Kim, Daniel Koss, Noah Nathan, Ruxandra Paul, Elizabeth Perry, Molly Roberts, Sparsha Saha, B. K. Song, Arthur Spirling, Kris-Stella Trump, and Hye Young You.

Field research and data collection were made possible thanks to generous funding and institutional support from the Harvard University Asia Center, the Asiatic Research Institute of Korea University, and the Taiwan Foundation for Democracy. My research and writing were also supported by the Laboratory Program for Korean Studies of the Ministry of Education of the Republic of Korea and the Korean Studies Promotion Service at the Academy of Korean Studies (AKS-2021-LAB-223002). I thank Park Munjin and Lee Horyong at the Korea Democracy Foundation and Mikyung Kang at the Harvard-Yenching Library for their assistance in locating and accessing archival materials and primary sources. For advice on field research, suggestions on source materials, and feedback on the project, I thank JungGie Choi, Rick Chu, Ming-sho Ho, Michael Hsaio, Chang-ling Huang, Jai Kwan Jung, Byung-Kook Kim, Sunhyuk Kim, Nae-Young Lee, Michael Lin, Bo Tedards, Hung-mao Tien, Hans Hanpu Tung, Chin-en Wu, and Erick Yu.

Acknowledgments xix

I came to Wesleyan University as an assistant professor after completing my PhD degree, and it was at Wesleyan that I made significant progress on this book. I am fortunate to work in an interdisciplinary environment with extremely supportive colleagues and bright students who help me to study and teach East Asian politics from different angles. Mary Alice Haddad, in particular, has been an incredible mentor and inspiring colleague in all aspects. I can only express my gratitude by paying it forward by becoming a colleague like her to others. I thank Steve Angle, Hyejoo Back, Lisa Dombrowski, Erika Fowler, and Bill Johnston for their advice and encouragement. I also thank Scott Aalgaard, Yu-ting Huang, Naho Maruta, Ying Jia Tan, and Takeshi Watanabe for their comradeship and for giving me a sense of belonging at the College of East Asian Studies. I am grateful to my undergraduate research assistants—Gloria Kang, Chaiyeon Lee, and Rosanne Ng—for their excellent work in helping me collect and analyze data for chapters 4 and 6. I also thank Fiona Chu (for her help in accessing books from the National Assembly Library of Korea) and the students who took my Social and Political Changes in Korea, Korean Politics Through Film, Democracy and Social Movements in East Asia, and Challenges to Democracy in East Asia courses for helping me better articulate my knowledge of the politics of Korea and East Asia. (Some of my lecture notes have been incorporated into this book.)

A book manuscript workshop held virtually in the spring of 2021 gave me the confidence to complete this book and helped me to find my voice in explaining South Korea's democratization. I am very grateful to Celeste Arrington, Mary Alice Haddad, Stephan Haggard, Elizabeth Perry, and Emy Matesan for their careful reading of the manuscript in its entirety and for their insightful feedback to help me make significant improvements to it. I also thank Masami Imai, Yu-ting Huang, Peter Rutland, and Ying Jia Tan for their participation and helpful conversations that preceded or followed the workshop. This book also benefitted from feedback from scholars at the George Washington University (GW Institute for Korean Studies), Harvard Kennedy School (Ash Center for Democratic Governance and Innovation), Harvard University (Politics and History Annual Workshop), Johns Hopkins University Paul H. Nitze School of Advanced International Studies (APSA-USKI Graduate Publication Seminar), Seoul National University (SNU-Harvard-UCLA Graduate Student Workshop), Taiwan Foundation for Democracy, University of British Columbia (Centre for Korean Research), University of Michigan (Nam Center for Korean Studies and Weiser Center for Emerging Democracies), Wesleyan University (Division II Faculty Lun-

xx   *Acknowledgments*

cheon), and Yale University (Council on East Asian Studies and Autocracy and Asia Workshop).

I also want to acknowledge the wider academic community that I have been able to be a part of and the ways in which colleagues outside of my institutional gates have also impacted me in researching and writing this book. My sincere thanks to Victor Cha and David Kang for their valuable career advice and for connecting me to a strong network of Korea specialists, including the U.S.-Korea NextGen Scholars network. I thank Erin Chung, Ji Yeon (Jean) Hong, Jae Yeon Kim, Yoonkyung Lee, Hyung Gu Lynn, Dan Slater, and Andrew Yeo for their insightful feedback at various stages of the writing process. I am especially grateful to Hyung Gu for his careful reading of the manuscript and the detailed comments and suggestions he provided. I thank Janum Sethi and Kyra Hunting for their accountability and support during the writing process. I also thank Todd Henry, Aram Hur (my "Korean academic sister"), Dan Mattingly, and Elvin Ong for their advice and encouragement in navigating the book publishing process. And special thanks to Lauren Rubenzahl, who helped me express my ideas clearly as a writer.

At the University of Michigan Press, I thank Elizabeth Demers, Haley Winkle, and Kevin Rennells for their guidance and help throughout the review and production process. I am incredibly grateful to Dan Slater, who has been generous in sharing his time and knowledge with me since my graduate school days and for shepherding this book at the University of Michigan Press for the Weiser Center for Emerging Democracies Series. I also thank Christopher Dreyer for the helpful conversations we had since the Nam Center's International Conference of NextGen Korean Studies Conference. And, finally, I thank the anonymous reviewers for their careful reading of the manuscript and their insightful comments and suggestions that allowed me to improve the initial manuscript in significant ways.

Last but not least, I am truly blessed to be born into a loving family, to be able to marry into another one, and to form one of my own. I would not be where I am now if it weren't for my parents—Hee Sang Cho and Kwang Ja Park—and the tremendous sacrifices they made to give me better opportunities to dream bigger. My parents-in-law—Un Jung Kang and Young Hae Kang—have been nothing but supportive and understanding. I am grateful to my brother John for the cheerfulness I needed during my graduate studies and for sharing his talent by making an amazing illustration for my book cover. I also thank Minjy and Vince for their support and encouragement. My children—Erin Surim and Noah Sejun—have brought me so much joy, and their existence in this world constantly helps me to keep my priorities straight. Finally, I would not have been able to turn my dissertation into this book if it were not for my husband, Michael Kang. He has emulated Christ's love in our marriage, and I am indebted to his patience, unconditional love, and unwavering support. Because of all these people I acknowledge, I count myself beyond blessed. I hope the insights generated from this book and what I have learned from writing this book will allow me to give back to my personal and academic communities.

ONE

Introduction

Reexamining South Korea's Democratization

On June 10, 1987, after almost three decades of repressive authoritarian rule, protestors poured into the streets of cities all over South Korea, shouting "Abolish the evil Constitution!" and "Down with dictatorship!" In addition to widespread street rallies held by student protestors and opposition politicians in Seoul, the capital city and often the center of such protests, mass demonstrations were held in cities such as Taejŏn, Pup'yŏng, Sŏngnam, and Kunsan, where such events had not been observed before. Altogether, approximately 240,000 people from 22 cities participated in mass demonstrations against the dictatorship on that day, thus marking the beginning of the "June Democratic Uprising."

Demonstrations continued to grow with each passing day: on June 15, students held them at 59 universities; on June 16, at 65 universities; and on June 17, at 70 universities. On June 18, approximately 1.5 million people in 16 cities, including Seoul, Pusan, Mokp'o, Sunch'ŏn, Chŏnju, Wŏnju, and Ch'unch'ŏn, participated in mass rallies to ban tear gas, which the police had been using to suppress the protests. On June 26, the "Great Peaceful March of the People for the Achievement of a Democratic Constitution" was held in 33 cities, and approximately 1.8 million people across the country agitated for "Direct election of the president!" Finally, on June 29, 1987, after almost three weeks of sustained mass protest, the ruling party announced the "June 29 Declaration." This eight-point democratization package included a promise to hold direct presidential elections and brought a dramatic end to the authoritarian era.

The nationwide protests throughout that month revealed not only South Koreans' widespread discontent but also their latent capacity to mobilize. For most of the preceding three decades, the authoritarian regimes had proven to be resilient—they had used coercion to quell dissent and successfully claimed political legitimacy based on the extraordinary economic development they achieved. The first military dictator, Park Chung Hee, had been credited with lifting the country out of poverty and bringing about economic growth so dramatic that it is known as the "Miracle on the Han River." His strong economic record, along with his use of repressive measures, had allowed him not only to maintain his grip on power but also to extend his rule by amending the constitution in 1967 and installing a new Yusin (revitalization) constitution in 1972, which transformed his presidency into a legal dictatorship. The second dictator, Chun Doo Hwan, had managed to get away with a bloody massacre in 1980, deliver economic growth amid the second global oil crisis, and successfully consolidate his new, coup-born regime. Although antiauthoritarian struggles by dissident intellectuals, religious leaders, students, and laborers had existed throughout the authoritarian period, none had ever reached the scale of the June 1987 protests or included so many ordinary citizens, including white-collar workers. Given the seeming durability and invincibility of those regimes, what could explain the explosion of antigovernment sentiment and, ultimately, the end of authoritarian rule?

This book answers that question by examining the long-term trajectory of South Korea's democratic transition and the contentious politics surrounding the process. It shows that although economic growth initially increased popular support for and thereby stabilized the authoritarian regimes, the autocrats' industrial and educational policies also contributed to the organization of social forces—and those forces facilitated the nationwide pro-democracy protests that ultimately brought about the democratic transition. Despite claims made in the existing literature, the country's democratization was not solely "from below" (i.e., through popular pressure, such as that generated by various social movements) or solely "from above" (i.e., due to policy changes coming from the incumbent elites)—rather, it resulted from a combination of the two. And, for this reason, this book argues that authoritarian development *itself* was a hidden root cause of democratic development in South Korea.

Introduction   3

What We Know—and Do Not Know—
about South Korea's Democratization

South Korea: A Model Case of Modernization Theory?

Political scientists have long sought to explain why and how countries become democracies, and they have identified several key determinants of such transitions: economic development (e.g., Lipset 1959) and income inequality (e.g., Boix 2003; Acemoglu and Robinson 2006), culture (e.g., Almond and Verba 1963; Inglehart and Welzel 2005) and cultural heritage (Bernhard, Reenock, and Nordstrom 2004), institutional (state) capacity (Fukuyama 2014; Huntington 1968), social capital and civil society (e.g., Putnam 1994), natural resources (e.g., Dunning 2008; Ross 2012), waves of democracy (Huntington 1991), and linkages with Western democracies (Levitsky and Way 2005). Of these determinants, the first—economic development—has received the greatest share of attention. As Seymour Martin Lipset puts it, "All the various aspects of economic development—industrialization, urbanization, wealth and education—are so closely inter-related as to form one major factor which has the political correlate of democracy" (Lipset 1963, 41). This conception is reflected in Lipset's modernization theory, which asserts that the more economically developed a nation is, the greater the chance that it will develop into a democracy (Lipset 1959). Indeed, as the theory predicts, many large-n studies in comparative politics have identified a positive relationship between per capita income (a commonly used measure of a population's standard of living and quality of life) and levels of democracy (e.g., Barro 1990; Boix and Stokes 2003; Bollen 1979; Burkhart and Lewis-Beck 1994; Epstein et al. 2006; Jackman 1973; Londregan and Poole 1990).[1]

South Korea (hereafter Korea) is one of the countries that conforms to this correlation between income and democracy. Known as one of the "East Asian Tigers" (i.e., newly industrializing countries in East Asia that achieved economic growth and industrialization between the 1960s and the 1980s), Korea is regarded as one of the most successful cases of "third wave democratization" (Huntington 1991) in the late twentieth century. It is one of the "dream cases of a modernization theorist" because it "developed under a dictatorship, became wealthy, and threw dictatorship off" (Przeworski and Limongi 1997, 162). Indeed, a vast literature on Korea's economic development and political development depicts a relatively smooth and peaceful capitalist transition toward modernity that brought about the expansion of the middle class and civil society—and, eventually, democracy.

What has happened there since democratization seems to support this label, too. First, Korea has continued to thrive economically since becoming a democracy; despite the effects of the 1997–98 Asian Financial Crisis, the country made a quick recovery and grew to be the tenth largest economy in the world. Additionally, although some scholars have argued that it is showing signs of democratic decline (e.g., J.-J. Choi 2012; Haggard and You 2015; W. Kang and Kang 2014; G.-W. Shin 2020), Korea passed Samuel Huntington's (1991) "two turnover test" when the 2007 presidential election marked the second peaceful transfer of power to the former opposition in the country's electoral history.[2] Most recently, the 2016–17 "Candlelight Revolution" led to the impeachment of President Park Geun-hye, who was found to be corrupt, unjust, and undemocratic. The international community praised this movement for showing the world "how democracy is done" (e.g., Caryl 2017; Tharoor 2017).

Despite the ways in which Korea seems to be a perfect case of modernization theory, however, the empirical facts deviate from the standard, broad-strokes narrative of Korea's economic and political development, revealing instead a country on a bumpier path to democracy. The First Republic, led by Syngman Rhee at the establishment of the Republic of Korea in 1948, became increasingly authoritarian and was overturned by the April Revolution in 1960. A parliamentary regime emerged but ended abruptly on May 16, 1960, when General Park Chung Hee carried out a military coup. Under Park's military dictatorship (1961–79) and then Chun Doo Hwan's (1980–88), the political system did not (as predicted by modernization theory) become increasingly democratic as the national economy grew—it instead became increasingly authoritarian. Party–based politics and representative government were restored in 1963, but in 1972 Park drastically increased executive power and effectively converted his own presidency into a legal dictatorship (H. B. Im 2011). In 1980, the incumbent regime was replaced by Chun's autocratic rule, which maintained and even increased the prior regime's level of repression (Hellmann 2018, 74). Figure 1.1, which graphs these joint dynamics of democracy and development over time, makes clear that Korea's transition dynamics are not as smooth and linear as they are commonly understood to be. Indeed, Goldstone and Kocornik-Mina (2013) show that such trajectories are often highly nonlinear and exhibit extreme irregularity: many countries "bounce" or "cycle" between dictatorship and democracy without achieving sustained economic growth. Additionally, the growth of the middle class—which has been proposed as a causal mechanism linking the two variables—does not adequately explain its successful transition from a poor authoritarian country to a wealthy democratic country.[3]

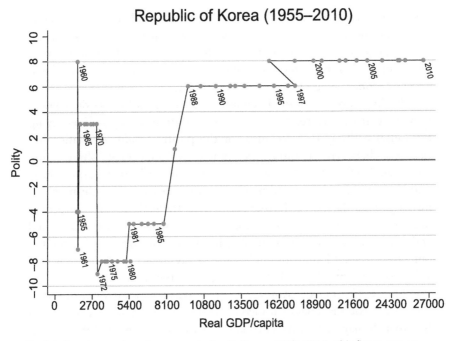

Fig 1.1. Development vs. democracy in South Korea, 1955–2010. This figure comes from Goldstone and Kocronik-Mina (2013). The horizontal axis measures real GDP per capita using the Laspeyres Purchasing Power Parity measure from the Penn World Tables 6.1 (Heston, Summers, and Aten 2002). The vertical axis measures levels of democracy using the 21-point Polity IV scale (Marshall, Jaggers, and Gurr 2003).

To better assess and understand the relationship between economic development and democracy, some recent studies in comparative democratization also seem to favor a more refined version of modernization theory. This "conditional version" of modernization theory suggests that (1) the "causal effects" of economic development emerge in the medium or long term (i.e., about 10 or more years) (Treisman 2020b; Boix 2018) and (2) economic development creates the contextual conditions under which other triggering factors—such as economic crisis (Kennedy 2010), elections (Knutsen et al. 2019), institutional weakness (M. Miller 2012), and leader turnover (Treisman 2015)—exert effect. Additionally, research shows that the income–democracy link depends on the choice of democracy measure (i.e., the aspects of democracy under examination), the time period in question, and control variables included in large-n analyses (Knutsen et al. 2019; Rød, Knutsen, and Hegre 2020). Thus, by examining when and how the positive relationship holds (and does not hold), these newer studies confirm the need to further enhance and engage with modernization theory. And given that cross-national large-n studies are sensitive to model specifications and data coding, single-country research may be useful in identifying the causal mechanisms that drive the conditional effect of economic development on democracy.

This book provides a single-country case study on Korea's democratic transition. It uses Korea to clarify modernization theory by identifying the causal pathway that accounts for the positive *nonlinear* relationship that exists between economic development and democracy. John Gerring (2007, 241) refers to such a case as a "pathway case"—that is, one whose purpose is to elucidate causal mechanisms rather than to confirm or dismiss a general theory. He further states that "the pathway case exists only in circumstances in which cross-case covariational patterns are well studied and in which the mechanism linking [the explanatory variable] X_1 and [the outcome variable] Y remains dim" (239); he says that a viable pathway case will be one in which "the addition of X_1 pushes the case toward the regression line" (243). Thus, if Korea is to be used as a pathway case, the addition of the country's national income should push it toward a regression line that displays a positive correlation between income and democracy. As discussed earlier, despite the nonlinear improvement in its "democracy score," Korea continued to exhibit economic growth and became more democratic even after the transition. The fact that this positive correlation existed both during and after democratization makes Korea a good candidate for a pathway case study to elucidate the causal mechanisms and thereby clarify modernization theory.

Democratization "from Above" or "from Below"?

There is no consensus regarding the mode of Korea's transition to democracy. Some scholars have classified it as a case of democracy "from above": although it is unclear whether there was a genuine split among the Korean ruling elites (S. Kim 2000, 4), earlier studies have applied the "transition" (or "elitist") paradigm (O'Donnell, Schmitter, and Whitehead 1986) to explain that Korea's democratization resulted from a series of elite calculations and interactions (e.g., T. Cheng and Kim 1994; H.-B. Im 1994). Even when compared with other East Asian polities (such as China, Indonesia, Malaysia, Singapore, and Taiwan), Korea has been identified as a case of authoritarian-led democratization in which the ruling party, the Democratic Justice Party, "conceded democracy" from a position of strength, "with the reasonable expectation it would survive, minimally, and, at best, continue to rule a democratic Korea" (Slater and Wong 2013, 726). Erik Mobrand (2019) goes further, arguing that Korea's democracy is a "top-down democracy" in which the earlier authoritarian structures, including exclusive political institutions, were not dismantled by popular movements and actually remain part of the postauthoritarian political system.

Other scholars classify Korea as a case of "bottom-up" democratization, in which pressure from civil society and social movements played a critical role in the transition from authoritarianism to democracy (e.g., S. Kim 2000; 2009; Haggard and Kaufman 2016). According to Sunhyuk Kim (2000, 4), "The elitist explanation of Korean democratization tends to neglect, either intentionally or inadvertently, that there had been a series of massive, intense, and protracted pro-democracy popular movements prior to June 29, 1987 [when the June 29 Declaration was made by the ruling elite]." Research on the authoritarian period also supports that idea, revealing that movements for democracy existed throughout the 1960s, 1970s, and 1980s, and that those movements played an important role in democratization (e.g., C. Kim 2017; N. Lee 2007; Koo 2001; P. Y. Chang 2015a).

However, Korea's process of democratization differed from the bottom-up transitions observed in the Western world, which were driven either by the capitalists (the "bourgeoisie"; Moore (1966)) or by the working class alone (Rueschemeyer, Stephens, and Stephens 1992; Therborn 1977). Additionally, despite the predictions of modernization theory, middle-class involvement in Korea's democracy movement was largely absent throughout the authoritarian period. Instead, the bottom-up pressure exerted upon the incumbent regime was uniquely empowered by the *cross-class alliance* that students and intellectuals formed with workers (N. Lee 2007, 200; Koo 2001). Given the dichotomous explanation of Korea's democratic transition (as either being "from above" or "from below") and the fact that the class-based theory of democratization fails to identify the main driver(s) of its transition process, there is no consensus regarding how Korea's transition occurred.

Thus, this book aims not only to clarify modernization theory by using Korea as a pathway case but also to reconcile the debate over Korea's democratization and its mode of transition. In doing so, the book will (1) analyze previously unexamined patterns in pro-democracy movements throughout the *entire* country, not just in Seoul; (2) examine numerous decades before and after 1987, rather than just a few years leading up to 1987; and (3) break down the macro-variable of economic development into meso-level phenomena (i.e., the geographical-spatial transformation of industrial complexes and student campuses), thereby proposing a middle ground between the analyses of Korea's democratization as strictly "top down" or "bottom up." By moving away from a focus on the national, Seoul-based politics surrounding the moment of democratic transition and the events that fit into a preexisting democratization narrative, this book's approach will yield a more nuanced and complete understanding of Korea's democratization and the impacts that authoritarian development had on it.

The Argument in Brief

Using South Korea as a pathway case, this book argues and demonstrates that economic development has contradictory effects on authoritarianism: modernization structures developed by autocrats can generate regime support, but they can also transform into sites of pro-democratic mobilization. The democratizing effect of development lags behind the initial stabilizing effect because the geospatial pattern of development only gradually facilitates the organization of social forces. In advancing these claims, I make three distinct but interrelated arguments.

My first argument is that the impact of economic development on democratization is nonmonotonic and curvilinear. As illustrated in figure 1.2, despite modernization theory's prediction that authoritarian regime stability will more or less consistently decrease with modernization, I posit that economic growth can actually stabilize authoritarian rule before it has democratizing effects. As argued by studies of the political economy of authoritarian rule that fall under the "performance legitimacy models," "authoritarian regimes will benefit from greater popular support if they provide high-quality infrastructure, rising incomes, and steady economic growth" (Albertus, Fenner, and Slater 2018, 11). For example, the industrialization and urbanization driven by these regimes create industrial jobs in urban areas and thereby provide opportunities for upward mobility among the poor rural population. The expansion of education used to bolster economic development, including vocational education and training, also provides the masses with the skills they need to find higher-paying jobs. Moreover, as autocratic countries promote tertiary education in pursuit of development, they are likely to balance these policies with good jobs, good benefits, and other perks that keep educated groups satisfied (Rosenfeld 2020, 15). Research on authoritarian regimes show that autocrats are able to remain in power by essentially buying support with such goods and services (e.g., Blaydes 2011; Greene 2007; Kim and Gandhi 2010; Lust 2006;

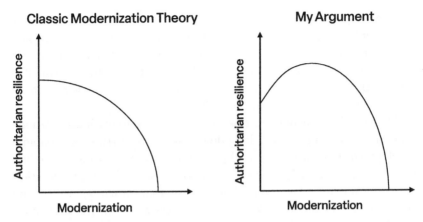

Fig 1.2. Graphical representation of the relationship between modernization and authoritarian resilience: Classical modernization theory vs. my argument.

Lust-Okar 2009; Magaloni 2006; Pan 2020; Schady 2000). These benefits are not only doled out selectively as rewards (to supporters) or as punishments (to dissenters) (e.g., Magaloni 2006; Stokes et al. 2013) but are also distributed more broadly as a way to establish state dependency among its citizenry (Albertus, Fenner, and Slater 2018).[4] Finally, recent empirical studies (including my own) on authoritarian South Korea have found that, in the short term, autocrat-led development buys political legitimacy with economic performance, and the expansion of mass media[5] successfully promotes loyalty to the state, as reflected in increased electoral support for the ruling parties (J. E. Cho, Lee, and Song 2017; 2019; Hong and Park 2016; Hong, Park, and Yang 2022). Taken together, these studies suggest that modernization and economic development may initially help stabilize authoritarian rule by increasing performance-based legitimacy, state dependency, and regime support.

Despite these initial effects, economic development gradually undermines authoritarian resilience because increasing income promotes democracy in the medium or long term (Treisman 2020b; Boix 2018). I will add that urbanization accompanied by economic growth and industrialization ultimately leads not only to increased national wealth but also to increased geospatial concentration of social actors, who are otherwise scattered across different parts of the country and disconnected from each other. Such dense concentrations of social actors can bolster their capacity to organize and engage in collective action against authoritarian regimes. As found in the social networks and collective action literature, such density also increases interactions (or ties) among these social actors, which provides opportunities to build linkages within and across groups and thereby enlarges the size and scope of the movement.[6] Increased frequency and wider spread of protests increase the threat of revolution and the cost of repression, which in turn increase the likelihood that autocrats will offer democratic concessions (such as voting rights) or full-scale democratization (Acemoglu and Robinson 2001; 2006).

My second argument is that this nonmonotonic and curvilinear relationship can be explained by breaking down the macro-variable of economic development into two meso-level phenomena: (1) the creation of industrial complexes and (2) the creation of vocational and tertiary education sites and campuses. These spatial-geographic transformations accompany economic development—indeed, both are necessary in the transformation from a low-income agricultural country to a middle- or high-income country (Doner and Schneider 2016). Many developing countries have sought such economic development by pursuing export-led growth strategies that hinge on the development of manufacturing industries and an abundant supply of labor. As a result, the development of multiple industrial plots in a single area—that is, an industrial complex (or industrial estate)—has emerged as an effective strategy for providing the infrastructure (such as water, electricity, gas, transportation, and telecommunication) needed to build new factories. Without such a strategy, the high cost associated with creating infrastructure deters individual firms from building new factories and hinders the growth of their industries. Similarly, tertiary education, including vocational training and education and higher education focused on science and engineering, are often expanded to produce a large, technologically skilled labor force within a short time frame to generate productivity growth. In these industrial and educational sites, humans interact with their political and economic systems and social structures to bring about economic development.

My third argument is that these industrial complexes and sites of tertiary and higher education are also ecological sites that have various social effects on the workers and students that inhabit them. The chief effect is the organization of social forces—that is, the creation and intensification of social ties and networks that facilitate organization, collective action, and antiregime mobilization through the establishment of labor unions, student organizations, and ecology-dependent protest strategies. As Stephan Haggard and Robert Kaufman (2016, 16) show, "longer-standing [or enduring] social organizations" (e.g., unions and civil society organizations) are important for "distributive conflict transitions," as they are "pivotal actors in turning people out in the streets and mounting sustained threats to authori-

Introduction

tarian rule." Building on this finding, I argue that the *national organization of social forces*—not necessarily the growth of the middle class, as posited by modernization theory—is the core causal variable that explains not only the contradictory effects of economic growth on regime stability but also why economic development leads to democracy in the long run. Social groups may include economic class actors, like the middle and working classes, but also nonclass collective actors, such as university students, human rights activists, church leaders, and regional elites. At the peak of this national organization of social forces, we will observe (1) an increased number and size of social organizations within each social group (e.g., student groups and labor unions), (2) horizontal coordination within and across groups (e.g., inter-/intracampus, inter-/intraunion, worker-student alliance), and (3) widespread protests across the country. The horizontal linkages formed within and across different social groups enlarge the size and scope of the pro-democracy movement. And when this phenomenon is not confined to a particular locality (or is not only observed in the country's capital) but is instead observed more widely across the country, the likelihood of a successful mass-initiated democratic transition increases. This time is when we are most likely to see a country reaching the inflection point in figure 1.2.

According to the "conditional modernization thesis," the effect of economic development is delayed, and its intensity varies across periods. As Daniel Treisman (2018, 33) states, "If some factor that occurs periodically triggers the political effect of economic development, then that trigger is more likely to show up within a 10-year spell than in any individual year." That is, triggering events such as economic crises, elections, and leader turnover may activate the effect of economic development, but they can do so without regard to any particular income threshold (M. Miller 2012; Kennedy 2010; Treisman 2015). I argue that, at its peak, the organization of social forces can also catalyze the effect. However, unlike "triggering events," which are more difficult to predict and sometimes occur randomly (Treisman 2020a), development-induced social changes—such as the organization of social forces—develop and reach their peaks gradually. As pointed out by Paul Pierson (2004, 13–14) in *Politics in Time*, causal processes may occur slowly because they are incremental (i.e., they take a long time to add up to anything), involve threshold effects (i.e., have little significance until they attain a critical mass, which may then trigger major change), or require the unfolding of extended causal chains (i.e., *a* causes *b*, which causes *c* . . .). Thus, even if they ultimately bring about a significant change, social organization initially has a modest or negligible impact and thus allows the stabilizing effect of economic growth to dominate for a while.

The destabilizing effect of economic growth—via the organization of social forces—may also increase the momentum of that growth and overwhelm its stabilizing effect when political opportunities (or openings) arise. The role that such opportunities play in movement emergence and success has been highlighted as essential in the social movement literature (e.g., della Porta 1996; Kitschelt 1986; Oberschall 1996; Tarrow 1996). Despite their importance, however, political openings are only potential rather than actual opportunities unless and until they are perceived and defined as such by a group of actors that is sufficiently well organized to leverage them (McAdam, McCarthy, and Zald 1996; D. Suh 2001). That is, political openings may be necessary but by themselves are not sufficient for mass mobilization to occur in an authoritarian environment. Rather, it is the organization of social forces that brings about democratic change. As the empirical chapters of this book will show, in Korea, Chun Doo Hwan's political liberalization policies in the 1980s provided political opportunities for students, workers, and opposition politicians to form linkages with one another—and to launch the nationwide mass demonstrations that resulted in the regime's capitulation to the public demand for democratic reforms. However, workers and students had to be sufficiently organized and aware of that political opportunity to engage in collective action and to coalesce with opposition politicians in that moment.

Indeed, as articulated in Doug McAdam's (1982) political process theory, three factors explain the onset and development of most political movements: expanding political opportunities, availability of mobilizing structures (defined as "the collective vehicles through which people initially mobilize and begin to engage in sustained collective action"), and the social psychological process of "cognitive liberation" (i.e., the ability of movement participants to recognize their collective strength and to take advantage of political opportunities as they arise). In Korea, mobilizing structures and cognitive liberation had to be in place—in addition to the political opening in the 1980s—for mass protests to overthrow the regime. And these two elements, I argue, were the by-products of autocrats' industrial and educational policies.

Mobilizing structures such as churches, schools, community organizations, and student groups that exist prior to the onset of a social movement can be activated for collective action (McAdam 1982). They provide solidarity, leadership, membership, and communication networks for the movement (Clemens 1996; McAdam 1982; Snow, Zurcher, and Ekland-Olson 1980). In the Korean case, the ecological conditions surrounding the industrial complexes and university campuses contributed to the formation of mobilizing structures, which were the already existing formal and informal organizations and networks found in their communities that workers and students used to organize and engage in collective action. The development of industrial complexes and the ecological conditions surrounding them led to the creation of small group-based networks of factory workers that facilitated the development of the labor movement, including the formation of workers' consciousness and labor unions (chapters 2 and 3). Similarly, the expansion of higher education resulted in an explosion in the number of students on university campuses across the country. These students created a nationwide student movement by rebuilding student councils on university campuses (chapter 4). As workers and students were brought together to work, study, and reside in close quarters, interfirm and intercampus networks as well as a worker-student alliance were created. Student activists strategically chose industrial complexes as sites of mobilization and organized small groups composed of workers from different firms (chapter 3). They also utilized national student organizations to mobilize students across regions and levels of university prestige and connect with opposition politicians to campaign against the incumbent regime (chapters 4 and 5).

The cognitive liberation of workers and students was also built over time inside the industrial complexes and on tertiary education campuses (chapters 3 and 4). And although the Park regime succeeded at hampering labor activism among heavy chemical industry (HCI) workers who were trained through the state-subsidized technical high schools and vocational training institutes, the subsequent regime's failure to maintain the vocational education and training programs weakened the state-dependent relationship between capital, government, and workers. This reduced dependence on the state—in addition to the small group networks that facilitated the development of workers' consciousness and solidarity among workers—contributed to the cognitive liberation among HCI workers who led the 1987 Great Workers' Struggle. Thus, although all three explanatory factors of the political process theory are evident in Korea's democratic transition, it was the industrial and educational policies pursued by the autocrats "at the top" that directly and indirectly created the "bottom-up" factors—including pressure from the social forces—that worked toward ending their rule.

These arguments and findings from Korea clarify modernization theory by demonstrating that economic development's impact on democratization is nonmonotonic and curvilinear: although economic development and democratization are causally associated over time, this relationship occurs in a nonlinear fashion. My work here also contributes to the emerging literature on conditional modernization theory by showing that the organization of social forces (which results from authoritarian development) is the variable that explains why the relationship between economic development and democracy differs in the short term versus the long term. Lastly, it reveals that Korea's mass-initiated democratic transition was facilitated by top-down factors—namely, the autocrats' industrial and educational policies.

Research Design and Methodological Approach

Examining Democratic Transitions

Democratization is the process through which a political regime becomes democratic. Although the term has been defined and measured differently by different scholars, most would agree that "liberal democracy is more than elections, but cannot be less" (Schedler 2001, 7). In other words, at a minimum, democracy is understood to be "the method by which people elect representatives in competitive elections to carry out their will" (Schumpeter 1942, 250). The most widely accepted definition of "liberal democracy" (put forth by Robert A. Dahl [1971] and labeled as a polyarchy) is a political system characterized by having fair elections under universal suffrage, offering citizens civil and political liberties, and allowing alternative (that is, nongovernment) sources of information, all of which enhance the democratic qualities of elections.[7]

Scholars typically conceptualize democratization as containing two phases: democratic transition (i.e., the initial transition from an authoritarian or semiauthoritarian regime to a democracy) and democratic consolidation (i.e., the process by which a new democracy matures and becomes unlikely to revert to authoritarianism). A democracy is not considered to be "consolidated" until after its democratic transition is complete. And, as stated by Juan Linz and Alfred Stepan (1996, 14), "A necessary but by no means sufficient condition for the completion of a democratic transition is the holding of free and contested elections (on the basis of broadly inclusive voter eligibility) that meet the seven institutional requirements for elections in a polyarchy that Robert A. Dahl has set forth." An important caveat is that such elections do not guarantee the completion of a democratic transition, and a transition does not always lead to consolidation. As demonstrated by Samuel Huntington (1991), waves of democratization historically have often been followed by reverse waves in which some of the newly democratic countries reverted to nondemocratic rule. This pattern is reflected in the many third-wave democracies in the post–Cold War era that later became hybrid regimes—that is, they combine elements of both democracy (e.g., democratic institutions such as elections) and authoritarianism (e.g., political repression).[8] Nevertheless, "elections as a constitutive feature of democracy provide transitions with a clear-cut institutional threshold: the holding of 'founding elections' that meet democratic minimum standards" (Schedler 2001, 7).

This book primarily focuses on the phase of democratic transition, which is understood to be the period between the breakdown of an authoritarian regime and the conclusion of the founding election that meet democratic minimum standards. Korea's democratic transition occurred in 1987. Surrendering to the June Democratic Uprising, the incumbent regime announced the June 29 Declaration and through it promised democratic reforms, including direct presidential elections. A constitutional bill was passed by the National Assembly on October 12, 1987, and on October 28 of that year, it was approved by 93% of the population in a national referendum. It took effect on February 25, 1988, when Roh Tae Woo—who had won the founding election on December 16, 1987—was inaugurated as president. Although the democratic reforms were not implemented until later, the democratic transition period in Korea is defined as having started on June 29, 1987, when authoritarian rule broke down, and having lasted until the founding election itself.

In examining Korea's nonlinear path to democratic transition, I adopt Daniel Ziblatt's (2017) long view of democratization: rather than focusing on the level of authoritarianism or democracy at a single moment in time, this view zooms out to encompass both democratic breakthrough and subsequent regime cycling. This approach differs from large-n studies that use regression analysis (which assumes a linear relationship between variables, including the one between wealth and democracy) and that engage measures that are strictly dichotomous (such as "democracy" vs. "autocracy") or that conflate the different dimensions (or, as Ziblatt [2006] calls them, "episodes of democratization") by focusing on the "snapshot" moments of democratization. This long-view approach builds on Paul Pierson's (2004, 3) argument for "placing politics in time—constructing 'moving pictures' rather than 'snapshots'" in understanding such complex sociopolitical dynamics. By adopting such a view of democratization, I will be able to account for the time-varying, contradictory effects that economic development had on Korea's democratic transition.

Examining the Contentious Politics of the Democratic Transition

By considering the entire trajectory of Korea's democratization process, I capture both the short-term and long-term effects of two autocrat-developed modernization structures—industrial complexes and institutions of vocational and higher education—on regime stability. As important as these structures were in facilitating the democratic transition, however, that transition grew out of Korea's rich history of social movements. Therefore, I focus not only on the regimes' industrial and educational policies but also on the contentious politics that surrounded the transition.

Such contentious politics was driven by the long-standing student movement, which was at the vanguard of the democracy movement and spanned more than 30 years—from the uprising in April 1960 through the 1990s. During this period, opposition politicians, intellectuals, religious leaders, journalists, and other groups were also active in social movements. Ordinary citizens actively engaged in the Masan and Seoul demonstrations during the April 19th Revolution of 1960, the Kwangju Uprising of 1980, and the June Democratic Uprising of 1987. And during the industrialization period, the labor movement developed alongside the growing working class as a democratic union movement, reaching its height during the Great Workers' Struggle of 1987. These last two—the June Democratic Uprising and the Great Workers' Struggle—were critical to Korea's democratic transition, and they were built on the groundwork laid by the democracy movement of the earlier periods.

Most studies on Korea's democratic transition focus on the June Democratic Uprising, which immediately preceded the authoritarian breakdown. However, analyzing protests that occurred both before and during the democratic transition reveals the groups and issues that were central to the democracy movement and their impacts on the transition. Thus, when considering the entire trajectory of the democratic transition, it is essential to examine the Great Workers' Struggle as well. This uprising erupted immediately after the June 29 Declaration. A cable from the U.S. Embassy in Seoul on July 3—four days after Roh Tae Woo announced the declaration—revealed that the Korean people's struggle for democracy was not over: the "student council leaders, professors, the RDP [Reunification Democratic Party (a splinter party from the opposition New Korea Democratic Party)] assemblymen and dissident figures [gathered at Yonsei University for the Grand National Debate on Nation's Politics] generally acknowledge[d] that a political 'breakthrough' [had] been achieved,

Introduction 17

but warned that *the ruling camp's 'verbal promises' would have to be followed by concrete action*" (National Museum of Korean Contemporary History 2018, 242; emphasis added). The June 29 Declaration had not addressed the issue of labor oppression or the prospect of guaranteeing basic labor rights, so during the months of July and August, workers continued their struggle for democracy and secured essential gains through their protests. New democratic unions proliferated across the country, and the level of real wages increased dramatically.[9] When we do not consider the Great Workers' Struggle in our examination of the impacts that mass protests had on democratic transition, we overlook both workers' collective efforts to achieve democracy in the workplace and the ways in which the autocrats' development policies impacted them and their capacity to organize. As this book will show, examining the various social movements and protests before and during the democratic transition, including the Great Workers' Struggle, helps clarify when and how the organization of social forces gradually reached its peak to bring about a regime change.

Multilevel Theory Building and the Subnational Approach

In examining the long-term trajectory of Korea's democratic transition and the contentious politics surrounding that process, I apply the subnational research method to build a multilevel theory that "combines national and subnational factors to offer strong explanations for outcomes of interest" (Giraudy, Moncada, and Snyder 2019, 19). According to Agustina Giraudy, Eduardo Moncada, and Richard Snyder (2019, 19), "bottom-up theories identify how national and even international phenomena are shaped by subnational factors. From this standpoint, national policies cannot be properly understood without paying attention to subnational institutions, actors, and events." In this book, such a theory of Korea's democratic transition is formulated by weaving together the findings derived from the subnational analyses offered in the empirical chapters. These chapters utilize qualitative and quantitative data to examine the relationship between economic development (as generated through industrial complexes and vocational and higher educational institutions) and regime support (revealed by citizens' voting and protest behavior) observed at the subnational (county; *si, gun, gu*) level. Quantified measures of the geospatial concentration of workers and students resulting from the industrial and educational policies are also included in the analyses to examine the role of this concentration as a causal mechanism. By obtaining the "average effect" in Korea from statistical analyses of counties, I build a national-level argument about

18 Seeds of Mobilization

how a national outcome (such as a democratic transition) resulted from the organization of the social forces that were developed locally and then spread across the country.

In conducting this subnational research, I use a mixed-method strategy. I analyze a wide range of new qualitative and quantitative data on Korea's socioeconomic development and its democracy movement. Qualitative sources include Korean-language primary sources and archival materials (e.g., pamphlets, reports, leaflets, and guidelines) and sourcebooks from the Korea Democracy Foundation (KDF; Minjuhwa Undong Kinyŏm Saŏphoe).[10] Primary sources are publications by the Korean government as well as by Christian, student, and labor activists in the 1970s and 1980s, including the Christian Institute for the Study of Justice and Development (Han'guk Kidokkyo Sahoe Munje Yŏn'guwŏn), the National Council of Trade Unions of Korea (Chŏn'guk Nodong Undong Tanch'e Hyŏbhŭihoe), and the National Council of Churches in Korea (Han'guk Kidokkyo Kyohoe Hyŏbŭihoe). The KDF sourcebooks include the *KDF Dictionary of Events Related to the Democracy Movement* (KDF Events Dictionary; *Minjuhwa undong kwallŏn sakŏn sajŏn*) and 11 volumes of the *KDF Reports on the History of South Korea's Regional Democracy Movement* (KDF Regional History Report; *Chiyŏk minjuhwa undongsa p'yŏnch'an ŭl wihan kich'o josa ch'oejong bogosŏ*), one for each region of the country: Ch'ungbuk, Taejŏn and Ch'ungnam, Wŏnju and Ch'unch'ŏn, T'aebaek and Ch'ŏngsŏn, In'chŏn, Kyŏnggi, Cheju, Chŏnbuk, Kwangju and Chŏnnam, Taegu and Kyŏngbuk, and Pusan and Kyŏngnam.[11] Additionally, I utilize the oral history interviews conducted with former student and labor activists archived at the KDF Open Archives.

I supplement these qualitative sources with subnational and Geographic Information System analyses of protest events. Using the abovementioned primary sources, KDF archival materials, and newspaper articles from the Naver News Library (https://newslibrary.naver.com), I created three novel event datasets.[12] The first dataset documents college student protests from 1980 to 1987, and it draws on data from the *KDF Events Dictionary* and newspaper articles from the Naver News Library. The second and third datasets document 1,285 events during the 1987 June Democratic Uprising and 1,194 events during the 1987 Great Workers' Struggle, respectively. Data on the June Democratic Uprising is drawn from the *KDF Events Dictionary*, the *KDF Regional History Report*, and *The Great June Democratic Uprising for Democratization* (Han'guk Kidokkyo Sahoe Munje Yŏn'guwŏn 1987a). Data on the Great Workers' Struggle also comes from the *KDF Events Dictionary*, the *KDF Regional History Report*, the *Timeline of the Korean Democracy Movement* (Minjuhwa Undong Kinyŏm Saophoe

2006), and *The July–August Mass Struggle of the Workers* (Han'guk Kidok-kyo Sahoe Munje Yŏn'guwŏn 1987b). I also consulted various primary and archival sources from the KDF archives (listed in the appendix) to either identify protest events that are not reported in the KDF sourcebooks or to obtain more detailed information on particular events.

These new datasets are significant because, unlike existing datasets on the country's democracy movement (e.g., the Stanford Korea Democracy Project Events Dataset), they contain comprehensive information on events in regions *throughout* the country—not only those that occurred in Seoul.[13] Such information allows us to examine previously unexplored spatial patterns of protests. Scholars have noted and acknowledged that both the June Democratic Uprising and the Great Workers' Struggle happened all across Korea. The students who were actively involved in pro-democracy protests (especially in the 1980s) came from a wide range of universities, not just from the elite ones in Seoul. Similarly, workers from all major sectors in many different areas, not just the Seoul-Kyŏnggi-Inch'ŏn area, were engaged in the strikes and protests during the Great Workers' Struggle. Despite scholars' knowledge of how widespread such engagement was, explanations for the mass-initiated democratic transition have not properly accounted for nationwide protests (i.e., protests not confined to a particular location or region) or the process by which they became a national phenomenon.

The original datasets used here provide information on the location of each protest event, thereby helping reveal the subnational patterns of protests and allowing rigorous testing of whether and how these patterns map onto subnational characteristics driven by the autocrats' industrial and educational policies. These patterns help explain how student and labor movements developed and spread as well as how alliances formed across different groups (e.g., workers, students, and opposition politicians) and the impacts that they had on the nationwide pro-democracy protests in 1987. In elucidating such patterns, this book reveals how various social movements developed during the authoritarian period. Whereas previous works on different social movements during the authoritarian period (e.g., the labor movement in the 1970s and 1980s by Hagen Koo, Christians in the 1970s by Paul Chang, and student movements in the 1960s and 1980s by Charles Kim and Namhee Lee, respectively) show the unique developmental trajectories of each movement and collectively demonstrate how the democracy movement as a whole developed over time, this book uses subnational research to reveal that *space* played an important role in that process by linking the different movements and allowing protests to spread on a nationwide scale.

Scope Conditions

The theoretical insights from the Korean case help clarify when and how economic development contributes both to authoritarian resilience and to democratization: the effects are different in the short term versus the long term, and it is the organization of social forces that destabilizes the regime over time. These insights tend to be most applicable to authoritarian regimes built around labor- or ethnically repressive economic projects, as such regimes are more likely to experience "bottom-up" transitions (Haggard and Kaufman 2016). However, they also apply to some authoritarian regimes that are more likely to experience elite-led transitions. As Dan Slater and Joseph Wong (2022) argue, some strong authoritarian states—specifically, those possessing "stability confidence" (i.e., the expectation that democratic concessions will not undermine either political stability or economic development) and "victory confidence" (i.e., the expectation among authoritarian incumbents that they can fare well, or even continue to dominate outright, in democratic elections in the post-transition period)—can preemptively "democratize through strength" when facing sudden shocks (or signals) to the authoritarian system, whether they are electoral, contentious, economic, or geopolitical.

These theoretical insights are not without limitations, as they will be less applicable to certain developing authoritarian countries. First, as pointed out by Richard Doner and Ben Ross Schneider (2016), today's middle-income economies in East and Southeast Asia (Malaysia, Thailand, and debatably China) face greater institutional challenges than those that became higher-income economies in the twentieth century, including Korea. It is more challenging to implement productivity-enhancing reforms and investments because there are more social cleavages (e.g., formal versus informal workers and domestic firms versus multinational corporations) that can interfere with collective action and coalition building. In these cases, it will take longer or even be impossible to reach the inflection point illustrated in figure 1.2.

Second, repression and co-optation in strong authoritarian regimes can shift the inflection point upward, as illustrated by the dashed line in figure 1.3. A higher inflection point means that (1) it will take longer for social forces to be organized nationally and to activate the destabilizing effect of development, and (2) it is possible that the threshold becomes too high to achieve, which would make the regime more likely to endure despite having undergone economic development. The Chinese case illustrates this point: despite its level of economic growth, the country remains

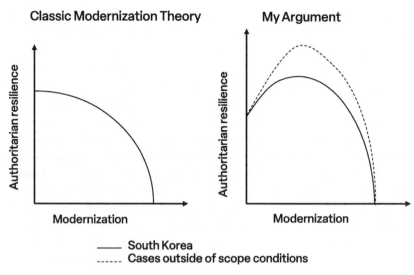

Fig 1.3. Graphical representation of the relationship between modernization and authoritarian resilience: Scope conditions

authoritarian. Scholars have explained that the state's coercive capacity (Y. Wang 2014) and consolidated state repression (Fu and Distelhorst 2018) allow the government to monitor and control the masses, thereby limiting contentious participation. There are also systems of top-down control underpinning coercive distribution in China—namely, the *danwei* (or work unit) system and the *hukou* household registration system[14]—that leave the Chinese populace too dependent on the state to undertake serious protest (Albertus, Fenner, and Slater 2018; Perry 1997). The Chinese Communist Party regime has also expanded the state-dependent middle class (i.e., the middle-class professionals who choose state employment, including state-owned enterprises), and members of that class are less likely to support democracy and participate in pro-democracy coalitions (Chen 2013; Nathan 2016; Rosenfeld 2020). Like China, the strong states in Singapore and Malaysia also have ample coercive and administrative power to coerce rivals, extract resources, register citizens, and cultivate dependence, thereby forestalling democratization (Slater 2012; Slater and Fenner 2011). The forms and arrangements of coercion and co-optation that we observe in these authoritarian countries help explain why social forces may not be sufficiently empowered by economic development to destabilize authoritarian incumbents.

Nevertheless, the causal mechanism linking the conditional effect of economic development on democratization—i.e., the organization of social forces stemming from ecological sites—still applies to other developing authoritarian countries. For example, returning to the Chinese case, despite the overall weakness of the nation's labor movement (especially under Xi Jinping), recent labor strikes by migrant workers suggest that the ecological conditions of industrial sites—alongside the gradual relaxation of the *hukou* system, especially in small- and medium-sized cities—is contributing to the changing nature of collective labor disputes among Chinese workers (Siu and Unger 2020). In the past, migrant workers in China typically voiced only immediate grievances and did not make long-term demands (regarding future wages and conditions) because, in the face of discrimination for having a rural *hukou* status while working in an urban area, so many of them left their factories within a year. With the relaxation of the *hukou* system, however, workers started to settle down near their factories. Then, starting in the 2010s, they began to protest for future work benefits. Examples include a 2010 strike at a Honda auto-parts factory close to Guangzhou and a 2014 strike of 40,000 workers at a large factory compound in Guangdong of Yu Yuen. The latter was "led by veteran workers in their 40s, many of whom had settled near the factory for many years and who were concerned about their futures" (Siu and Unger 2020, 775).

The ecological conditions surrounding the industrial sites in China also helped build a (precarious) worker-student alliance (i.e., the Jasic Workers Support Group) during the Jasic Incident, a labor dispute that occurred from July to August 2018 at Shenzen Jasic Technology. Chinese students who joined the Jasic Workers Support Group—just like the Korean students in the 1980s—were exposed to labor issues at student-run university clubs and reading groups. Similar to the students-turned-workers in Korea during the 1970s and 1980s (discussed in chapters 2 and 3), Shen Mengyu, the key media spokesperson of the Jasic Workers Support Group, graduated with a master's degree from a top Chinese university (Sun Yat Sen University) in 2015 and deliberately went to work at an auto parts factory in Huangpu district, Guangzhou. There, she and her coworkers developed friendships on the factory floor and in the factory dormitory. Like the Korea Student Christian Federation students (introduced in chapter 3), Shen carried out an in-depth survey to collect workers' opinions on their working conditions. After she was fired for her labor activism, Shen formed the Jasic Workers Support Group, which was joined and supported by numerous students from China's top universities. About 50 of these students traveled to the city of Huizhou and rented accommodations near the

Jasic factory while they protested in solidarity with the workers seeking to form a union.

These recent developments in China—a case that seems to defy my theoretical argument the most—suggest that although there are developing (or developed) authoritarian countries that have not reached the inflection point, and although that point might be higher and thus more difficult for them to reach, the main causal mechanism derived from the Korean case—that is, the organization of social forces—still seems to hold. And even in those contexts, ecological sites such as industrial complexes and university campuses can empower social groups and organizations to exert their influence and, potentially, destabilize authoritarian regimes.

Plan for the Book

The remainder of the book is organized as follows. Chapter 2 examines whether and how the industrial policies pursued by the South Korean autocrats affected the stability of their regimes. Specifically, it focuses on the development of industrial complexes, which played a crucial role in actualizing the authoritarian regimes' export-led industrialization strategy for economic growth. The first part of the chapter explains that the development of industrial complexes initially had a stabilizing effect because it generated electoral support for the ruling party. The chapter then presents a statistical analysis of the industrial complexes' long-term effects on labor activism, showing that the counties that housed these facilities exhibited more labor protests during the Great Workers' Struggle than those that did not. The counties that housed these facilities for a longer time also exhibited more protests. Additionally, the analysis demonstrates that the geospatial concentration of manufacturing firms played a role in the causal mechanism that mediated the long-term effect of industrial complexes on labor protests.

Chapter 3 builds on the findings from chapter 2 and explains *how* the industrial complexes facilitated the gradual development of the labor movement. It argues that the ecological conditions of the industrial complexes—especially the living conditions of workers inside factory dormitories and rooming houses—enabled labor mobilization within and across firms and facilitated the entry of social activists (specifically, Christians and students) into the labor movement. The chapter also demonstrates that, in moments of expanded political opportunity, the ecology surrounding the industrial complexes eased the spread of protests and facilitated the formation of ecology-dependent strategies of collective action. These strategies ultimately contributed to the regional interfirm solidarity struggles in the 1980s, including the 1987 Great Workers' Struggle.

Chapter 4 explores the multifaceted effects of education on authoritarian regime stability by analyzing the ways in which vocational and higher education impacted the development of the labor and student movements. It also shows that the vocational education and training programs contributed to regime stability by hampering labor activism—but only until the government failed at the upkeep stage in the 1980s. At the same time, the expansion of higher education had a destabilizing effect on the regime because it provided mobilizing structures—including student councils (*haksaenghoe*), department student organizations (*hakhoe*), and national student organizations—through which student activists created a nationwide movement and formed alliances with workers (chapter 3) and opposition politicians (chapter 5). These alliances strengthened the pro-democracy movement vis-à-vis the incumbent authoritarian regime.

The significance and effectiveness of the relationships formed between students and opposition politicians in the 1980s are explored further in chapter 5. Utilizing an original dataset on the 1987 June Democratic Uprising, the chapter shows that the areas that were more supportive of the new opposition party (i.e., the New Korea Democratic Party) during the 1985 National Assembly election exhibited more protests during the June Democratic Uprising—but only in areas with a high concentration of college students. The findings of this chapter underscore the critical role of student organizations serving as mobilizing structures in destabilizing the regime by linking electoral activities to antigovernment protests. And as demonstrated in chapter 4, such organizations and coalitional protests proliferated across the country as higher education was expanded under Chun Doo Hwan's rule.

Whereas the preceding chapters examine how economic development affected Korea's democratic transition, chapter 6 explores the enduring effects of that process in the democratic period. It specifically explores whether and how the time-varying, contradictory effects of economic development on democracy are reflected in the generational differences in civic and political engagement in the post-transition period. Using Korean General Social Survey data from 2003 to 2012, the chapter argues and demonstrates that the intergenerational differences in Korea are explained by each generation's relative prioritization of economic development versus democracy, which is heavily shaped by their different formative experiences (or lack thereof) of economic growth and authoritarian rule. The findings of this chapter suggest that economic development not only has a democratizing effect on the regime through generational replacement in civil society but also has continuous impacts on people's political attitudes and behavior in the democratic period.

The concluding chapter summarizes the main findings of the book regarding how Korea's transition occurred and discusses how they help clarify modernization theory. It introduces Taiwan (Republic of China) as a reference case to help illustrate how the causal mechanism linking economic development and democracy varies across different transition paths. The comparison highlights the importance of examining the *geospatial pattern* of development to better understand how democracy emerges in a developing country. Additionally, the chapter addresses the implications of the authoritarian legacy for Korea's democracy in the post-transition period. It illustrates that, just as autocrat-led economic development initially acted as a double-edged sword by stabilizing dictatorship first but bringing it down later, it continues to do so even post-democratization by leaving behind authoritarian baggage that creates challenges to the newly emerging democracy.

TWO

Industrialization as a (De)stabilizing Force

The development of Modern Industry, therefore, cuts from under its feet the very foundation on which the bourgeoisie produces and appropriates products. What the bourgeoisie therefore produces, above all, are its own grave-diggers.

—Karl Marx, *Communist Manifesto* (1848)

In the 67 years between the end of the Korean War (1950–53) and 2020, the Republic of Korea (South Korea) underwent a dramatic shift in its economic situation: it transformed from one of the poorest countries in the world—poorer even than its war-torn counterpart the Democratic People's Republic of Korea (North Korea)—to the fourth largest economy in Asia and the tenth largest economy in the world. The country is acclaimed by scholars of (but not limited to) political economy for this rapid export-led economic growth, which is known as the Miracle on the Han River (Han'gang ŭi kijŏk). This explosive growth was driven by two coup-born authoritarian regimes, which seized political power illegally and then sought and obtained both political legitimacy and regime support through economic performance. In many ways, the approach worked: despite his regime's repressive nature and extensive human rights violations, former dictator Park Chung Hee continues to be revered by many South Koreans for his strong leadership and role in creating this so-called miracle.[1] However, this economic miracle also contributed to the downfall of authoritarianism and to democratization through the growth of civil society. How can we make sense of these seemingly contradictory accounts of the relationship between economic growth and democratic political development in South Korea?

This chapter examines whether and how the industrial policies pursued by South Korean autocrats affected the stability of their own regimes. In particular, it focuses on the development of the industrial complexes that were critical in actualizing the autocrats' export-led industrialization strategy for economic growth. Although the short-term political effects of this and other industrial policies have received some attention, to my knowledge their long-term effects have not been examined before. This chapter will fill that gap. Its findings will demonstrate that although the development of industrial complexes initially stabilized the regime by generating electoral support for the ruling party, such development also had a destabilizing effect in the long run because it facilitated the labor protests that were a key part of the larger pro-democracy movement.

To make this case, I first empirically investigate whether the development of industrial complexes during the authoritarian period in South Korea affected regime support in the long term and, if there is evidence of such an impact, what kind of impact it was. Specifically, I examine whether the development of industrial complexes had an effect on labor protests that were considered disruptive to the economy and to regime stability. Utilizing a novel dataset on the 1987 Great Workers' Struggle (which occurred during the country's democratic transition and was the first nationwide protest cycle by workers since industrialization), I use a two-stage regression estimator, the sequential g-estimator (Joffe and Greene 2009; Vansteelandt 2009), to estimate the controlled direct effect of industrial complexes on these labor protests. The results of this analysis reveal that the *presence* and *duration* of an industrial complex in a given county were associated with increased protests in that county during the Great Workers' Struggle. They also demonstrate that the concentration of manufacturing firms—which resulted from the development of industrial complexes—mediated the effect of industrial complexes on labor protests. By revealing the different impacts that industrialization had on regime stability at different moments in time, this chapter helps reconcile the seemingly divergent accounts of economic growth and democratic political development in South Korea.

South Korea's Industrialization under Authoritarian Rule

Korea was a largely agrarian society before its colonization by Japan, which lasted from 1910 to 1945. When industrialization began during this period of colonial rule, it was used as a strategy to buttress the Japanese Empire and its war effort during World War II. To that end, it focused on mining resources like gold, coal, copper, tungsten, graphite, and other minerals in the northern part of the country (present-day North Korea), whereas the southern part of the country (present-day South Korea) was treated as the "rice basket," supplying Japan with rice and other food products. When colonial rule ended in 1945, separation from the Japanese economy and social unrest brought about a 40%–75% decline in manufacturing from its height in the 1930s (Han'guk Ŭnhaeng Chosabu 1985; Shim and Lee 2008, 74), and the economic divide within the country solidified with the division of the Korean Peninsula in 1948: the North was left with most of the important minerals, metal and chemical industries (including fertilizers), and major sources of power, and the South, which lacked mineral resources, was left with agriculture and light industries such as textiles, printing, and food manufacturing. This put South Korea at a disadvantage compared to North Korea in jump-starting industrialization. Moreover, during the Korean War just a few years later (1950–53), much of the physical infrastructure and many of the industrial facilities built by the Japanese in both the North and the South were destroyed, so those resources could no longer help bolster the economy. As a result, the country became heavily dependent on foreign grants and loans (mostly from the United States), and its per capita Gross Domestic Product lagged behind those of many developing countries in Africa, Asia, and Latin America.

The new South Korean government immediately worked to improve the country's economic situation. In 1954, the first South Korean president, Syngman Rhee, launched postwar reconstruction plans. He focused on restoring and expanding physical infrastructure with U.S. assistance and initiated the import-substitution industrialization strategy for major nondurable consumer goods such as textiles, sugar, and food processing. The goal was to reduce the need for imports by creating local businesses that produced products for domestic consumption. However, these import substitution policies did not generate economic growth—instead, the government-run businesses became inefficient monopolies that avoided risk, innovation, and improvement in productivity. Moreover, the allocation of resources such as foreign aid, which was the main source of government revenue at that time, was driven by collusive ties between politicians and businesses. Corruption was widespread, and the state bureaucracy could not implement their own ideas and plans for economic development, as they were subject to political interference from the executive and the ruling Liberal Party (Chayudang).

As a result, South Korea's industrialization did not start to take off until the 1960s after General Park Chung Hee seized political power through a military coup in 1961 and launched a series of Five-Year Economic Development (FYED) Plans. After unsuccessful attempts at implementing import-substitution industrialization (as Rhee had done) from 1961 to 1962, the Park government officially adopted *export*-oriented industrialization in 1963.[2] As a result of this strategy, exports increased dramatically, from $87 million in 1963 to $835 million in 1970, with Gross National Product increasing by approximately 10% each year (Koo 2001, 28). Then, in the early 1970s, the global competitive power of the light industries weakened while trade deficits continued to increase, so, in 1973, Park announced an industrial upgrading plan to heavy and chemical industrialization. The government pursued what was called the Heavy Chemical Industry (HCI) Drive, which focused on steel, nonferrous metals, shipbuilding, machinery, electronics, and chemicals.[3] As a result of this change, Park's government achieved an annual growth rate of 7.8% from 1971 to 1980, and the manufacturing sector grew at an annual rate of 14.8% (Koo 2001, 30).

To achieve such rapid economic growth, the Park government mobilized workers with ideologies of nationalism and developmentalism. Slogans such as *choguk kŭndaehwa* ("modernization of the fatherland"), *minjok chunghŭng* ("restoring national glory"), and *chal sara bose* ("let's try to live well") exemplify the government's appeal to nationalism in linking individual sacrifices to the greater cause of national development. In particular, the "economy first" (or "growth first") ideology was propagated to legitimize the government's prioritization of economic development over democratic values and thus to justify authoritarian rule. In a 1972 speech, Park defined his top priority as follows:

> The priority of politics in a developing country such as Korea should be placed, above all, on economic construction. It is the fundamental condition for the growth of democracy in a developing country to achieve economic construction first to the extent where people are freed from worry about dietary life and clothing. (Pak 1972, cited in Y. J. Kim 2011, 98)

Along the same lines, Park claimed that developing nations sometimes "have to resort to undemocratic and extraordinary measures in order to improve the living conditions of the masses . . . One cannot deny that people are more frightened of poverty and hunger than totalitarianism" (Oh

1999, 53, cited in Chang 2015a, 26). Based on this ideology, the Korean people—especially those working in the industrial sector—were asked to cooperate with the central government, accept authoritarian rule, and make personal sacrifices for the export-oriented economy.

Park also compelled every citizen to work hard to construct a prosperous welfare state (Park 1979, 188–202). The New Village Movement (or New Community Movement; Saemaŭl Undong, 1971–79), which originally began as a top-down rural development plan, functioned as a "social mobilization mechanism" to induce such work in rural areas (Han 2004). In 1973, the Factory New Village Movement (Kongjang Saemaŭl Undong) brought to factories the same "Saemaŭl spirit" of diligence, self-help, and teamwork while also emphasizing increased productivity and labor-management cooperation. In his Export Day Speech that year, Park explicitly emphasized the "family-like atmosphere" and "complete harmony between employees and employers" to strengthen the firm-as-family motif of this movement (C. H. Park 1979, 216, 251–52). With "Treat employees like family. Do factory work like your own personal work!" as its major slogan, the movement promoted ideological conformity and a compliant worker mentality to improve productivity and encourage the capital-labor cohesion deemed necessary for a successful export-led industrialization (J.-J. Choi 1989). In these ways, the Park regime also engaged heavily in ideological mobilization to actualize the goals of export-oriented industrialization, which was to generate economic growth through exports and ultimately lift the country out of poverty.

Industrial Complexes and Export-Oriented Industrialization

Scholars have long argued that market forces alone cannot adequately explain South Korea's economic "miracle." The South Korean state was not a minimalist state envisioned by neoclassical economists—rather, the government made strategic interventions in the economy through industrial targeting and selective allocation of resources in strategic sectors. In other words, the successful implementation of Park's export-oriented strategy (which hinged on the economy-first ideology) relied not only on the abundant supply of labor but also on the state-led development of manufacturing industries. According to Alice Amsden (1992), the South Korean miracle was a product of the state intervening in the market to deliberately get the relative prices "wrong" (providing subsidies to private firms that distorted the relative prices of goods) rather than getting the prices "right" (in accordance with market forces), and in doing so allowed industries (targeted for development) to grow and become globally competitive. It was the relative autonomy of the "developmental state" (Amsden 1992; Deyo 1989; Haggard 2018; Johnson 1982; Jones and Sakong 1990; Woo-Cumings 1999) and its competent and meritocratic bureaucracy that facilitated the formulation of efficient, coherent, and consistent economic policies and their effective implementation.[4]

The Economic Planning Board (Kyŏngje Kihoegwŏn), which was a state bureaucratic agency created by Park in 1961, had unprecedented power over developing economic plans (i.e., the FYED plans), allocating resources and budgets, and attracting foreign capital. The Economic Planning Board was headed by the deputy prime minister and staffed by bureaucrats known for their intellectual capabilities and educational background in business and economics. It was through the first three FYED plans (1962–76)—under the auspices of the Economic Planning Board—that the development policy changed from import-substitution industrialization to export-oriented industrialization. And this shift to export-oriented industrialization in the 1960s accompanied the development of industrial complexes.

Development of Industrial Complexes

Korea's successful export-led industrialization relied on the construction of massive industrial complexes beginning in the early 1960s. The government's plan for the development of industrial complexes was conceived at the onset of Park's rule. One week after the government's announcement of the First FYED Plan on January 13, 1962, the Special Act for Expropriation of Land for Manufacturing Zone Development was enacted, promptly beginning the development of industrial complexes or industrial estates (*kongŏp tanji*). Defined as "complexes planned and developed according to a comprehensive plan for the collective establishment and development of factories" (Industrial Location and Development Act, article 2, clause 2), these complexes were a focal point in the Korean government's export-led industrialization strategy. Earlier industrialization efforts had left the country with little infrastructure of this kind—as mentioned earlier, although industrial development first began under Japanese colonial rule in the 1930s and 1940s, it was designed to aid Japan's war efforts, not to serve Korea. In addition, much of the physical infrastructure built during that time was destroyed during the Korean War.[5] The new industrial complexes were designed to fill that void. Additionally, concentrating factories in designated areas was intended to yield several benefits: synergic effects among related industries, increased exports and employment opportunities, and the free exchange of technology.

The development of industrial complexes reflected the government's industrial strategy that first focused on light manufacturing industries followed by heavy industries. As Korea's original comparative advantage was cheap and abundant labor, light manufacturing sectors such as textiles, garments, footwear, and simple electronics—all of which took advantage of this resource—were the key sectors for the expansion of industrial exports in the 1960s. In order to establish this competitive advantage on a global scale, the Development of Export Industrial Complexes Act was enacted on September 14, 1964, and based on this legislation, Korean Export Industrial Complex No. 1 was developed in the Kuro district of Seoul, followed by No. 2 and No. 3 in Seoul and No. 4, No. 5, and No. 6 in Pup'yŏng and Chuan of Inch'ŏn. These industrial complexes focused on textile and sewing industries to foster export industries in the 1960s.

The export industrial complexes were the first of many industrial complexes, and they were not the only kind. The Ministry of Commerce and Industry worked with local governments to establish general (or regional) industrial complexes in provincial capital cities in inland areas such as Kwangju, Taejŏn, Chŏnju, Ch'ŏngju, Taegu, and Ch'unch'ŏn. Subsequently, industrial complex development expanded to small- and medium-sized regional cities such as Iri, Wŏnju, and Mokp'o. Finally, private industrial complexes were set up to regulate the preexisting individual sites of private enterprises in Kyŏnggi, Inch'ŏn, Pusan, and Taegu. Such industrial complexes included the Yŏngdŭngp'o Mechanical Industrial Complex, Korean Plastic Industry Complex, Inch'ŏn Mechanical Industrial Complex, Inch'ŏn Non-ferrous Metal Industrial Complex, and Korea Materials Corporation.

To support the government's HCI Drive, the Industrial Complex Development Promotion Act was enacted in 1973, and additional large-scale industrial complexes were built in coastal areas that had the ports, water supply, and land availability needed to support the factories' production capacity. Developed as part of new industrial cities, these complexes specialized in particular industries: chemical industries were assigned to Ulsan and Yŏsu, steel to Pohang, electronics industries to Kumi, mechanical industries to Ch'angwŏn, and shipbuilding to Pusan, Ulsan, and Kŏje.[6]

The development of these complexes led to regional economic imbalances. In 1977, the government aimed to correct these imbalances with the launch of the Fourth FYED Plan (1977–81) and the enactment of the

Distribution of Industry Act, both of which suppressed the overconcentration of industries in large metropolitan areas and promoted distribution to other regions. The government also passed the Regional Industrial Development Act, which limited new industries in the already industry-rich Seoul and the surrounding areas. It aimed to disperse Seoul's population and industry by creating Regional Industrial Development Enterprise Zones and developing more industrial complexes, such as the Panwol Special Zone and Namdong Industrial Complexes. In 1983, the Act on Promoting the Development of Income Sources for Agricultural and Fishing Villages led to the development of agricultural industrial complexes in rural areas. Finally, from 1986 to 1990, the government aimed to reduce regional economic disparities caused by the uneven patterns of industrialization in the preceding two decades: they built additional industrial complexes in areas that did not yet have any.

These government-built industrial complexes were constructed all over the country, fostering manufacturing activity and employment. And in order to cope with the dramatic increase in demand for technicians and skilled workers in these large-scale industrial complexes, especially in heavy and chemical industry, the government was compelled to make other changes as well: it expanded vocational educational schools and the vocational training system, and it improved the technical qualification system. (The educational policies and their impacts will be discussed in more detail in chapter 4.) Table 2.1 provides information on the number of industrial complexes built between 1961 and 1987 and their combined sizes in each administrative region of the country.[7]

TABLE 2.1. Number and Size of Industrial Complexes by Administrative Region, 1963–1987

Administrative Region	Number of ICs	Total Size of ICs ($1,000m^2$)
Seoul	3	2,185
Inch'ŏn and Kyŏnggi	11	50,138
Kangwŏn	5	5,786
Ch'ungbuk	2	4,032
Ch'ungnam and Taejŏn	3	2,115
Chŏnbuk	7	12,434
Chŏnnam and Kwangju	11	26,575
Kyŏngbuk and Taegu	13	42,968
Kyŏngnam and Pusan	12	124,466
Cheju	—	—

Source: Sanggongbu (Ministry of Commerce) (1989).

State-Business Relations and Labor Repression
for Export-Led Industrialization

Korea's miraculous export-led economic growth—facilitated by the development of industrial complexes—was possible not only due to its developmental state and meritocratic bureaucracy but also due to its close relationship with the domestic capitalists that emerged under the protection of the state. The government's effort to promote export industrialization, especially in the HCI sector in the 1970s, contributed to the development of large conglomerates, known as the *chaebŏls*,[8] that worked closely with the state authorities in carrying out economic plans.[9] To encourage such firms to expand and take risks in state-designated industries (e.g., automobiles, ships, electronics, and electrical parts in the 1970s), the state provided low-interest loans, tax cuts, and foreign capital to those in the business sector that engaged in those industries. The government supported *chaebŏls* that had a proven track record of risk-taking, managerial capability, and high performance; it also allowed failing *chaebŏls* to go under (E. Kim and G.-S. Park 2011). The government also offered these businesses favors based on their export performance, and it was able to control and discipline them through financial institutions: the state (specifically, the Ministry of Finance) had nationalized all commercial banks and made the Bank of Korea subordinate to the government. Thus, though they were technically private firms, the *chaebŏls* were under quite a bit of government control.

Over time, however, the *chaebŏls* and business associations did increase their power vis-à-vis the state because they drove a significant portion of the national economy. For instance, in 1977, 100 *chaebŏl* companies made up 48.3% of the nation's gross national product in terms of total sales, and the top ten companies accounted for 25.6% (J.-J. Choi 1989, 58–59). Although the state was initially in a commanding position in the formulation and implementation of industrial policies such as the export-oriented industrialization policy and HCI Drive, the government (starting under Park's rule, but even more so in the postauthoritarian period) increasingly found itself in an interdependent relationship with the *chaebŏls*. These companies ultimately became "too big to fail," and the government often had to accommodate their demands for bailouts in times of economic crisis.

Given their increasingly close relationship, domestic capitalists and the government shared an interest in achieving the national export target during the industrialization period. To do that, both wanted to keep costs down and maintain export competitiveness, and so both were motivated to repress labor and any demands for improved working conditions. Accordingly, throughout industrialization, working hours were long and wages were low by international standards.[10] Workers also had no effective organization to advocate for and protect their rights. The authoritarian governments established firm control over unions, all of which were required to affiliate themselves with the Federation of Korean Trade Unions (FKTU; Han'guk Nodong Chohap Ch'ongyŏnmaeng). Developed under Syngman Rhee (1948–60) as a quasi-government organ to combat left-wing unionism prior to the Korean War (1950–53), the FKTU was revived and reorganized by the Park government in 1963. It would be placed under further restrictions during Chun Doo Hwan's rule (1980–87) and would remain the only officially sanctioned umbrella organization for workers in Korea throughout the authoritarian period and even after political democratization in 1987 (i.e., until the Korean Confederation of Trade Unions was officially recognized in 1999). Throughout the authoritarian period, the FKTU had no genuine interest in promoting workers' welfare (Koo 2001, 26–27); workers often referred to the FKTU-affiliated unions as *ŏyong* unions, meaning antilabor, pro-company, and antidemocratic.

This initial shift occurred during the Park regime, when all labor policies became increasingly authoritarian and repressive. The 1963 amendment of the labor laws banned unions from participating in political activities and from establishing a second union (which would allow there to be one at both the plant and national levels). In 1969, the government announced the Provisional Exceptional Law Concerning Labor Unions and the Settlement of Labor Disputes in Foreign-Invested Firms, which imposed severe restrictions on labor organizing and prohibited strikes at foreign-invested firms. Furthermore, in 1971, the Law Concerning Special Measures for Safeguarding National Security suspended two of the three basic rights of workers guaranteed by the constitution: the right to bargain collectively and the right to engage in collective action. Subsequently, under Chun's rule, with the revised Trade Union Act in 1980, the government decentralized the union structure, thereby eliminating industry-wide collective bargaining. The revised labor law also prohibited "third-party intervention," making bargaining possible only between a company and a plant union and thereby preempting any linkage between labor and political opposition groups. Building on these drastic changes in policy, the South Korean authoritarian governments relied heavily on repression to manage and discipline labor. Rather than imposing discipline via legal or bureaucratic institutions (such as the Ministry of Labor or regional labor councils), the autocrats often resorted to coercive institutions such as the police, the Korea Central Intelligence Agency (Chungang Chŏngbobu),

36 Seeds of Mobilization

and military security forces to suppress labor activism. And, as pointed out by Hagen Koo (2001, 28), the labor policies of the authoritarian era not only reflected the regime's attempt to mobilize workers economically as an element of production but also reflected its goal of demobilizing them politically as a possible threat to regime stability. As shown in the rest of the chapter, this very repression sowed the seeds of the regime's downfall.

The Short-Term Effect of Industrial Policy
on Authoritarian Regime Stability

Despite the regime's repressive practices, a significant portion of Korean society embraced the country's economic growth and the regime's narrative about what was necessary to sustain it. To generate this kind of loyalty, the regime equated economic growth with fighting both poverty and the threat of Communism (from North Korea). This framing was successful: many workers became loyal to the state and embraced their state-propagated identity as industrial warrior-citizens. The Park regime launched the Saemaŭl Factory Movement and used the rhetoric of nationalism and developmentalism to shape workers' motivation and self-identity. Factory workers were called *sanŏp ŭi chŏnsa* (industrial warrior), *sanŏp ŭi yŏkkun* (builders of industry), and *such'ul ŭi yŏkkun* (chief producers of exports), as illustrated in Park's Labor Day Speech delivered on March 10, 1966:

> Each and every one of the Korean workers who are right now work-ing busily in factories, in mines, or on a railroad or harbor, or in other workplaces across Korea, is the true pillar and warrior in our effort for the modernization of our homeland. (Park 1966, cited in W. Kim 2016, 212)

Female factory workers had particular motivations for embracing this identity. As the majority of the factory workers in light (labor-intensive) industry, they were traditionally looked down upon by society at large and were often referred to using the derogatory term *gongsuni* ("little miss factory"). In an interview with the *Korea Times* (2015), Han Myŏnghŭi, a union leader of Control Data Company from 1980 until its closing in 1982, said that she hated being called *gongsuni*, which she described as "a term for a less educated young female manufacturing worker." Against this background, these workers began to embrace the state-propagated identity, which commanded greater respect than was usually granted to them. Even some of those at Dongil Textile Company—a workplace that was famous for labor activism during the 1970s, when labor activism wasn't prevalent—called themselves "pillars of industry" because doing so "made them to feel like valuable and productive members of society and contributors to the national economy" (W. Kim 2016, 214). Yi Chaesŏn, a female worker at this company, illustrated this attitude:

> I've worked for Dongil Bangjik [Dongil Textile] for two years now. Still a young girl when I first entered this place, now I am a grown woman and *I became a pillar of industry* [emphasis added] who pours all my care into cloth-weaving. . . . Some of my colleagues tease me sometimes, calling me the stingy one. But I couldn't care less about what they say. I just know too well the contempt that awaits me if I do not have money, and the fool I will be treated as. So, no matter what others said around me, I saved and saved, at all costs. (Yi 1976, cited in W. Kim 2016, 213)

As this quote demonstrates, workers—even those at firms where independent anti-FKTU unions had formed—were susceptible to the economic development slogans of the Park regime.

Although they did not have the same motivations as female factory workers, male skilled workers in the heavy and chemical industry likewise conformed to Park's nation-building HCI program as patriotic and obedient "industrial warriors" and remained "voluntarily docile" even after Park's demise in 1979 (H.-A. Kim 2020, 12). This embrace of the state-propagated identity of industrial warriors meant that Korean workers—both female and male, in both light manufacturing and HCI firms—internalized the state's goals as their own personal goals. They were mobilized by the state in a manner that compelled them to accept the regime's values, thereby legitimizing the Park regime's economy-first ideology.

Regime support was cultivated not only among factory workers but also on a broader scale. Like other authoritarian regimes in Latin America (e.g., Mexico under the Institutional Revolutionary Party) and the Middle East and North Africa (e.g., Jordan, Syria, and Egypt), Korean autocrats were able to garner popular support by providing economic and material benefits to targeted groups.[11] Proximity to industrial complexes benefited local residents by (1) expanding employment opportunities, (2) increasing the local population and tax revenue, (3) motivating significant investment in

38 Seeds of Mobilization

infrastructure such as transportation, facilities, sewage systems, electricity, and housing clusters, and (4) providing welfare benefits to workers in the manufacturing sector, including injury insurance and medical insurance (Han'guk Ŭnhaeng 1970; Hong and Park 2016, 6). Such benefits encouraged popular support for the regimes.

This relationship between industrial policy and regime support is borne out in a study conducted by Ji Yeon Hong and Sunkyoung Park (2016). It shows that the construction of industrial complexes generated popular support for the authoritarian regimes, as evidenced by electoral gains for Park's Democratic Republican Party (Minju Konghwadang) and Chun's Democratic Justice Party (Minju Chŏngŭidang).[12] In the 1978 National Assembly election, despite winning fewer overall votes than the opposition New Democratic Party (Sinmindang) in the aggregate (at the national level), Park's Democratic Republican Party gained 12%–14% more votes in areas chosen as sites for industrial complexes. This finding suggests that some Korean voters supported the authoritarian regime by voting for the incumbent party in return for the successful implementation of an industrial policy that generated (or was anticipated to generate) economic growth for their local communities.

Interestingly, however, the study also reveals that the political effect of these industrial complexes disappears as the construction of industrial complexes approaches completion. Although the authors of the study find that constituents increased their support for the ruling party in the election immediately following the government's announcement that it would build an industrial complex in their areas, they do not find an additional positive effect on ruling party vote share when the construction of industrial complexes began or was completed. They even observe stagnation of support during the construction period. The results of Hong and Park's (2016) study suggest that although the construction of industrial complexes did initially help the ruling party garner electoral support to maintain its control of the National Assembly, the political effects of industrial complexes on regime support—exhibited in voting behavior—decreased over time.[13]

To sum up this section, the development of industrial complexes initially had a stabilizing effect on autocratic rule by allowing the autocrats to legitimate the economy-first ideology, buy political legitimacy, and increase regime support with economic benefits and performance derived from the industrial complexes. The subsequent section empirically investigates the long-term effect on the labor movement that destabilized the regime.

The Long-Term Effect of Industrial Policy
on Authoritarian Regime Stability

Although we have empirical evidence of the short-term effect (i.e., increased regime support) of the industrial policies on regime stability, there has not been an empirical investigation of the long-term impact of these policies. To fill that gap, this section examines the long-term impact of industrial policy on labor activism. Given that incumbent party vote share has been used as a proxy for measuring more support for the incumbent regime, levels of antigovernment protest (regarding industrial and labor issues) should effectively measure dissent or less regime support. It will be the measure used for that purpose here.

The Development of the Labor Movement under Authoritarian Rule

During the authoritarian period, labor had little power, and workers are understood to have largely remained submissive, unorganized, and politically quiescent. Frederick Deyo (1989, 3–5) describes this lack of power and influence, saying that "organized labor [in newly industrialized East Asian countries] played a politically marginal role and insignificant role in national affairs. . . . Rapid, sustained industrialization has not altered the weak political position of labor . . . [and] despite the creation of a vast factory work force over a period of three decades, labor movements in general remain controlled and inconsequential." Although labor organizations did emerge in the 1920s under Japanese colonial rule as well as briefly during the postliberation period (1945–48), the leftist unions were completely destroyed by right-wing forces and U.S. military forces during and after the Korean War. Labor disputes also reemerged after the fall of the Rhee regime (1948–60) but were immediately repressed by the newly established Park regime in May 1961. The consistency of labor weakness during the authoritarian period is often explained by the colonial legacy (e.g., Kohli 2004),[14] strong anticommunist regimes that emerged in the postwar period and wiped out preexisting leftist labor movements, and the authoritarian governments' use of a security-oriented approach to labor exclusion and repression (Koo 2001; 2011).

Despite brief interludes in which labor tried to regain power, Korean labor was weak overall throughout the 1960s,[15] and it was not until the 1970s that the labor movement began to grow through the formation of anti-FKTU independent labor unions.[16] These unions started to form first among female workers in small, light manufacturing industries in the highly urbanized Seoul and Inch'ŏn areas.[17] Because this struggle focused on forming independent unions, it is often referred to as the "democratic union movement" (*minju nojo undong*). This movement was important but was limited in the sense that (1) only a minority of individuals opted for collective resistance, (2) it was geographically concentrated in the Seoul-Kyŏnggi-Inch'ŏn area, and (3) their demands were mostly focused on economic issues such as wage increases and better working conditions. Despite its growth in the midst of a repressive, anticommunist climate, the movement did not criticize the government's developmentalist policy or the state-led economic development (W. Kim 2016, 214), and the labor struggles were confined to a single firm or union.

In contrast, the labor struggles of the mid- to late 1980s were characterized by interfirm solidarity strikes, which gave them increased collective power. This power was first exhibited on June 22, 1985, at the Kuro Industrial Complex (officially the Korea Export Industrial Complex Zones 1–3, located in the Kuro district of Seoul). On that date, the arrest of three union leaders at Daewoo Apparel, a small manufacturer of women's clothing, sparked a weeklong strike that was joined by workers at nine other companies inside the industrial complex and by students and dissident (*minjung*) groups, who staged sympathetic street demonstrations outside the factory gates. This tactic of engaging in solidarity struggles, in which workers across several factories in the same industry or region acted collectively, laid the foundation for the democratic labor movement.

Labor struggles of the 1980s had another distinctive characteristic as well: they were transformed into political struggles (K. Yu 2002). Workers in the 1980s no longer limited their demands to economic issues and no longer only targeted their employers—instead, they started to challenge the existing system of state-led economic development.[18] During the Kuro Solidarity Strike (discussed in detail in chapter 3), for example, workers began to make political demands, shouting slogans such as "Stop repressing the labor movement," "Revise the labor law," and "The minister of labor should step down" (K. Yu 2002, 135). Following that strike, labor activists (many of whom were students-turned-workers) became interested in forming broader and more politically oriented labor organizations that focused outside the confines of enterprise unions. Two such regional (or area-based) political organizations—the Seoul Council of the Labor Movement (Sŏnoryŏn) and the Inch'ŏn Council of the Labor Movement (Innoryŏn)—were established to overcome enterprise unionism and pursue broader political goals.

In addition to expanding its goals, the labor movement formed alliances with other opposition groups in society, including progressive Christian groups in the 1970s (Chang 2015a) and college students in the 1980s (N. Lee 2007) (see chapter 3 for more on these alliances). These alliances were crucial to the development and growth of the movement. The product of this cumulative growth in workers' capacity to systematically organize and engage in collective action became visible during the democratic transition. In the wake of democratization in 1987 (indicated by the vertical dashed line in figure 2.1), there was an explosion of strikes and protests on a scale unseen before in Korea. It involved approximately 1.2 million workers (about a third of the regularly employed workforce) from most major industries, including the mining, manufacturing, shipbuilding, transportation, and service sectors. These protests, now referred to as the Great Workers' Struggle (or the Great Labor Uprising), erupted from July to August 1987 and represented the largest labor protests since the founding of the Republic of Korea in 1948.

The demands raised during this first nationwide labor movement were not limited to economic issues; they also focused on the democratization of the workplace (S. Kim 2000). The issues raised at these sit-ins and strikes included labor rights, wage issues (e.g., guaranteed minimum wage, paid vacation, overtime pay), improvement of labor conditions, and liquidation of the existing state-corporatist unions and establishment of democratic unions. As explained by Kyung Moon Hwang (2017), "The laborers who had so long sacrificed for their employers would not have made the breakthrough toward gaining their fair treatment and recognition of their economic rights. . . . Without the Great Labor Uprising, the democratization of 1987 would have been incomplete, perhaps even meaningless." Many of the independent unions that were established during and after the Great Workers' Struggle went on to form regional trade union councils. They led the movement to establish an independent federation of trade unions—as an alternative to FKTU—that resulted in the launch of the Korea Trade Union Congress (Chŏnnohyŏp) in January 1990.[19]

As this section has shown, Korea's labor movement grew gradually throughout the authoritarian period. And, given its history, it would be misleading to think that the Great Workers' Struggle in 1987 was an isolated incident from previous struggles. The labor movement also evolved under export-led, labor-intensive industrialization. Alongside the development of industrial complexes, we witnessed the growing solidarity among workers within *and* across factories.

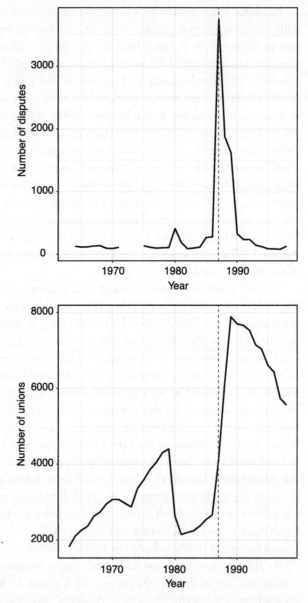

Fig 2.1. Number of labor disputes and labor unions, 1963–91. Figures are produced using table 7.1 in Koo (2001, 159).

Data and Methodology

In examining the long-term impact of the industrial policy on labor activism, I focus on the subnational variation found in the 1987 Great Workers' Struggle (GWS). The dependent variable, *Great Workers' Struggle Protests*, is the number of protests in a given county (*si*, *gun*, *gu*; note that this is the administrative division below provinces[20]) during the Great Workers' Struggle of July and August 1987. "Protests" include strikes, sit-ins, street demonstrations, and rallies, including union formation rallies (*nojo kyŏlsŏng taehoe*). The data is from an original dataset of 1,285 events during the GWS that I created using archival materials from the Korea Democracy Foundation Archives, *The July–August Mass Struggle of the Workers* published by the Christian Institute for the Study of Justice and Development (Han'guk Kidokkyo Sahoe Munje Yŏn'guwŏn), and the *National Trade Union Council White Paper* published by the National Trade Union Council White Paper Publication Committee (Chŏn'guk Nodong Chohap Hyŏbŭihoe Paeksŏ Palgan Wiwŏnhoe) and the Labor Movement History Archives (Nodong Undong Yŏksa Charyosil) (see the appendix for the detailed data description).

Following Hong and Park's (2016) approach to empirically measuring the effect of industrial complexes,[21] I construct two main independent variables: (1) *Presence of IC* (industrial complex) is a dummy variable indicating whether a given county contains at least one industrial complex in 1987 and (2) *Duration of IC* is the number of years since a given county has had at least one industrial complex. The first measure gets at the treatment effect of industrial complexes (presence effect) and the second measure captures the temporal dimension of the treatment effect (intensity of the treatment effect), allowing me to explore the short-term versus long-term effect of industrial complexes on labor activism. These measures are created using data on 62 industrial complexes that existed and were in operation in 1987, found in *An Overview of Industrial Complexes* (*Kongŏp tanji hyŏnhwang*) published by the Chungso Kiŏp Hyŏptong Chohap Chunganghoe (Korea Federation of Small and Medium Business) in 1989.

Figure 2.2 displays the subnational variation in protest intensity (with darker shades of gray representing greater intensity) in each county, along with sites of completed industrial complexes in 1987 (represented by the dots). The figure shows an apparent link between industrial complexes and intensity of labor activism—it shows that counties surrounding industrial complexes witnessed more labor protests during the GWS than did those without such complexes.

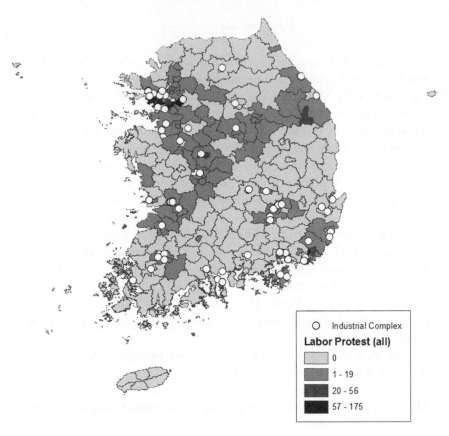

Fig 2.2. Level of protests during the 1987 Great Workers' Struggle and the location of industrial complexes. Data on industrial complexes are from Sanggongbu (Ministry of Commerce) (1989) and Maeil Kyŏngje Shinmunsa (Maeil Business Newspaper) (1987). Protest data are from the author's dataset.

Before I rigorously examine the link between industrial complexes and these labor protests, I have to confirm that these labor protests were prodemocratic. In doing so, I use an ordinary least squares (OLS) regression to regress the total number of protests during the GWS on the opposition candidates' vote shares in the first free direct presidential election since 1971, which was held in December 1987.[22] As table 2.2 shows, the coefficient of *Great Workers' Struggle Protests* is statistically significant and positive. It shows that counties with more GWS protests had a higher vote share for the opposition candidates in the presidential election that was held two months after the Great Workers' Struggle than did counties with fewer GWS protests. The estimate suggests that having experienced one

TABLE 2.2. The Great Workers' Struggle Protests and Electoral Support for the Opposition Candidates in the 1987 Presidential Election

	Opposition Vote Share (1987)
Great Workers' Struggle Protests	0.135***
	(0.045)
NKDP Vote Share (1985 Legislative)	11.777*
	(6.029)
Urbanization	7.620***
	(1.526)
(Log) College Student Population	1.439**
	(0.628)
Honam Region	48.113***
	(1.836)
Yŏngnam Region	0.249
	(1.748)
N	211
R^2	0.805
Adjusted R^2	0.799
Residual Std. Error	10.082 (df = 204)
F Statistic	140.265*** (df = 6; 204)

Note: Standard errors are in parentheses.
$^*p < 0.1$, $^{**}p < 0.05$, $^{***}p < 0.01$

additional protest during the GWS is associated with 0.14% more votes for the opposition candidates.

In estimating the average causal (or treatment) effect of industrial complexes on labor activism in 1987, I follow Acharya, Blackwell, and Sen (2016) and use a two-stage regression estimator called the sequential g-estimator (Joffe and Greene 2009; Vansteelandt 2009) to estimate the controlled direct effect of industrial complexes, which is the causal effect of industrial complexes when the mediator is fixed at the same value for all units. I do so because estimating the treatment effect while controlling for post-treatment covariates may introduce post-treatment bias into the analysis. In this case, the proposed mechanism (the moderating variable or the moderator) driving the treatment effect of industrial complexes on labor protests is the concentration of manufacturing factories, *Manufacturing Firms (1987)*, which is a post-treatment covariate that is directly or indirectly affected by the treatment itself (i.e., construction of industrial complexes). Previous research supports the argument for this mechanism, showing that workers in large, heavy-industry companies concentrated in industrial complexes are better able to organize unions and engage in confrontational strategies than are workers who are dispersed through numer-

46   Seeds of Mobilization

ous small firms (Huang 1999; J. Kim 1993, 199; Orru, Woosely Biggart, and Hamilton 1997; G.-Y. Shin 1994). Additionally, in *Korean Workers: The Culture and Politics of Class Formation*, Hagen Koo (2001) identifies the concentrated pattern of industrialization as one of the features that contributed to the development of working-class identity in Korea—here I suggest that its role expanded into other realms, too.

To measure the concentration of factories in each county, I use the number of manufacturing firms found in the *Report on Mining and Manufacturing Survey* (*Kwanggongŏp t'onggye chosa pogosŏ*) published by Kyŏngje Kihoegwŏn (Economic Planning Board) in 1987.[23] This measure, which is the most comprehensive one that I was able to locate at the county level, captures the mediating role that the concentration of manufacturing firms (resulting from the government's construction of industrial complexes) would play in the causal pathway. That is, although a county may contain manufacturing firms regardless of whether it also contains an industrial complex, the number of manufacturing firms is likely to increase with the presence of an industrial complex. As the summary statistics (in table 2.3) show, the number of manufacturing firms ranged from 2 (minimum) to 3,394 (maximum), with a mean of 243 firms and a standard deviation of 492 firms.

TABLE 2.3. Summary Statistics

Statistic	N	Mean	St. Dev.	Min	Max
Outcome Variable					
Labor Protest Events (1987)	214	5.178	20.449	0	253
Industrial Complex Variables					
Presence of Industrial Complex	214	0.196	0.398	0	1
Duration of Industrial Complex	214	2.752	6.164	0	26
Pretreatment Covariates					
Distance to Nearest Port (*m*)	214	52,419.410	33,699.910	971.486	148,125.500
Prop. Rural Households (1960)	214	55.818	27.449	0.012	86.460
Prop. Employed in Manufacturing (1960)	214	7.052	7.672	0.858	55.203
Population (1960)	214	117,026.300	76,319.300	8,866	702,863
1987 Covariates					
Manufacturing Firms (1987)	214	243.379	492.305	2	3,394
Unemployment (1985)	214	0.395	0.105	0.161	0.723
Population Density (1985)	214	0.138	0.427	0.003	4.102
Population (1985)	214	185,726.300	233,925.800	17,281	2,029,853
June Democratic Uprising (1987)	214	0.318	0.467	0	1

The analysis also includes post-treatment control variables for the mediator-outcome relationship, which are unemployment, population density, and population in 1985.[24] In addition to these controls, I include a dummy variable for counties that experienced protests during the June Democratic Uprising, a nationwide pro-democracy protest in 1987 that occurred one to two months before the GWS. This variable is important to include because the uprising could have provided a political opportunity for the GWS protestors (Koo 2001, 162). Lastly, I include four pretreatment confounders: distance to the nearest port, proportion of rural households, proportion of employed population in manufacturing, and population in 1960.[25] These confounders capture the geographic conditions and locational efficiency that the government considered in allocating industrial complexes, especially during the early phase of the development of industrial complexes. These confounders are included in the analysis to examine whether the presence of an industrial complex— not these geographic conditions—has a causal effect on the dependent variable—labor activism.

Empirical Analysis

To estimate the direct effect of industrial complexes on labor protests and ensure that it is not completely driven by the mediator, I follow Acharya, Blackwell, and Sen (2016) and estimate the average controlled direct effect (ACDE). This measure indicates that the industrial complexes had an actual direct effect on the outcome (i.e., labor protests) when it is statistically significant and greater than zero. The difference between ACDE and the total effect (or the average treatment effect; ATE) would tell us the extent to which a mediator participates in a mechanism, either through (1) indirect effects or (2) the (causal) interaction between the treatment and mediator at the individual (in this case, county) level.[26]

Table 2.4 displays the total effect of industrial complexes in columns (1) and (3) for *Presence of IC* and *Duration of IC*. Columns (2) and (4) report the average controlled direct effect of industrial complexes setting *Manufacturing Firms (1987)* to its mean value. The estimated ACDEs for both *Presence of IC* and *Duration of IC* are statistically significant and positive, suggesting that there is a strong direct effect of industrial complexes on labor protests (that is not completely driven by the mediator). As illustrated in the table, during the GWS, there were approximately eight more protests in counties with industrial complexes than in those without industrial complexes, holding everything else at constant and fixing the mediator at its mean.

48 Seeds of Mobilization

TABLE 2.4. Effects of Industrial Complexes

	Labor Protests, 1987			
	(1)	(2)	(3)	(4)
Presence of IC	11.924***	7.636***		
	(1.770)	(2.650)		
Duration of IC			0.885***	0.560***
			(0.112)	(0.094)
Province Fixed Effects	✓	✓	✓	✓
1960 Covariates	✓	✓	✓	✓
1987 Covariates		✓		✓
Bootstrapped SEs		✓		✓
Model	OLS	Seq. g-est.	OLS	Seq. g-est.
N	214	214	214	214
R^2	0.823	0.822	0.834	0.828

Note: Baseline estimates are reported in columns (1) and (3). Columns (2) and (4) report the average controlled direct effect (ACDE) under Manufacturing Firms (1987) = mean of Manufacturing Firms (1987). Columns (2) and (4) use sequential g-estimator of Joffe and Greene (2009) and Vansteelandt (2009) to estimate the ACDE of industrial complexes. First-stage estimates from the sequential g-estimation model are reported in the online appendix A2.1.

$^*p < 0.1, ^{**}p < 0.05, ^{***}p < 0.01$

And, ceteris paribus, a five-year increase in the duration of industrial complexes is associated with an increase of three protests, with the mediator set at its mean for all units. These results demonstrate that industrial complexes directly and indirectly contributed to the increased labor activism, and that counties that had industrial complexes for a longer period of time had more protests during the GWS.

To ensure that these results are not driven by the modeling assumptions in sequential g-estimation, I also perform nearest-neighbor Mahalanobis distance matching and find that there is a statistically significant and positive effect of the presence of industrial complexes on labor protests in 1987. The full results are reported in figure A2.1 and table A2.2 in the online appendix.

To assess the strength of the causal mechanism, I examine the difference between the ATE and ACDE. As seen in table 2.4, the estimated ACDEs in columns (2) and (4) are smaller than the estimated ATEs in columns (1) and (3) (assuming that there is no interaction between the treatment and the mediators at the individual levels). In fact, fixing the mediator eliminates about 36% and 25% of the ATE of *IC Presence* and *IC Duration*, respectively. Figure 2.3 further shows that the effect of industrial complexes (for both *Presence of IC* and *Duration of IC*) on labor protests

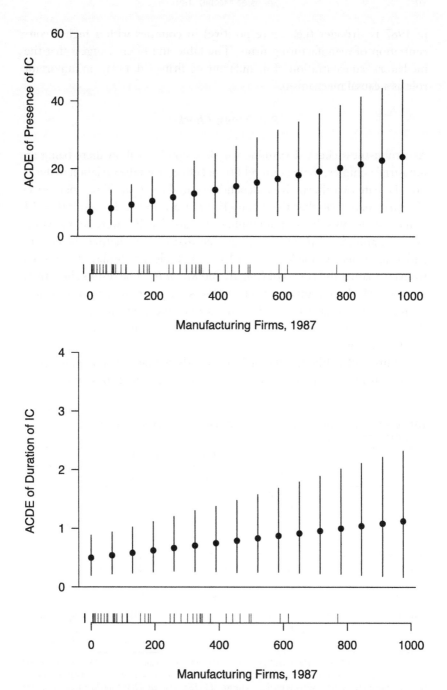

Fig 2.3. The average controlled direct effect (ACDE) of industrial complexes as a function of the fixed level of manufacturing firms. The vertical lines are 95% confidence intervals from 1,000 bootstrapped replications.

50   Seeds of Mobilization

in 1987 is stronger (i.e., more positive) in counties with a higher concentration of manufacturing firms. The table and figure suggest that the mediator—concentration of manufacturing firms—did play an important role as a causal mechanism.[27]

Robustness Checks

As a robustness check, I examine whether, conditional on there being an industrial complex, there is any additional effect from the variation in duration. I create two alternative independent variables, *Long IC* (a binary variable that marks whether the county had at least one IC for more than 14 years—the mean value of the number of years that ICs were in operation in 1987) and *Recent IC* (a binary variable that marks whether the county had at least one IC for less than 14 years). Table 2.5 displays the results from estimating the effects of *Long IC* and *Recent IC*. The results show that, as expected, the treatment effect of ICs is stronger (based on statistical significance) and larger (based on the size of the coefficient) in counties that had ICs for a more extended time compared to those that had ICs for shorter amounts of time.

Additionally, although the main results show that the geographic concentration of firms played a significant role as a causal mechanism, one

TABLE 2.5. Additional Effects from the Variation in the Duration of Industrial Complexes

	Labor Protests, 1987			
	(1)	(2)	(3)	(4)
Recent IC	4.340*	3.468*		
	(2.304)	(2.803)		
Long IC			16.578***	9.681***
			(2.417)	(4.147)
Province Fixed Effects	✓	✓	✓	✓
1960 Covariates	✓	✓	✓	✓
1987 Covariates		✓		✓
Bootstrapped SEs		✓		✓
Model	OLS	Seq. g-est.	OLS	Seq. g-est.
N	214	214	214	214
R^2	0.786	0.800	0.824	0.818

Note: Baseline estimates are reported in columns (1) and (3). Columns (2) and (4) report the average controlled direct effect (ACDE) under Manufacturing Firms (1987) = mean of Manufacturing Firms (1987). Columns (2) and (4) use sequential g-estimator of Joffe and Greene (2009) and Vansteelandt (2009) to estimate the ACDE of industrial complexes.

$^*p < 0.1$, $^{**}p < 0.05$, $^{***}p < 0.01$

may wonder whether the effect of industrial complexes on labor protests in 1987 was driven by some other factor, possibly even to a greater extent. The most obvious and plausible such factor is population change resulting from the construction of industrial complexes. Rural-urban migration became a common phenomenon during industrialization, and it is likely that the construction encouraged such migration. The resulting changes in population makeup and size could have impacted the level of labor protests. Another external factor that could have plausibly impacted the GWS protests was the political opportunity presented by the aforementioned June Democratic Uprising. As documented by scholars of social movements, political opportunity has been one of the major factors that explain the mobilization of movement participants as well as the success and failure of social movements (e.g., Kitschelt 1986; McAdam 1982; McAdam, Tarrow, and Tilly 2012; Meyer 2004).

To address the concerns that such factors could have been driving the observed effect, I use sequential g-estimation to estimate the ACDE of industrial complexes while fixing each mediator—(log) population and June Democratic Uprising—at a certain value for all counties.[28] Showing that there is a nonzero ACDE would suggest that the effect of industrial complexes is not exclusively due to population change or political opportunity. I also separately compare the ATE and ACDE for each mediator to estimate support for the preferred mechanism. As shown in figure 2.4, the estimated ACDEs are statistically significant, positive, and greater than zero, suggesting that the effect of industrial complexes on labor protests is not completely driven by these two factors.[29] Additionally, while fixing the number of manufacturing firms eliminates about 36% of the ATE, fixing the population eliminates about 20% of the ATE, and fixing the June Democratic Uprising eliminates only about 7% of the ATE.[30] These results suggest that the concentration of manufacturing firms appears to play a greater role as a causal mechanism than do the two alternative factors.

Conclusion

The results of the statistical analyses of this chapter demonstrate that there is indeed a strong direct effect of the industrial complexes built during the authoritarian era on labor protests during the democratic transition period. It also shows that the proposed causal mechanism—concentration of factories—plays a significant role in the causal pathway between the two. Moreover, the analyses reveal that the presence of at least one industrial

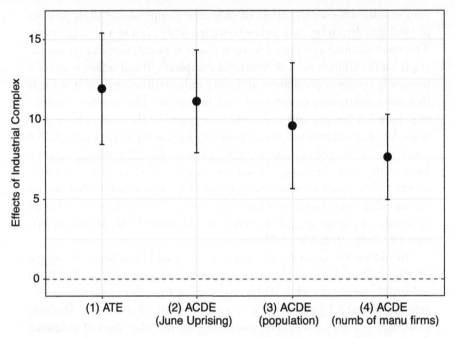

Fig 2.4. Coefficients on Presence of IC compared. The vertical lines are 95% confidence intervals from 1,000 bootstrapped replications.

complex in a given county and the *longer* duration of such a presence are associated with a greater number of labor protests during the 1987 Great Workers' Struggle. This finding is significant because it demonstrates that the level of labor activism exhibited in 1987 was not a spontaneous outcome. Rather, it was reflective of the accumulated growth of the labor movement that was shaped by the ecological conditions surrounding the complexes (to be discussed in chapter 3).

In Korea, the majority of manufacturing industries in the 1970s were located in large urban areas around the major axis connecting Seoul and Pusan. By 1984, approximately 50% of all manufacturing workers were located in the Seoul-Kyŏngin area (Seoul, Inch'ŏn, and the surrounding areas in Kyŏnggi Province). Another 40% were located in the southeastern Yŏngnam region, which was closely tied to the Heavy Chemical Industry Drive in the 1970s that led to the creation of industrial complexes in Ulsan, Masan, Ch'angwŏn, Kumi, and Okp'o. Figure 2.5 shows the concentration of workers in different regions of Korea over time, measured by the number of workers per factory. First, it shows that the concentration of

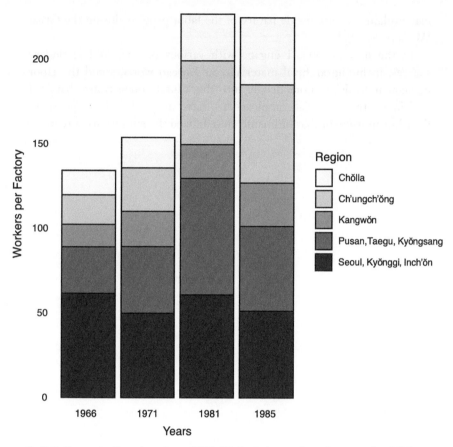

Fig 2.5. Concentration of workers, 1966–85. Statistics are from Sanggongbu (Ministry of Commerce) (1989).

workers increased over time, as demonstrated by the increasing heights of the bars across the *x*-axis. Second, the concentration was highest in the Seoul-Kyŏngin region (marked by black) in the 1960s and 1970s, when (lower levels of) labor activism (predominantly by female workers) was observed in small light manufacturing firms. The concentration of factory workers in the Yŏngnam region (marked by the darkest shade of gray) was also higher in 1981 compared to that in 1971, which is consistent with the expectation that the concentration of workers would increase in this region with the HCI Drive that began in 1973. Lastly, the figure shows that by the mid-1980s, when labor activism was much stronger overall, the concentration of workers was relatively even across the country, which may explain the nationwide nature of the labor protests during the Great Workers' Struggle.

In the next chapter, I engage with various primary and secondary sources, including archival materials, on Korean workers and the labor movement to delve more deeply into this causal connection—that is, I explain *how* the industrial complexes facilitated the gradual development of the labor movement that ultimately destabilized the authoritarian regime.

THREE

Manufacturing Protests

*Ecology of Industrial Complexes and
the Labor Movement*

Despite the overall weakness of the labor movement vis-à-vis the strong authoritarian state, Korean workers developed a stronger movement than their counterparts in other newly industrialized East Asian economies (Deyo 1989; Huang 1999; Y. Lee 2011). The strength of the movement was reflected in the 1987 Great Workers' Struggle and, as the statistical analysis in the preceding chapter has shown, the intensity of labor protest in any given area was driven not only by political opportunity (presented by the 1987 June Democratic Uprising) but also—and to a greater extent—by the presence of the government-built industrial complexes. This finding underscores the impacts of industrial policy and the underlying strength of the labor movement, which had to be in place for external circumstances (such as increased political opportunities) to trigger further action.

In this chapter, I argue that the ecological conditions surrounding the industrial complexes played a critical role in facilitating the labor movement's gradual growth and in building its underlying strength. The physical gathering of large numbers of people in a given space or place is an important feature of nearly every form of contentious politics, including but not limited to the South Korean labor movement. This notion has been reflected in studies that employ an ecological perspective on contentious politics and social movements.[1] Due to variations in the contexts where such social movements emerge and develop, scholars have focused on different aspects of spatiality and their impacts on social movements, and this empirical reality is reflected in the literature. For example, Elizabeth Perry's (1980) study of Chinese peasant rebellions in the 19th and 20th centuries showed that the harsh environment of the Huai-pei region shaped not only the collective survival strategies of the peasants but also their participation in rebellions and revolutions. Roger V. Gould's (1991, 1995) research on the nineteenth-century Paris uprisings found that, unlike the 1848 insurgence that was mobilized around class identity, the 1871 Paris Commune was based on neighborhood solidarity. He explained this change in organization ecology by showing that Baron Haussmann's urban construction project in Paris (1852–80) created cross-class neighborhoods on the outskirts of the city, where a geographically based identity became the new basis of social solidarity. Dingxin Zhao's (1998) study of the 1989 pro-democracy movement in Beijing also demonstrated that campus ecology not only nurtured student networks that were essential to student mobilization but also produced ecology-dependent strategies of mobilization (such as hanging posters in a centrally located area on campus and chanting around dormitories before going out to the streets) that increased students' participation in protests. Likewise, Joel Stillerman (2003) found that the characteristics of the built environment and the everyday spatial routines of metal workers and coal miners in Chile shaped the mobilizing structures of strikers. This somewhat eclectic line of research demonstrates that social movement mobilization and outcomes are shaped by the movement's ecological conditions, which should be understood as "the spatial characteristics of a physical environment and the accompanying density, distribution, composition, place-based relations, and routine special activities of a given population" (Zhao 1998, 1523).

In the case of South Korea, the ecological conditions surrounding the industrial complexes facilitated the formation of mobilizing structures—defined by Doug McAdam (2017, 194) as "the collective vehicles through which people initially mobilize and begin to engage in sustained collective action"—that were critical to the development of the labor movement. Such ecological conditions included, for example, the high concentration of factories in related industries within each industrial complex, which contributed to the formation of a relatively homogeneous labor force inside those industrial complexes. The built environment—especially the shared living arrangements within and close to the factory compounds—nurtured small group-based networks, which facilitated the development of workers' consciousness and solidarity among workers. Such development was essential for any kind of labor activism (including the establishment of independent unions and the organization of strikes) to occur in a given firm. These ecological conditions were also put to good use by social activists, who took advantage of the ways they made it possible to mobilize workers within and across firms. Lastly, when political opportunities arose, the ecological conditions contributed to the spread of protests and led to the development of ecology-dependent strategies of collective action. These strategies were central to the interfirm solidarity struggles in the 1980s, including the 1985 Kuro Solidarity Strike and the 1987 Great Workers' Struggle, which showcased the increased mobilizational capacity of the workers. A close examination of the ways in which the ecology of industrial complexes fostered networks and solidarity among workers as well as movement strategies and protest tactics that generated cross-class, intra- and interfirm mobilization—offered in this chapter—demonstrates *how* the autocrats' industrial policy inadvertently strengthened labor vis-à-vis the authoritarian regime.

This chapter draws on primary qualitative data and secondary literature published in Korean to demonstrate how exactly the ecological conditions surrounding the industrial complexes contributed to the development of ecology-dependent strategies by workers and social activists. Archival data comes from the Seoul Museum of History and the Korea Democracy Foundation archives, including its oral archives. Other qualitative sources used and triangulated are the various publications by Christian and student organizations that were involved in the labor movement during the authoritarian period. These include the Korea Student Christian Federation (Han'guk Kidok Haksaenghoe Ch'ongyŏnmaeng) and the Urban Industrial Mission (UIM; Tosi Sanŏp Sŏn'gyohoe).

An Ecological Approach to Examining the South Korean Labor Movement

The impact of the industrial environment on South Korea's labor movement has not gone unnoticed—various researchers have noted that the highly concentrated pattern of industrialization (dense concentration of factories) within the urban areas (Koo 2001) and dormitory living and leisure time activities (W. Kim 2004; Koo 2001; Won 2006; J.-C. Yu 2010; K. Yu 2001) contributed to the development of working-class identity and solidarity. However, the existing studies do not explicitly spell out the design factors of industrial complexes and their spatial arrangements, which played a significant role in that process, and they don't explain the

58   Seeds of Mobilization

ecology-dependent process of mobilization that occurred among workers and social activists as a result of those arrangements. This chapter explores the ecology of industrial complexes and demonstrates the ways in which the living and working environment of the industrial complexes gradually shaped the labor mobilization process in the 1970s and 1980s by providing a structural foundation for the formation of independent unions, the emergence of interfirm solidarity struggles, and social activists' involvement in the labor movement.

The Ecology of Industrial Complexes in South Korea

The well-known idiom that "there is strength in numbers"—that "a group of people has more influence or power than one person" (Merriam-Webster 2021)—resonates strongly with social movements. In the case of the South Korean labor movement, it was the physical features of the government-built industrial complexes that not only resulted in the high concentration of workers in each industrial complex but also in the homogeneity of the industrial workers' working and living experiences that had significant implications for labor organizing.

The government-built industrial complexes in Korea were massive in scale and concentrated a large number of workers—often in related industries—into a single designated area. By 1987 (the year in which the Great Workers' Struggle erupted), there were 58 industrial complexes operating in the country (Chungso Kiŏp Hyŏptong Chohap Chunganghoe [Korea Federation of Small and Medium Business] 1989).[2] While variation existed across industrial complexes, a single industrial complex contained up to 2,065 firms and more than 140,000 workers (see table 3.1).[3] The Herfindahl-Hirschman Index (HHI; a commonly accepted measure of market concentration in economics) calculated for each industrial complex (using data on industrial complexes from 1987 found in the 1989 publication by the Korea Federation of Small and Medium Business) also shows that the industrial complexes were populated by workers from the same or related industries. The HHI ranges from 1 (least concentrated market) to 10,000 (most concentrated), and according to the U.S. Department of Justice,[4] HHI values of less than 1,500 represent low concentration, between 1,500 and 2,500 represent moderate concentration, and more than 2,500 represent high concentration. The closer a market is to a monopoly, the higher the market's concentration and the lower its competition. In my case, the closer an industrial complex is dominated by one or few indus-

TABLE 3.1. Size and Number of Firms and Employees of Industrial Complexes

	Mean	St. Dev.	Min	Max
Size (thousand m^2)	3,787.41	8,117.95	42	50,781
Firms	135	295	1	2,065
Employees	16,025.52	26,457.09	80	142,920

Source: Chungso Kiŏp Hyŏptong Chohap Chunganghoe (Korea Federation of Small and Medium Business) (1989).

Note: Agricultural industrial complexes are excluded.

tries, the higher the industrial complex's concentration of workers from few/similar industries. If, for example, there were only one industry in an industrial complex, the HHI of that industrial complex would be 10,000. The calculated HHI values of Korea's industrial complexes in 1987 ranged from 1,700 to 10,000, with an average of 4,988.[5] These values imply that the government-built industrial complexes in Korea were indeed concentrated with only a few industries, creating a relatively homogenous labor force that could better relate with one another in their workplace struggles and grievances.

In addition to the relatively homogenous labor force that was formed within these industrial complexes, the physical structure of the industrial complexes intensified interactions among workers during and outside of working hours. The industrial complexes were physically separated from the surrounding community by a gate, a wire fence, or a brick/cement wall. The management office (*kyŏngbisil*) was located at the front gate of an industrial complex, and its security officers strictly guarded the entrance. Moreover, in addition to factory buildings, industrial complexes typically (but not always) contained other housing and welfare-related facilities such as dormitories (*kisuksa*), cafeterias, welfare centers (*pokchigwan*), health clinics, and communal grounds (*undongjang*). The dormitories imposed strict discipline on workers, including limiting outside trips and staying outside overnight. Consequently, the workers of industrial complexes not only shared similar working experiences (by laboring in close proximity to one another in the same or related industries) but also spent their limited leisure time and recreational activities together at these additional facilities. As the subsequent section will show, the ecology of the industrial complexes that encompassed workers' living arrangements provided favorable conditions for workers to develop class consciousness and engage in collective action.

The Physical Structure of the Workers' Living Environment

During the industrialization period, workers' living arrangements were designed to control them and to benefit the companies that employed them as well as the authoritarian regime that derived its regime legitimacy from economic performance. While these arrangements did both of those things, they ultimately contributed to the building of the labor movement as well.

Among the most common living arrangements were factory dormitories. Starting in the 1970s, when mass production of export goods at larger factories required better workforce management, these modern-looking buildings were built either inside factory compounds or in close proximity to the industrial complex in question. Some tenant companies had their own dormitories, and others shared a dormitory building for their workers: for example, at the Korea Export Industrial Complex, some dormitories housed employees from and were managed by single companies (such as Daewoo Apparel), whereas others (such as the Ch'ŏlsan Apartment, which was built by the government-owned Korea National Housing Corporation [Han'guk T'oji Chu'taeg Kongsa]) served as the dormitory for workers of various tenant companies of the Korea Export Industrial Complex. At the Masan Free Export Zone, the government provided a dormitory that housed 2,050 workers from 31 tenant companies (in 1987) in addition to a welfare hall and a health clinic (S. Kim 1997, 37).

During the industrialization period, such arrangements were in the interest of the state, capitalists, and laborers. Providing accommodation inside or close to the factory compound allowed both the state and the capitalists to control and retain labor, guaranteeing that workers reached government-set export goals. To these ends, dormitory living was accompanied by long working hours, body searches, strict curfews, and oversight by head residents (*sagam*) to prevent the loss of labor hours and productivity.

As for the workers, there were many compelling reasons to seek factory employment in the city, especially at a large factory (*taegyumo kongjang*) that provided housing accommodations. Despite the restrictions it imposed on their autonomy, such employment represented a chance to escape poverty and achieve upward mobility for many young men and women in the countryside. For these migrant workers, dormitory living reduced not only housing costs but also time and transportation costs, and such savings were essential given that monthly wages could barely cover the rent anywhere else—even for skilled, experienced workers. In June 1979, for example, the average monthly wages were ₩59,000 for an experienced worker at the

Kuro Industrial Complex (located in Seoul) who was in their third year at a company and who worked 48 hours overtime and two overnight shifts (and between ₩30,000 and ₩40,000 for an unskilled worker); in comparison, the average monthly rent for a room in nearby industrial complexes in Seoul and its surrounding areas around that time was ₩50,000 (DongA Ilbo 1980; Seoul Yŏksa Pangmulgwan 2013, 119). However, Kuro Industrial Complex workers living in factory dormitories only paid ₩9,000 for room and board and spent ₩16,000 on living expenses, leaving them with about ₩20,000 for savings (DongA Ilbo 1980). Similarly, outside of Seoul, factory workers at the Masan Free Export Zone (in Masan city, South Kyŏngsang Province) living outside the dormitory spent three times more on room, board, and transportation costs than those living in the dormitory (S. Kim 1997, 27).

In addition to these relatively low costs, workers were attracted to the well-equipped facilities and amenities inside factory dormitories. The dormitory building of Dongil Textiles Company, for example, had a game room, a meeting room, a music room, a reading room, a resting room, and a washing room.[6] Workers who visited Dongil Textiles described the factory compound as a "beautiful university campus," and they were especially impressed by the dormitory (W. Kim 2016, 205).

Living arrangements were particularly valuable for female workers, who received little or no formal education due to a patriarchal family structure that prioritized raising and investing in sons and who therefore needed more support to move into the workforce.[7] This is reflected in the numbers: in the 1970s, when female workers contributed heavily to the country's export-led industrialization (which at that point focused on light manufacturing), more than half of female workers resided outside their own house. These workers often lived communally in dormitories; such arrangements were most prevalent among female workers in the textile (43.4%), clothing (24.1%), and transportation (30.9%) sectors (Nodongch'ŏng 1973, 65). In the dormitories run by large factories, there were typically about 20 workers sharing one large room (Ko 2002, cited in J.-C. Yu 2010). At smaller factories, four workers shared a small room, and five to seven workers shared a larger room (Song 2002, cited in J.-C. Yu 2010).[8]

Although such living arrangement was more common among female workers, male migrant workers also resided in dormitories or housing provided by the company, which were proximate to the industrial complexes. Many opted to live in these housing accommodations to maximize the use of their limited leisure time due to their long working hours, including overnight work and overtime work on weekends (Won 2006, 316). For example, male workers of the *chaebŏl* Hyundai-affiliated companies at the Ulsan Mipo Industrial Complex (e.g., Hyundai Heavy Industries, Hyundai Mipo Dockyard, and Hyundai Wood Industries) lived together in dormitories and apartment buildings provided as company housing. The dormitory buildings were typically five stories tall, and each floor was divided by a corridor with ten rooms on each side (for 20 rooms total per floor). Two to three workers shared a room that was 3–5 *p'yong* (equivalent to 10–17 square meters) in size. Each floor contained a shared public bathroom and bath. Although there is no comprehensive data available for individual firms and industrial complexes, there were approximately 24,000 workers at Hyundai Heavy Industry in 1987, and more than half of the (predominantly male) employees are known to have lived in dormitories and company housing buildings (Won 2006, 305–321).

Dormitories were not the only option for housing near the industrial complexes, however. For workers who were employed at factories without housing accommodations or who wanted to escape the regulated dormitory life, it was possible to rent tiny rooms in rooming houses surrounding the industrial complexes. According to the Seoul Museum of History's publication on the history of Karibong-dong—a neighborhood in the Kuro district of Seoul, where the Korea Export Industrial Complex No. 1–3 (or the Kuro Industrial Complex, KIC) was located—a dire housing shortage caused by a significant increase in the number of workers at the KIC prompted the growth of private-sector rental homes (Seoul Museum of History 2015). These units (represented by the dots in fig. 3.1) were referred to as "beehive houses" (*pŏlchip*) or "chicken coop houses" (*takchangjip*) because the homes they contained were tiny and rented out in great numbers—each of these two- to three-story buildings of tiny rooms and shared bathrooms housed as many as 50 households. Additionally, to reduce living costs, many workers adjusted their working hours to share a single "beehive unit," usually consisting of a room, a kitchen, and a shared bathroom. There were typically three to four people—usually two with day shifts and two with night shifts—who pooled their money to share one room that was approximately 1.5 to 3 *p'yŏng* in size (5–10 square meters). In the worst cases, a single bathroom was shared by up to 65 people (W. Kim 2015, 56).

The physical structure of these rooming houses was similar to that of factory dormitories. These houses were usually U-shaped or L-shaped. Although these buildings looked like regular single-family houses from the outside, as shown in figure 3.2, as one entered the house, one would see a

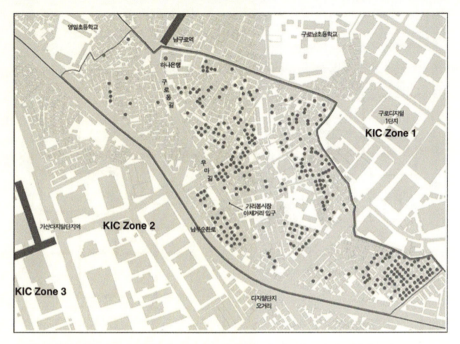

Fig 3.1. Beehive houses in Karibong-dong in Kuro district, Seoul. Credit: Seoul Museum of History (2013, 135). English text is added by the author.

corridor and doors for each main unit. Each of these units was equipped with a tiny living room and a small kitchen. In some units, the kitchens had a briquette furnace and a water faucet, but those without running water or sewers had to use the water in the courtyard that was located in the middle of the house. And all tenants shared public bathrooms. Given this similar physical structure of the rooming houses and factory dormitories, including room-sharing and bathroom-sharing arrangements, Korean factory workers—whether they lived inside or outside the industrial complex—had very similar living arrangements and experiences.

How Dormitories and Rooming Houses Provided the Foundation for Labor Activism

In Korea, class consciousness and solidarity among workers were essential for any kind of labor activism to occur (especially under a repressive authoritarian regime that prohibited or severely controlled protests), and the physical structure of the working and living environment surround-

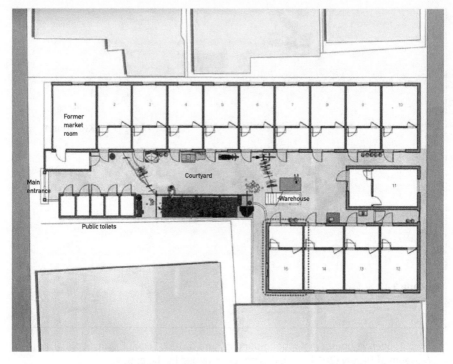

Fig 3.2. Floor plan of the ground floor of a beehive house in Karibong-dong. Credit: Seoul Museum of History (2015, 65).

ing the industrial complexes fostered both. Research has shown that, other factors being equal, the closer together people live, the greater the chance of unintentional contact and active group-making (e.g., Case 1981; Festinger, Schachter, and Back 1950; Michelson 1976; Whyte 1956), especially when there is a homogenous population (e.g., Gans 1967; Michelson 1976; Newcomb 1961). And as described in the previous section, whether they were living in factory dormitories or in rooming houses near the factory compounds, workers were living semipublic, homogenous lives. The lack of privacy enabled them not only to better relate to one another but also to become cognizant of their class position, given that they shared the same working and living experiences. For some groups of workers, this class consciousness was also derived from class inequality that was built into the physical structure of their living environment. For example, plant workers of the Hyundai-affiliated companies in Ulsan were placed in small apartments (as small as 4.5 *p'yŏng*), whereas senior managers were given large apartments (as large as 45 *p'yŏng*).[9] Hyundai plant workers—

Manufacturing Protests   65

who later initiated the Great Workers' Struggle—were thus able to form
a common identity based on their shared experiences with each other and
how dramatically they contrasted with the experiences of management and
managerial workers (Won 2006, 326).

Workers also connected with each other during their (limited) leisure time. Because their working hours were so long, workers typically
engaged in leisure activities within the confines of their immediate environment. They formed various "small groups" (*somoim*) based on hob-
bies, such as hiking, singing, *talchum* (mask dance or play), *pungmul*
(peasant band music and dance), writing *hanja* (Chinese characters used
in writing Korean), cooking, and flower arranging; they also created a
mutual aid society and book clubs. These small groups met regularly
inside and outside the factory compounds and also organized outings and
retreats. Regardless of where they occurred, though, small group meetings brought together workers from different divisions or shifts, or both,
and allowed them to share their working experiences and grievances
(Koo 2001; W. Kim 2004; Won 2006; J.-C. Yu 2010). At these gatherings, workers also had the opportunity to learn about labor laws and
discuss ways to improve poor working conditions. According to Hagen
Koo (2001, 75), "Some of these small groups remained primarily friendship or recreational groups, but most of them eventually turned into loci
where workers acquired a sharper class awareness and learned about the
importance of unions."

Although both male and female workers participated in such small
groups, one common leisure activity that was reserved specifically for male
workers was social drinking. Drinking mostly happened at pubs (*sŏnsulchip*)
and street stalls (*p'ojangmach'a*) right outside the factory compounds and
in the open spaces between the workers' residential buildings (Won 2006,
334–39). Because such places were easy to access from workers' living and
working quarters, social drinking provided male workers with opportunities to meet and communicate with many other workers—including those
from different divisions within their own company and those from other
companies. They shared not only their discontentment (regarding their
workplaces) but also information regarding their working conditions and
wage levels. This way of connecting people was so effective that Hyundai
Heavy Industries workers even organized a small group named *mŏkjahoe*
(translated as "let's eat group"). Although the group did explore the various
restaurants and pubs in Ulsan, it had an ulterior motive: to use the small
group network for democratic union activities (Won 2006, 339). In these
ways, the informal and formal small-group-based networks formed among

66 Seeds of Mobilization

workers in their working and living environment became the mobilizing structures for labor activism.

As workers became increasingly connected with each other and thus gradually developed class consciousness, they also started to devise *ecology-dependent strategies* for their democratic union movement—that is, they took advantage of the physical structure of the living environment in multiple ways. First, union leaders recruited members through networks formed inside dormitories. The independent union at Y.H. Trading Company (formed in 1975) created such a network and used it to recruit about 500 members (Han'guk Nodongja Pokchi Hyŏbŭihoe 1984, 45–46). In fact, of the few manufacturing firms that were able to form their own independent unions in the 1970s (e.g., Dongil Textiles, Wonpoong Textiles, Bando Trading Company, and Y.H. Trading Company), all had their own factory dormitories—and they were often used in this way. According to Chu Yŏn-ok, who organized the first union at the Han'guk Tongkyŏng Chŏnja (Korea Tongkyŏng Electronics) located inside the Masan Free Export Zone, the dormitory was a "reservoir" of potential union members:

> In order to organize a union [in the 1980s], we needed signatures of a minimum of thirty people. We agreed that each of us should bring three workers next time. . . . When we met on the evening of the 17th [of August 1987], we still didn't have thirty people. . . . I remember that Sun-hui *ŏnni* [older sister] did a lot of things for us at that time. She brought in a South Korean flag, placard, other things. But most importantly, she provided workers needed to organize the union since we did not have the necessary 30 workers. She went off to the Auxilium dormitory for Catholic workers and recruited any KTE [Korea Tongkyŏng Electronics] workers who were willing to come. At last we had thirty-six workers and we could organize. (S. Kim 1997, 116–17)

Similarly, in the 1980s, the union organizers of Karibong Electronics (located in Zone 1 of the Kuro Industrial Complex) and Rom-Korea (KIC Zone 3) visited the Ch'ŏlsan Apartment (the dormitory for workers of various tenant companies of the KIC) with the intention of increasing their union membership (KDF interview with Yun Hyeryŏn, August 2005). Workers from these two firms later joined the historic Kuro Solidarity Strike in 1985, which will be covered in detail later in this chapter.

Another ecology-dependent mobilization strategy adopted by workers was to exert control over the physical structure of their dormitories for union organizing. In order to use their factory dormitory buildings to form an independent union and carry out union activities, workers at Y.H. Trading Company fought to secure control over dormitory operations. In doing so, they formed their own dormitory operations committee (*kisuksa unyŏng wiwŏnhoe*) and ousted the existing head resident (*sagam*) of their dormitory (who the company originally had selected to monitor the workers) by electing their own representatives for each room and each building. Similarly, at Wonpoong Textiles, the unionized workers formed their own dormitory council (*kisuksa chach'ihoe*), ousted their *sagam*, and the union leaders—as the head of the dormitory council—operated the factory dormitory autonomously (W. Kim 2004, 121–22). The Wonpoong Textiles' 1982 "Dormitory Council Regulations" listed various living rules, specified the rights and duties of each dormitory member, and outlined the selection process for the president and executive leaders of the dormitory council (KDF Open Archives No. 00853553). Thus, factory dormitories not only housed potential union members but also themselves became political spaces for unionization.

Not surprisingly, both the companies and the government were aware of the role that dormitory living played in facilitating the democratic union movement, and they worked to weaken that movement in various ways. Companies tried to reduce the ecological benefit of dormitories—for example, Bando Trading Company reduced dormitory capacity (and provided their workers with bonuses so they would be less likely to become involved with the union) and the Dongil Textiles management separated union organizers from each other when assigning rooms (W. Kim 2004, 126). The police did not directly intervene with the dormitories in this way, but when surveilling labor activism, they closely monitored dormitory residents. An example is found in a police report produced by Seoul Nambu (Southern) Police Station in 1981 when the Chun Doo Hwan government was severely cracking down on labor. The "Research Report on the Collective Activity of Wonpoong Textiles Dormitory Members" states the following:

> We are reporting on a collective activity involving singing and dancing by approximately 120 workers on August 26th from 6:30 AM to 9:05 AM led by dormitory-living union representatives Yi Oksun (age 27) and Pak Chŏngsuk (age 23). . . . While approximately 60 workers living in the dormitory have given their statements that they were in Kwanak Mountain just for a morning hike, one could tell that they were engaged in collective resistance regarding vari-

68 Seeds of Mobilization

ous grievances they had since last March, including issues related to wage, union merger, and layoffs. (KDF Open Archives No. 0854038)

These accounts from primary and secondary sources illustrate that the factory dormitories and rooming houses surrounding the industrial complexes provided the structural foundations for workers to develop workers' consciousness and engage in labor activism. The workers as well as their employers and the state became aware of the mobilization potential that the workers' shared living arrangements had for labor activism.

Social Activists and the Development of the Labor Movement

In explaining the development of class consciousness among workers in Korea, scholars have emphasized the role of intellectuals in aiding the workers who were suffering from economic exploitation and political exclusion. Two groups of such intellectuals played key roles in the labor movement: Christian activists in the 1970s and college students in the 1980s. These groups helped mobilize workers by becoming factory workers themselves, setting up churches and welfare organizations for them, jump-starting the small groups mentioned earlier, and educating them through night schools. The remainder of this section first describes each of these two key groups and the nature of their involvement in and contribution to the labor movement. Subsequently, it shows the ways in which both groups deliberately considered the ecological conditions of industrial complexes in mobilizing the workers not just within each firm but across firms, thereby creating the mobilizing structures for future solidarity struggles that enhanced the collective power of the working class.

Christians

Progressive Christian groups were integral to the labor movement starting in the late 1950s and early 1960s, when they first became involved with labor as a way of sharing the gospel and expanding church membership. Their exposure to labor issues during evangelical work led them to link the attainment of religious salvation with the concern for social justice that was inherent in their faith (Cho 1981). Later in the 1960s and 1970s, both Catholic and Protestant groups—including the Young Catholic Workers (Jeunesse Ouvrière Chrétienne; JOC), the Methodist Urban Industrial Mission, and the Christian Academy—set up churches and social welfare organizations near the industrial complexes to increase their interactions with factory workers. They provided programs to educate workers about their rights and to help them form independent unions. A few dedicated Christian activists even lived and worked as factory workers—for example, Reverend Cho Sŭnghyŏk worked at Taesŏng Wood Industry as a laborer and aided the labor movement through the Inch'ŏn UIM. Reverend Cho Wha-Soon was another Methodist minister affiliated with the Inch'ŏn UIM. She worked at Dongil Textiles Company and, throughout the 1970s, played a critical role in the Dongil Textiles labor struggle, which later became a rallying point for the larger democracy movement (Koo 2001).

This progressive segment of the Korean Christian church was the only ally available to the workers during Park Chung Hee's repressive Yusin period (1972–79) when the official union structure (which might otherwise have offered support) was completely co-opted by the government. The church functioned as a shelter and "protective shield" (*pangŏbyŏk*) for the worker-activists (interview with the Inchon UIM staff worker Ch'oe Yŏnghŭi quoted in W. Kim 2006, 539; KDF interview with Pang Yongsŏk, November 2010). The authoritarian government considered such support of workers to be troublesome and so began repressing the JOC and UIM in the mid- to late 1970s. Following the 1979 Y.H. Incident (or the Y.H. Worker Protest),[10] the state-influenced media publicly targeted these organizations, such as by publishing articles containing the phrase "if the UIM comes, the company will go bankrupt" (*tosani tŭrŏ omyŏn tosan handa*).[11] The Park regime accused these organizations of being procommunist and then arrested, jailed, and tortured their leaders on charges of procommunist activities.[12] These repressive tactics, as well as the movement's turn to the radical left after the Kwangju Massacre in 1980 (which will be discussed in more detail in the next section) and the more violent and disruptive protest tactics of the 1980s (such as street demonstrations and the use of Molotov cocktails), resulted in the diminished role of Christians in the movement (G.-W. Shin et al. 2011, 25).

Despite this reduced participation, Christians left a lasting mark on the movement. Although Won Kim (2006) states that it is important not to exaggerate their achievements, as the effects of Christian organizations were not uniform across all firms,[13] Kim points out that they introduced the small group system that facilitated the formation of workers' class consciousness and the establishment of independent unions early in the labor movement. As we will see in the rest of the chapter, small groups continued to play an important role in mobilizing workers during and after the democratic union movement of the 1970s.

College Students

In the 1980s, as the role of Christian activists faded, college students played a significant role in politicizing the labor movement. As will be discussed in more detail in chapter 4, the expansion of student enrollment in universities in the 1980s contributed to the development of a nationwide student movement. More and more university students came from provincial lower- and middle-class households and the influx of working-class students increased the vigor of student activism (Cheon 2018, 44). Although there had been a few college students who individually dropped out of school to become disguised workers in the 1970s, it was in the 1980s that college students participated in the labor movement in a more systematic and collective manner.

The turning point of the student movement occurred in the wake of the 1979 assassination of Park Chung Hee, which ended the repressive Yusin era and ushered in a brief period of political openness called the "Spring of Seoul." The rising sense of hope for a more democratic society was crushed during the repressive response to the antigovernment protests in the city of Kwangju in South Chŏlla Province on May 18–27, 1980, when Chun Doo Hwan's new military regime killed upwards of 200 people (M. Lee 1990, 6).[14] The 1980 Kwangju Massacre heightened the militant antigovernment sentiment among students and was a defining moment for the larger democracy movement, also known as the *minjung* (people's) movement.[15]

In the aftermath of this uprising, the student movement became radicalized (Dong 1987; N. Lee 2007). Many college students were critical of the U.S. role in the massacre and became disenchanted with Western liberal democracy.[16] The early 1980s was also when intellectuals were "hit by a wave of socialism" (N. Lee 2005, 918). Student activists began to seriously study the writings of Karl Marx, Vladimir Lenin, and Kim Il Sung; this study led them to them see revolution as the goal of the student movement and to understand the working class as the main historical agent of revolution (Park 2005).

At this point, a newly enacted government policy presented students with a novel way to organize workers: becoming factory workers. The labor law of 1980 prohibited "third-party intervention," making it illegal for a local union to receive assistance from its industrial union or the FKTU when bargaining with the company. Because this change meant that labor bargaining was now only possible between the company and the plant union, anyone, including students, wishing to aid the workers in their labor negotiations had to become one of the workers (N. Lee 2005, 918). University students were thus "reborn as revolutionary workers" (N. Lee 2007, 256–57). In this new role, students both promoted workers' rights and began to mobilize workers to achieve the larger political goal of ending Chun's authoritarian rule and achieving a "just society."

The student movement at this time adopted labor praxis (*hyŏnjangron*) as its major strategy.[17] They entered factories disguised as workers and aimed to help politicize workers by creating the worker-student alliance (*nohak yŏndae*). Students considered such factory work (*kongjang hwaldong; konghwal*) to be an essential part of their movement (Han'guk Kidok Hak-saenghoe Ch'ongyŏnmaeng 1984, 9). They researched working conditions, formed small groups, and instilled political consciousness among workers through study, debate, and recreational activities. Because it was illegal for them to take factory jobs at that time, such work established one's willingness to risk prison and torture and thus demonstrated their political commitment (S. Kim 1997, 132). This "infiltration" or "bodily intervention" by students peaked in the mid-1980s when more than 3,000 college students became students-turned-workers (*haksaeng ch'ulsin nodongja; hakch'ul*); in 1985–86 alone, the police arrested "671 such agitators" (Ogle 1990, 99). According to Yu Kyŏngsun (2006, 201), "There was almost no factory without students-turned-workers. . . . The exact numbers are unknown, but they were at almost every single factory," and the estimated number of students-turned-workers was around 10,000 or more.

This alliance was instrumental in bringing labor power to the forefront of the democracy movement (Koo 2001; N. Lee 2007), and by the mid- to late 1980s, workers became more powerful and independent as a class and as a collective force. College students from across the country were directly participating in the labor movement en masse, and workers, professionals, and general citizens were now joining intellectuals, dissident politicians, students, and religious groups in the pro-democracy protests that ultimately resulted in democratic reforms in 1987.

Social Activists and Their Ecology-Dependent Strategies of Labor Mobilization

Both Christian and student activists studied the government's industrial policies and deliberately considered the ecological conditions of the industrial areas in their efforts to engage with workers and aid the labor movement. As illustrated in a 1976 report produced by the Inch'ŏn UIM, the Christian organization was cognizant of the government's industrial poli-

72 Seeds of Mobilization

cies and planned its mission work so that it would reach workers at the newly constructed industrial complexes:

> We first focused our activities in the heavy industry zone surrounding Inch'ŏn. As new industrial complexes are being built in accordance with the government's export-led economic development policy, we now have no choice but to spread out our team members to these new industrial zones to carry out our mission work. We have created mission plans for each industrial area and reorganized the teams that are currently carrying out mission work to achieve freedom, justice, and peace in these areas. (KDF Open Archives No. 00441922)

The JOC likewise reflected this approach in its 1972 motto: "Let's build churches inside the factories." At this point, both organizations expanded their focus beyond the few union leaders who were Christians and members of the JOC or UIM churches by reaching out to non-Christian workers at individual factories (W. Kim 2005).[18]

To this end, all UIM pastors and staff members were newly required to work at a factory for more than a year, during which they aided the workers by providing physical spaces for the recreational and cultural small-group activities described earlier in this chapter. Inside the Kuro Industrial Complex, for example, there were more than ten so-called *minjung* churches (i.e., churches that supported people's social movements, including the labor movement); these churches offered mission programs such as the Kuro Labor Counseling Center, the Labor Human Rights Center, and the South Seoul Worker Support Center (Seoul Museum of History 2015, 43). At the Masan Free Export Zone, the JOC Catholic Women's Center and its Labor Counseling Office greatly assisted the factory workers by hosting small group meetings (four to five workers in each group) and providing classes on how to organize unions (S. Kim 1997). The Yŏngdŭngp'o UIM alone organized 70 small groups in 1974, 80 in 1975, and 100 in 1979. Alongside this growth in the number of UIM small groups, the frequency of small group meetings increased from 1,648 in 1973 to 5,200 in 1979, and the number of participants likewise increased dramatically, from 11,536 in 1973 to 22,564 in 1977 to 62,400 in 1979 (Yŏngdŭngp'o Sanŏp Sŏn'gyohoe 40-yŏnsa Kihoek Wiwŏnhoe 1998, 135–37).

In addition to providing space and structure for the small groups, Christian organizations also set up night schools near industrial complexes. Night schools (*yahak*) were initially set up to help prepare workers for mid-

Manufacturing Protests 73

dle and high school Graduation Equivalency Examinations (*kŏmjŏng kosi*).[19] They usually met two hours a day, four or five times a week. Starting in the mid-1970s, night schools were usually taught by university students, and they started to focus more heavily on labor issues by teaching workers about labor laws and workers' rights, which contributed to the development of class consciousness and solidarity among workers. The "Guidelines for Night School Activity" (*Yahak hwaldong annaesŏ*), published by the Korean Student Christian Federation in 1981 (KDF Open Archives No. 00871651),[20] provided ecology-based information regarding site selection for night schools:

> First choose places that are conveniently situated and facing numerous social issues [resulting from the rapid industrialization], such as slums, industrial complexes, and shoe shine places. [In Seoul] areas with industrial complexes such as Karibong-dong, Kuro-dong, Yangnam-dong, [and] Yŏngdŭngp'o-dong are the best places [to set up night schools] as they have the potential [for night schools] to flourish. Once you have decided on an area, you need to secure a venue [to host the night school]. As venues, you could use church buildings, public institution buildings, rental rooms, and tents, but Catholic churches that are members of the JOC would be great. (Han'guk Kidok Haksaenghoe Ch'ongyŏnmaeng 1981, 25)

Similarly, the "Guidelines for Factory Work" (*Kongjang hwaldong annaesŏ*), also produced by the Korean Student Christian Federation in 1984 (KDF Open Archives No. 00063840), emphasizes the importance of carefully choosing industrial sites based on the ecology of a given industrial area for "successful" factory work:

> Industrial complexes are the most ideal places for factory work as a worker-specific culture has been formed in these areas, which would allow us to gain a more holistic understanding of the lives of the working class. However, because the application process and labor management system are more elaborate at large factories and firms inside the industrial complexes, it might be difficult to find jobs there for short-term factory work (that lasts about a month). For short-term factory work, it is more realistic to consider working at smaller manufacturing firms (with 30 or more employees) in the industrial areas surrounding the industrial complexes. Although the ecological factors are similar to the industrial complexes, the

74 Seeds of Mobilization

employment process and labor management system are more sim-
plified. (Han'guk Kidok Haksaenghoe Ch'ongyŏnmaeng 1984, 16)

As this excerpt implies, industrial complexes and their surrounding
areas were generally considered to be the ideal places for college students to seek factory employment in the 1980s. When choosing which
factories to enter, student activists considered ecological factors such as
the density of factories in a given area and the distance to night schools.
If possible, students were encouraged not to live at home and instead to
rotate between living in factory dormitories and living together with other
students-turned-workers in rooming houses shared by factory workers;
this would serve to deepen their experience as workers and to strengthen
their relationships with fellow workers (Han'guk Kidok Haksaenghoe
Ch'ongyŏnmaeng 1984, 18–19).

Especially after the Chun government changed the union structure
from industrial unionism to enterprise unionism in the 1980s, students-
turned-workers and labor activists (i.e., those who were fired from organizing democratic unions in the 1970s) intentionally made efforts to find
employment in large factories inside industrial complexes. By this time,
they understood the far-reaching ripple effects that labor activism at a large
factory could have on many other factories inside the industrial complex
(KDF interview with Kim Chisŏn, July 2009; KDF interview with Kim
Yŏngmi, September 2005).[21] By capitalizing on the ways that these spaces
brought people together, these social activists turned industrial complexes into complicated spaces that intertwined government and corporate
manufacturing goals with worker communities and cross-group alliances
between Christians and students. In other words, the ecology of industrial
complexes—originally designed by the state to control labor and bolster
the popularity of the regime—actually enhanced the organizational and
coalitional capacity of the labor movement.

Interfirm Solidarity Struggles of the 1980s

The increased mobilization of workers within and across firms—resulting
from the ecological conditions surrounding the industrial complexes,
including the entry of social activists—became evident in the 1980s
through the two interfirm solidarity struggles that took place inside the
government-built industrial complexes. The first of these was the Kuro

Solidarity Strike, which occurred June 24–29, 1985, inside the Kuro Industrial Complex (Zones 1–3 of the Korea Export Industrial Complex, located in the Kuro district of Seoul). It was the *first* struggle in South Korea's labor history (since the Korean War) in which workers from *different* companies participated in a joint solidarity strike.

The second of these interfirm solidarity struggles—and the first *nationwide* labor struggle—was the Great Workers' Struggle, which began in July 1987 in Ulsan. Home to Ulsan Petrochemical Complex, Ulsan Mipo Industrial Complex, and Onsan Industrial Complex, Ulsan was also known as the center of Hyundai conglomerate companies (including Hyundai Shipbuilding, Hyundai Heavy Industries, Hyundai Automobile, Hyundai Machinery, and their subsidiaries). The strikes, which started at Hyundai firms, spilled over into large street demonstrations and ignited labor disputes at smaller firms affiliated with Hyundai. The wave of strikes then spread to other major industrial centers in the southern coastal region, including Pusan, Masan, and Ch'angwŏn. By mid-August, the strike wave reached Seoul and its surrounding region (Kyŏnggi and Inch'ŏn) before spreading to smaller cities to the southwest. By late August, labor conflicts had spread all over the country. Figure 3.3 displays the number of new labor protests each day from July 5, 1987, to September 30, 1987. The data confirms that protests spread from the southeastern coastal area (i.e., Pusan and Kyŏngnam region, which includes Ulsan, Masan, Ch'angwŏn, and Kŏje) to the rest of the country.

Together, the 1985 Kuro Solidarity Strike and the 1987 Great Workers' Struggle demonstrated the increased strength of the labor movement. They proved to the government and to society that the movement had overcome the isolated, localized nature of labor disputes and unionism that had characterized it in the 1970s.

Several key factors enabled these interfirm solidarity struggles to develop: (1) the formation of class consciousness and solidarity among workers (facilitated by the homogenous workforce found within an industrial complex, the semipublic living environment, and ecology-nurtured leisure activities), (2) small-group networks that were organized by workers and social activists within and across firms, (3) expanded political opportunities, and (4) the use of ecology-dependent protest tactics. Although the ecological factors played a more prominent role during the Great Workers' Struggle due to that struggle's spontaneous nature, these factors (to varying degrees) drove the success of interfirm solidarity struggles of the 1980s.

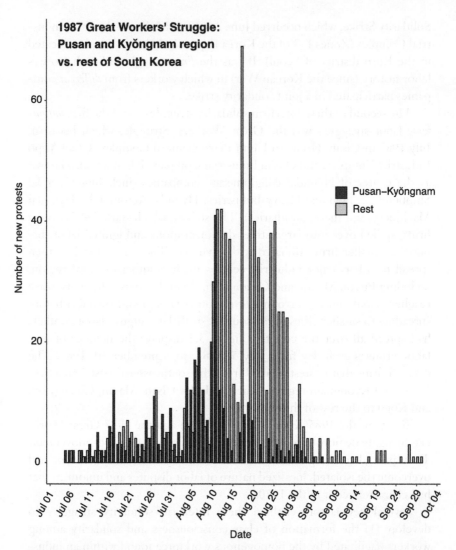

Fig 3.3. Diffusion of protests during the Great Workers' Struggle: The number of new protests in Pusan and Kyŏngnam vs. the rest of South Korea. Statistics are from the author's dataset.

The 1985 Kuro Solidarity Strike

The democratic union movement in the Kuro area (and specifically in the Kuro Industrial Complex) emerged under the harsh political conditions of the 1970s. In particular, the Young Catholic Workers and the Urban Industrial Mission (UIM Yŏngdŭngp'o and Kyŏnggi-Suwon branches) supported workers' efforts to unionize at Tongkwang Textiles in 1970, Crown Electronics in 1972, Korea Marvell Co. in 1975, Daehyup in 1976, and Dae Dong Electronics in 1978 (Han'guk Kidokkyo Kyohoe Hyŏbŭihoe 1984). After experiencing a brief period of political openness during the Spring of Seoul (from the October 1979 assassination of Park Chung Hee to the May 1980 Kwangju Massacre), the nascent labor movement was completely neutralized during the first three to four years of the new military regime under Chun Doo Hwan.

The movement was revived when Chun began to loosen his tight control over society. Starting in December 1983, the regime reinstated students and university professors who had been dismissed for their involvement in antigovernment activities and allowed them to return to their schools. It also lifted the ban on political activities for 202 former politicians, and it pardoned or rehabilitated about 300 political prisoners (S. Kim 2000, 80).[22] Although these conciliatory measures were most relevant to the middle class, workers—with help from the students-turned-workers—took advantage of the expanding political opportunities and "released their accumulated discontentment" toward their employers and the government (K. Yu 2001, 13). From June to July 1984, workers at the Kuro Industrial Complex (which housed Daewoo Apparel, Hyosŏng Products, Sŏnil Textile, and Karibong Electronics) unionized, and by June 1985, there were 33 unions formed inside the KIC (K. Yu 2001, 35).

On June 22, 1985, the government arrested the union president and two union officers of Daewoo Apparel (Kim Chunyŏng, Kang Myŏngja, and Ch'u Chaesuk) for having organized overnight sit-ins (which had resulted in a wage increase) during the wage-negotiation period the previous April; the sit-ins were deemed to be "illegal" for violating the Law on Assembly and Demonstration, Labor Disputes Adjustment Act, and the Basic Press Law.[23] In response to these arrests, the union officers of four KIC firms—Daewoo Apparel, Hyosŏng Products, Karibong Electronics, and Sŏnil Textile—collectively organized an interfirm solidarity strike to commence on June 24 (for which they had to obtain approval from their respective union members at their provisional general meetings). Thirteen hundred workers from these four firms participated. From

78 Seeds of Mobilization

June 25 to 26, three additional firms—Namsŏng Electronics, Sejin Electronics, and Rom-Korea—organized protests in solidarity; these protests took place after regular working hours. And, on June 28, workers at Samsung Pharmaceutical Company also protested in solidarity, and Puhŭngsa workers joined the solidarity strike with the original four firms. This strike gained additional support from students, a total of 26 different social organizations—including a federation of dissident (*chaeya*) groups called the People's Movement Coalition for Democracy and Reunification (Minju T'ongil Minjung Undong Yŏnhap or Mintongnyon)—and workers from other regions of the country (e.g., union leaders of T'ong'il Industry, located inside the Ch'angwŏn Industrial Complex in South Kyŏngsang Province).

In addition to garnering wider support than earlier struggles, the Kuro Solidarity Strike made larger-scale demands. Unlike the struggles in the 1970s, which mainly targeted employers and focused on economic issues such as wages and poor working conditions, the Kuro Solidarity Strike made demands that were political, and they were directed toward both employers and the government. The joint declaration by the unions at Hyosung Products, Karibong Electronics, Sejin Electronics, Chŏnggye Garments, and Sunil Textiles included such demands as these: "Immediately release Kim Chunyŏng, the union leader of Daewoo Apparel, and others who are currently arrested," "Get rid of all unjust laws hindering the labor movement, such as the Assembly and Protest Law, Press Law, and Labor Law," "Immediately reinstate all fired workers," and "The Minister of Labor Cho Ch'ŏlgwŏn, who has been destroying democratic labor unions, should resign" (Minjuhwa Undong Kinyŏm Saophoe 2006, 439). Although ultimately the strike was forcibly broken up and ended with 43 arrests, forced resignations, and more than 700 layoffs, the Kuro Solidarity Strike "shaped the direction of the subsequent movement by demonstrating the power of using interfirm solidarity strikes and of transforming a labor dispute into a political struggle" (J.-L. Nam 2000, 99).[24] Indeed, interfirm solidarity struggles became a new strategy in the labor movement in the 1980s and were widely observed during the Great Workers' Struggle, in which interfirm solidarity struggles were taking place within each industrial complex on a nationwide scale.

Ecology of the KIC and the Kuro Solidarity Strike

The close proximity of the firms inside the Kuro Industrial Complex facilitated the development of a network structure that enabled workers

Manufacturing Protests 79

to coordinate the Kuro Solidarity Strike. The union leaders of the different firms there were able to come together and decide quickly (within 30 minutes) to go on a solidarity strike because they had already been collaborating for some time. They had exchanged information and devised strategies together both before and after the establishment of their independent unions in 1984. They had also organized various interunion activities by inviting one another to the celebrations of their unions' founding anniversaries, overnight trainings for union officers, and cultural or athletic activities.[25] Similarly, students-turned-workers (who were also union organizers and members) had worked with grassroots labor leaders (who had previously been fired or blacklisted due to their involvement in the democratic union movement) to create interunion small groups. Each of these small groups had been composed of six workers from different firms, and they had published and disseminated a newsletter (*Kongdan sosik*; as many as 3,000 copies of each issue) to raise workers' consciousness and develop an area-based political union movement (Koo 2001, 121). According to Sim Sang-jung, a student-turned-worker who led Kuro's clandestine network of labor activists, students-turned-workers of the early 1980s had identified industrial complexes as an organization unit for their labor activism, and they had purposefully found employment at different textile and electronics factories inside the KIC to promote interfirm union activities (K. Yu 2001, 51). Together, these small group and interfirm union activities, as well as the relationships between union leaders, created a network structure for the Kuro-area workers that was easy to activate in June 1985.

The tactics used to spread this strike from one firm to the next also relied heavily on the ecology of the industrial complex—specifically, they took advantage of the high concentration of workers and their proximity to each other. On June 24, which was the first day of the strike, Daewoo Apparel workers listed their demands (including "Revise the evil labor laws," "Release the arrested union leader," "Guarantee workers' three basic rights," "The minister of labor should resign") on banners and placards and hung them in the second-floor window of their factory building. On that same day, they heard gongs (*kkwaenggwari*) from the opposite building, which signaled that the Hyosŏng Products workers had started their strike (see fig. 3.4). Daewoo workers rushed to the windows facing the Hyosŏng factory and noticed a big placard stating, "Daewoo fighting!"[26] They also saw Hyosŏng workers dancing the "liberation dance" (*haebangch'um*; a popular dance among students and workers in the 1980s) on the second-floor veranda (Koo 2001, 114; K. Yu 2002, 131). As seen in figure 3.5, Daewoo Apparel workers posted in their window a sign that

Fig 3.4. Layout of the Kuro Industrial Complex. English text is added by the author. Credit: Kyung-Min Kim.

read "Stay strong Hyosŏng" (*Hyosŏng himnaera*). Both groups of workers shouted encouragement and waved at each other.

On the next day (June 25), 300 Namsŏng Electronics workers and 250 Sejin Electronics workers (both in KIC Zone 3) gathered on their factory communal grounds (*undongjang*), where they chanted and sang songs during their sit-ins to show their support for the striking Daewoo Apparel workers (T. Yi 1986, 488). Rom-Korea workers (in Zone 2, where Hyosŏng and Daewoo were located) also posted a placard ("Release the arrested [union leaders of Daewoo Apparel]") outside the second floor of their building, where 70 of them were gathered at the cafeteria to protest in solidarity (T. Yi 1986, 488). On June 26, there were demonstrations both inside and outside the industrial complex near the KIC entrance and at the

Fig 3.5. Sit-in strike organized by Daewoo Apparel workers on June 24, 1985.
Credit: Pak Yongsu (provided by the Korea Democracy Foundation).

Karibong five-way intersection, and two Seoul National University students climbed up the smokestack of the Hyŏptong Sewing factory building that was facing the Daewoo Apparel building and shouted, "Stop the crackdown on democratic unions!" (Minjuhwa Undong Kinyŏm Saophoe 2006, 439).[27] In these ways, the spatial ecology of the KIC shaped protest strategies and facilitated the spread of protest. It was the high density and close proximity of the factories and workers inside the industrial complex that made it possible for gongs to be audible, for signs to be visible, and for workers to witness the protests of their peers at other firms.

Moreover, although the preexisting network structure enabled the initial coordination of the solidarity strike on June 24, 1985, it was the ecology of the KIC that facilitated the spread and development of the subsequent strikes and protests. An interfirm committee had been formed by the union representatives from Daewoo Apparel, Hyosŏng Products, Karibong Electronics, and Sŏnil Textiles to orchestrate the strike, but they were able to meet and exchange information only once—on the first day of the strike (June 24)—as employers and the police took repressive measures and each factory became isolated from the others. They were not even able to communicate with one another using a landline phone (Yu Kyŏng-sun's interview with then union president of Hyosŏng Products Kim Yŏngmi; K. Yu 2002, 119).

Then, without any direct communication with the four firms that were on strike, four other factories inside the industrial complex—Namsŏng Electronics, Sejin Electronics, Rom-Korea, and Samsung Pharmaceuticals—organized sit-in demonstrations and hunger strikes (lasting from June 25 to 28) to demonstrate their support and solidarity. The union leaders of Namsŏng Electronics, Sejin Electronics, and Rom-Korea had participated in interfirm union activities in the past, but the Samsung Pharmaceuticals union had not. Still, all union members of Samsung Pharmaceuticals participated in the hunger strikes. Additionally, Puhŭngsa had originally been asked to join the solidarity strike, but they did not join it until June 28—four days after the four firms went on solidarity strike, and with no direct line of communication with the other firms.

What drove such solidarity despite the lack of direct communication was the proximity of the firms inside the industrial complex. Because they could see and hear each other, the firms were able to generate awareness and sympathy from workers from other firms, which ultimately influenced their decision to join the solidarity strike. Kong Kyejin, a former student-turned-worker at Puhŭngsa, shared the following in an interview regarding how the Puhŭngsa union ended up participating in the Kuro Solidarity Strike:

> The Puhŭngsa union could not come to a decision as to whether they should join the solidarity strike. . . . Then, on June 26, street demonstrations were happening [in the KIC area]. This was when the two firms [Daewoo Apparel and Hyosŏng Products] were on strike . . . and university students were protesting on the smokestack of the sewing factory next to Daewoo Apparel. It was very dynamic. I purposefully took the union officers there so that they would change their minds [to join the strike] from seeing [the protests in action]. The union leaders saw [what was happening] on June 26, and during the executive committee meeting on June 27, they decided to also join the strike. (KDF interview with Kong Kyejin, October 2005)

As illustrated here, it was the ecology of the industrial complexes that allowed for the gradual formation of workers' consciousness, the creation of small group networks within and across firms, and the development of the worker-student alliance, all of which Kuro-area workers capitalized on in orchestrating the Kuro Solidarity Strike. Due to the high concentration of electronics and textile industries inside the KIC, the Kuro area housed a relatively homogenous labor force—which meant that the KIC workers shared similar working experiences and were able to better relate to each other's plights and grievances. The close proximity and frequent interaction between workers who lived in the same or proximal dormitories or rooming houses also facilitated networks. The independent democratic unions of the KIC firms were formed through these small group networks.[28]

Interfirm union networks formed not only due to the close proximity of the firms inside the KIC but also as a result of the mobilization efforts by students, who deliberately considered the ecological conditions of the area in deciding whether and how to participate in the labor movement. Students-turned-workers (like Sim Sang-jung) intentionally found employment at firms inside the KIC to raise workers' political consciousness, and they then organized interunion small groups to create the interfirm network that union members and leaders relied on to coordinate the Kuro Solidarity Strike. Lastly, the high density and close proximity of the firms also introduced ecology-dependent protest tactics and facilitated the spread of protests inside and outside the KIC.

The 1987 Great Workers' Struggle

The Great Workers' Struggle from July through September 1987 is commonly understood to have been a product of the political opportunity created by that year's June Democratic Uprising. The uprising generated mass protests from June 10 to June 29, 1987, and it provided the workers with opportunities to directly participate in mass street demonstrations and to witness the outcome of those actions: the June 29 Declaration, in which the ruling party promised democratic concessions, including direct presidential elections.

These experiences contributed directly to the Great Workers' Struggle, during which about a third of the regularly employed workforce from all major industries engaged in labor unrest. In Ch'angwŏn, where labor unrest erupted soon after the initial strikes by the Hyundai workers in Ulsan, 40,000 factory workers (approximately 60% of the total number) at the Ch'angwŏn Industrial Complex went on strike, and on August 10, two-thirds of the firms inside the industrial complex experienced sit-in strikes (H. Kim and Mach'ang Noryŏnsa Palgan Wiwŏnhoe 1999, 51).

T'ong'il Industry was the third-largest factory plant (employing 2,800 workers) in this industrial complex, and it was one of the few firms not in the Seoul-Kyŏngin area in which the workers had been active in the democratic union movement since the early 1980s. It was also the first firm in the defense industrial base sector to organize a strike (in 1985). Mun Sŏnghyŏn, a graduate of the prestigious Seoul National University and a well-known student-turned-worker, had spearheaded T'ong'il Industry's democratic union

84 Seeds of Mobilization

movement in 1985. He had then co-led the Kyŏngnam (South Kyŏngsang Province) branch of the National Movement Headquarters for Democratic Constitution, which organized a series of massive pro-democracy demonstrations during the June Democratic Uprising. Along with students and other workers in Ch'angwŏn, T'ong'il workers had participated in the protests, shouting "Down with the dictatorship!" and "Achieve direct (presidential) elections!" And their participation in the pro-democracy protests in June had inspired them to again attempt to transform the union from one that was *oyŏng* (company controlled) into one that was genuinely representative of workers' interests (C. Kim 2015, 41–43). Chin Yŏngkyu, who later became the union president of T'ong'il Industry, gives an account of how the workers' participation in the June Democratic Uprising was quickly channeled into the Great Workers' Struggle:

> When the rallies [during the June Democratic Uprising] were over, we usually met at Yangsanbak [a famous lamb barbeque restaurant in Ch'angwŏn]. We shared our own hero stories over drinks. We evaluated [how the rally went that day] and discussed struggle tactics for the next protest rally or exchanged information on the political climate. It was then that we naturally started talking about forming a democratic union by saying, let's turn the union upside down! We need to rise up! We shared our determination [to engage in democratic union activism] by raising our glasses to one another. Such determination culminated in the formation of the Council of National Democratic Unions (Minju Nojo Ch'ujin Wiwŏnhoe) and later the Great Workers' Struggle in July and August. (H. Kim and Mach'ang Noryŏnsa Palgan Wiwŏnhoe 1999, 38)

As shown in the statistical analyses presented in chapter 2, the workers' exposure to the June Democratic Uprising protests was indeed statistically significant and positively associated with the intensity of protests during the Great Workers' Struggle less than a month later (see table A2.1 in the online appendix). I also showed that the political opportunity arising from the June Democratic Uprising functioned as a causal mechanism, eliminating about 7% of the total effect of industrial complexes on the number of Great Workers' Struggle protests. However, the concentration of manufacturing firms played an even greater role as a causal mechanism, eliminating about 36% of the total effect. These findings regarding the strength of the causal mechanism suggest that the political opening during the June Democratic Uprising may have been necessary but not sufficient to explain workers' participation in the Great Workers' Struggle. Other factors related to the construction of industrial complexes had to be involved as well.

Such factors were in development long before the June Democratic Uprising. First, workers developed class consciousness and comradeship through their shared living arrangements inside and near the factory compounds. For example, as mentioned earlier in the chapter, workers from Hyundai subsidiaries shared dormitory/apartment rooms and corridors with workers from different subsidiary companies and built relationships within these spaces. Workers also engaged in—and connected with each other through—a variety of small groups. At Hyundai Engine, where the first union was formed during the Great Workers' Struggle, a factory worker named Kwŏn Yŏngmok (who later led the Hyundai Workers Struggle of 1987) began organizing small-group activities, such as visiting sites of cultural heritage on the weekends. As in other small groups mentioned earlier in this chapter, members of Kwŏn's small group discussed problems in their workplace and studied labor laws and Marxist literature. Then, in 1986, Kwŏn and his fellow Hyundai Engine workers took control of the labor management council, transforming the council from a promanagement one to a more worker-representative organization, and subsequently organized a union during the Great Workers' Struggle (Koo 2001; Kwŏn 1988; S.-W. Lee 1994). There were similar small group activities happening in other Hyundai firms in Ulsan, including Hyundai Motors, Hyundai Heavy Electrics, and Hyundai Heavy Industries (Lee 1994).

Workers in the neighboring industrial cities of Masan and Ch'angwŏn likewise developed class consciousness through small groups, many of which were affiliated with religious and social organizations such as the *minjung* churches, JOC, Young Men's Christian Association, and Young Women's Christian Association (H. Kim and Mach'ang Noryŏnsa Palgan Wiwŏnhoe 1999, 35). They also belonged to various social groups, including hobby groups, hometown groups (*hyanguhoe*), and high school and vocational training center (*chigŏp hullyŏnwŏn*) alumni groups (*tongmunghoe*), which brought together workers from different firms. From 1985 to 1987, one particular interfirm small group that consisted of grassroots labor activists and workers from Masan and Ch'angwŏn (including T'ong'il Industry, Han'guk Heavy Industry, and Paejŏng Transportation) met regularly to study and discuss labor union laws, labor union activities, and various political, economic, and social issues that were pertinent to raising class consciousness (H. Kim and Mach'ang Noryŏnsa Palgan Wiwŏnhoe 1999, 34).

These preexisting small-group-based networks that were formed among workers *prior* to the June Democratic Uprising served as mobilizing structures for them to swiftly engage in labor actions when the opportunity arose in the summer of 1987. However, unlike the Kuro Solidarity Strike, which was coordinated by a group of union leaders from a single industrial complex, no central organization could lead or organize the Great Workers' Struggle. Instead, it was an unorganized and uncoordinated explosion of labor conflicts that were led by ordinary workers and that occurred throughout the country.[29] Although students-turned-workers were involved in unionization efforts at their respective factories, the Great Workers' Struggle itself was neither initiated nor directly guided by the students-turned-workers and received little support from outside organizations (Koo 2001, 161–62). Still, area-based solidarity struggle (worker solidarity across firms located in the same geographic area) became a key feature of the Great Workers' Struggle, as displayed in protest visits, street demonstrations, collective strike funds, and sympathy strikes (Koo 2001, 176–77).

In the absence of premeditation and organizational leadership, the ecological conditions of the industrial complexes—in particular, the built environment of factory housing—played a key role in facilitating the labor unrest that characterized the Great Workers' Struggle. In Ulsan, where the Great Workers' Struggle began, workers from various Hyundai-affiliated companies were living in the same dormitory buildings (usually for unmarried workers) and apartment complexes (usually for married workers and their families) built by Hyundai. According to Young-Mi Won (2006), the unprecedented, long, and explosive labor uprising among Hyundai workers, which lasted until September 1987, was possible due to the workers' underlying sense of homogeneity and social bonds—both of which were developed through the collective residential living and drinking gatherings around the industrial complex.

The residents of the Ojwabul dormitory-building complex (which consisted of eight five-story buildings for unmarried workers) acted as the main force of the labor strikes at Hyundai Heavy Industries during the Great Workers' Struggle: they guarded the strike scene until the very end of the struggle, thereby gaining the name "freedom community" for the complex.[30] On September 4, 1987, when the Hyundai management cut off Ojwabul's water and electricity and shut down its cafeteria, 20 Ojwabul residents started protesting around the neighboring Ilsan ("Man Saedae"; 10,000 households) apartment complex where married workers and their families lived. The protest grew to 5,000 people, and the residents of the

Ilsan apartment complex set up an outdoor kitchen and provided food to the Ojwabul residents (Won 2006, 330). Residents of other apartment complexes (Toran, Myŏngdŏk, and Chŏnha Complexes 1 and 2) also actively supported the struggle, collecting strike funds and providing goods and products for workers who were on strike (Won 2006, 324–331).

In addition to having these effects on the movement, the ecological conditions of the industrial complexes facilitated the development of region-based interfirm solidarity struggles that contributed to the spread of the Great Workers' Struggle (i.e., an increasing number of new protests) within a geographic region. According to my Great Workers' Struggle data (shown in fig. 3.2), the number of *new* instances of labor unrest (not including the ongoing strikes and protests) in the Pusan-Kyŏngnam area reached its peak on August 11, with unrest occurring at all of the industrial complexes in the region. In the industrial town of Ch'angwŏn in Kyŏngnam (South Kyŏngsang Province), spontaneous sit-ins and strikes had been happening at *individual* firms from July 21 to August 10. Then on August 11, for the first time, workers from different firms in different zones of the Ch'angwŏn Industrial Complex participated in an unplanned interfirm solidarity struggle (H. Kim and Mach'ang Noryŏnsa Palgan Wiwŏnhoe 1999, 46–48).

First, 200 workers from Kŭmsŏngsa (Gold Star Company located in Zone 1) protested around the industrial complex in their forklifts for an hour. Soon after, workers of Daelim Motor Company (Zone 2) protested outside their main factory gate for two hours, holding a banner saying, "We want to live like humans, guarantee a living wage." Three hundred workers from Ch'angwŏn Carburetor Company (Hagu [river mouth] Zone) also participated in the street demonstration before holding a sit-in in front of the Ch'angwŏn City Hall. And 400 workers from Poongsung Electric Company (Zone 1) followed suit by protesting all around Ch'angwŏn in their company commuter buses. When 250 Kŭmsŏngsa (Zone 1) workers came out again on their forklifts late in the afternoon, 200 workers from Poongsung Electric Company (Zone 1), 100 workers from Dongwoo/Kia Machine Tool Company (Zone 1), and workers from Osŏngsa (Zone 1) and Donghwan Industries (Zone 2) displayed their solidarity by cheering on the Kŭmsŏngsa workers.[31]

For the remainder of the Great Workers' Struggle, Ch'angwŏn workers continued to join street demonstrations and engaged in solidarity/sympathy struggles with neighborhood firms and other affiliated firms (H. Kim and Mach'ang Noryŏnsa Palgan Wiwŏnhoe 1999, 52; Koo 2001, 176–77). This interfirm solidarity formed among workers in Ch'angwŏn and in its

88 Seeds of Mobilization

neighboring industrial city, Masan, during the Great Workers' Struggle resulted in the establishment of the Council of Masan and Ch'angwŏn Unions in December 1987. In the spring of 1988, other regional councils formed in the Seoul, Inch'ŏn, and Sŏngnam areas, and by the end of that year, 11 regional councils had formed, incorporating 403 local unions and 113,500 union members (Huh 1989, 162). Various national federations of the group-level interfirm unions also formed at Daewoo, Sŏnkyung, and Ssangyong *chaebŏl* groups.

Conclusion

In the preceding chapter, I showed that although industrial policy initially stabilized the regime by producing "industrial warriors" and generating regime support, the construction of industrial complexes also had a destabilizing effect in the long run because areas that housed these facilities saw increased labor protests during the Great Workers' Struggle. In this chapter, I demonstrated *how* the concentration of factories—which resulted from the industrial policies pursued by the authoritarian governments—facilitated the gradual development of the labor movement. In doing so, I highlighted the ecological conditions surrounding the industrial complexes that contributed to the formation of class consciousness and solidarity among workers, the entry of social activists, and the development of ecology-dependent mobilization strategies. The small-group-based networks formed among workers and social activists in areas surrounding these industrial complexes served as mobilizing structures for the emergence of interfirm solidarity struggles in the 1980s, including the first nationwide struggle in 1987.

What remains to be explained is the *timing* in which such a mass mobilization of workers occurred at the national level. What explains the effectiveness of the worker-intellectual alliance in the 1980s? Why did the workers in the late 1980s no longer embrace their state-propagated identity as industrial warriors and rise up against the state? The next chapter engages with these questions by analyzing how the government's educational policies weakened and then strengthened the labor and student movements in the 1970s and 1980s.

FOUR

Learning to Dissent

Education and Authoritarian Resilience

Education is widely acknowledged to have been a driving force in South Korea's rapid economic growth and democratization, and that relationship seems to echo classical modernization theory.[1] Immediately after liberation in 1945, the country achieved nearly universal primary education. It then expanded and standardized secondary education in the 1960s and 1970s, thereby aiming to provide equal opportunities for education regardless of socioeconomic background. Finally, it focused on vocational and tertiary education (including higher education), which helped develop the human resources and human capital that were crucial to generating economic growth in a country that was essentially devoid of natural resources. This expansion of education paralleled the country's rapid industrialization, which resulted in a structural shift from light to heavy industries within the manufacturing sector. That shift drove the growth of the working and middle classes, which are understood to have played such a pivotal role in Korea's democratic struggle that the Korean media referred to it as a "middle-class revolution" (Koo 1991, 491).

A closer examination of the South Korean case, however, complicates the notion that Korea's path to modernity and democracy was relatively linear. Chapters 2 and 3 illustrated the contradictory effects that industrial policies had on authoritarian regime stability—that is, although the development of industrial complexes did generate regime support, it also concentrated manufacturing firms and workers in ways that ultimately facilitated social activists' entry into the labor movement and increased labor activism within and across firms. This chapter and the following chapter will show that the development of educational institutions had similarly contradictory effects on the country's path to democracy.

These chapters will show that, like industrial complexes, educational institutions helped stabilize authoritarian rule to a certain extent, but they did so in a different way—they trained skilled workers to help the regime achieve its national economic development goals. According to Mason et al. (1980, 378), education aimed to foster "the basic attitude of compliance with a strong central government . . . [and] education did play a critical role in . . . assisting a strong government with 'modernizing' policies to impose its will upon its nation." And as stated by the United Nations Education Scientific and Cultural Organization (UNESCO) mission in 1980, "The remarkable and rapid economic growth that has occurred in [South] Korea . . . has been based to a large degree on human resources, and education has assisted in the production of a literate and industrial people" (Mason et al. 1980, 342). Further highlighted by Alice Amsden (1992), a well-educated workforce was crucial for continuing Korea's successful "late industrialization," which required "industrial learning."[2] Even as they created the labor force that drove the economy's growth, however, these educational institutions also became hotbeds of political activism, and their students were at the forefront of the democracy movement that ultimately toppled the authoritarian regime. They also became the foundations for a nascent civil society, which was manifest in various social movements that were part of the larger democracy movement in the 1970s and 1980s (J. Cho and Chang 2017).

The trajectories of the labor and student movements mirrored each other in similar ways. As described in earlier chapters, only a minority of workers in the 1970s opted for collective resistance, and their labor struggles mostly occurred in areas surrounding Seoul, including Kyŏnggi and Inch'ŏn. Heavy chemical industry (HCI) workers—who had been educated and trained through the technical high schools and vocational training institutions set up in the 1960s and 1970s—largely remained acquiescent throughout the 1970s and early 1980s,[3] and *inter*firm solidarity struggles did not appear until the mid-1980s (as described in chapter 3). The labor movement reached its pinnacle in 1987 with the eruption of the Great Workers' Struggle, which involved 1.2 million workers (about a third of the regularly employed workforce at that time) from most major industries, including the HCI.

The student movement displays similar temporal and spatial patterns.

Learning to Dissent 91

Student demonstrations during the early 1970s were "brief affairs" (N. Lee 2007, 171)—they were small, one-off campus protests (Minjuhwa Undong Kinyŏm Saophoe 2010, 217) and "venturing into the streets outside the campus gate did not occur until the late 1970s" (N. Lee 2007, 171). Like labor protests at this time, on-campus and street demonstrations mainly occurred in Seoul, as "the universities clustered in Seoul created a very dense population of politically conscious, idealistic students" (Robinson 2007, 125). Then, starting in the mid-1980s, the student movement was no longer dominated by the "elite" schools (such as Seoul National, Yonsei, and Korea Universities) or by the "movement-prone" universities (such as Chonnam National University in Kwangju, South Chŏlla Province) (N. Lee 2007, 179).[4] Finally, in 1987, the June Democratic Uprising occurred in 22 cities across the country—and was driven largely by college students (C. Chung 2011, 174).

This chapter focuses on the role that education played in shaping these trajectories. It seeks to understand why the destabilizing (rather than the stabilizing) effects of economic development dominated in the 1980s and ultimately resulted in democratization. It will show that labor activism became conceivable to HCI workers at that time because the regime failed to sustain the vocational education training programs that had previously kept these workers in a state of so-called coercive dependence. Using an original dataset of 3,032 Korean student protests from 1980 through 1987 (drawn from the *Korea Democracy Foundation Dictionary of Events Related to the Democracy Movement*, the *Timeline of the Korean Democracy Movement* (Minjuhwa Undong Kinyŏm Saophoe 2006), and news articles from *Chosun Ilbo*, *Dong-A Ilbo*, *Kyunghyang Sinmun*, and *Maeil Kyŏngje* (found in the Naver News Library),[5] this chapter will also show that the regime's expansion of higher education created the ecological conditions for students to organize and mobilize into intercampus student organizations, ultimately creating a nationwide student movement.

Education and Economic Development in Authoritarian South Korea

Education was intended to legitimize authoritarian rule in several ways, perhaps the most obvious of which was by serving as political indoctrination. Under the authoritarian tenures of Syngman Rhee (1948–60), Park Chung Hee (1961–79), and Chun Doo Hwan (1980–88), education was used as ideological training to create loyalty to the state and the regime that ruled it (Seth 2012). Through this training, the autocrats appealed to

92 Seeds of Mobilization

nationalism and anticommunism[6] to mobilize the population and to justify political repression and violation of human rights in the name of national security. The subject of moral education (*todŏk*), which had existed during the Japanese colonial period, was reintroduced under Rhee not only to teach ethical conduct but also (and more importantly) to propagate nationalism and anticommunism. In 1968, the Ministry of Education mandated that anticommunist lessons be conducted each week, and military-style training and drills became an essential part of education. Schools used corporal punishment and emphasized militaristic discipline (including dress code and hair regulations) and obedience to authority (i.e., teachers to principal, students to teachers, and younger students to older students). Moreover, in addition to singing the national anthem and pledging their allegiance to the Korean flag, students were required to memorize and recite the Charter for National Education (Kungmin Kyoyuk Hŏnjang; also promulgated in 1968), which stipulated that education was a means of achieving the "revival of the Korean nation" and was printed on the first page of all textbooks. In 1974, the Park Chung Hee government also replaced the previous system of government-authorized or approved textbooks and introduced a single, nationalized Korean history textbook that emphasized national pride and economic strength. This system remained in place long after Korea democratized—it was 2003, under Roh Moohyun (2003–8), before contemporary high school Korean history textbooks were again published by private publishing houses.

Although education was used overtly as a tool of political indoctrination, however, that was not its only task—the autocrats also promoted education in their pursuit of economic development. They created educational policies that were closely aligned with national development plans (see table 4.1), which, in a country devoid of natural resources, relied on human resources to achieve economic growth. Education's role was therefore to produce a skilled workforce for industrial development, and each regime approached that task in its own way.

Education as Vocational Training

During the First Republic, the Rhee government (1948–60) prioritized literacy improvement and focused on elementary and secondary education. The government implemented the Six-Year Compulsory Education Completion Plan (1954–59) and, in 1957, successfully universalized primary education. This education "contributed to social cohesion and provided a literate workforce with the skills needed for a newly industrializing economy" (Seth 2012, 15).

Learning to Dissent 93

TABLE 4.1. Educational Development and Economic Development in South Korea

	1945–1960s	1960s–1970s	1980s–early 1990s
Major Economic Development	Liberation, postcolonial/postwar reconstruction, and establishment of the Republic of Korea	Export-oriented industrialization and rapid development	Economic reconstruction and stable growth
Major Educational Development	Establishment of an education system and the universalization of primary education	Expansion of secondary education and vocational education and training	Quality improvement in secondary education and rapid expansion of higher education
Key Education Policies	– Establishing the basis of an education system – Universalization of primary education – Literacy movement	– Expanding secondary education – Developing vocational education and training – Securing education revenue – Creating teacher training programs	– The July 30 (7.30) Education Reforms – Expanding higher education sector – Quality improvement in primary and secondary education – Enhancing local educational autonomy

Source: J. Chae (2013, 174).

The subsequent government, led by Park Chung Hee (1961–79), established the Five-Year Economic Development (FYED) Plans and adopted educational policies based on its assessment of industrial demand. Early in its regime, for example, when it began pursuing export-oriented industrialization, the Park government emphasized technical education: at the onset of the First FYED Plan (1962–66), the government announced the Promotion of Industrial Education Act to meet the increasing demand for semiskilled workers in light and labor-intensive industry. Then, at the end of the First FYED Plan in 1967, the government introduced the Vocational Training Act to establish vocational training institutions and provide subsidies to existing vocational institutes to transform unemployed youth into skilled laborers for export industries. As a result of this act, the number of trainees in public training institutes tripled, from 10,738 in 1967 to 30,588 in 1970. The number of in-plant training programs also grew, from 16 in 1967 to 59 in 1971, with the number of trainees increasing from 3,890 to 14,303 (Jeong 2008, 44–45).

In addition to introducing technical education through vocational training, the Park government expanded opportunities for secondary education. The universalization of primary schools in the 1950s and 1960s had dramatically increased demand for secondary education, which had placed tremendous pressure on and created competition among young students—

94 Seeds of Mobilization

they had to take school entrance examinations to access such education, and many of them had sought private tutoring to prepare. When the Park government standardized secondary (middle and high school) education through the 1968 Middle School Equalization Policy and 1974 High School Equalization Policy, however, it abolished these compulsory entrance examinations and started randomly assigning students among all (private and public) middle and high schools near their residences. These changes created equal educational opportunities for all students, regardless of socioeconomic background. They "normalized [secondary] education by ending excessive competition caused by 'education fever' [to get into highly ranked elite schools], especially among the affluent Korean middle class, but more notably broadened educational opportunities" (H.-A. Kim 2020, 28).[7]

With the launch of the Third FYED Plan (1972–76), also known as the heavy chemical industrialization plan (discussed in chapter 2), the Park government focused on strengthening vocational education at the upper secondary level by providing elite technical skills training within the high school education system. Through the Specialization Initiatives at Technical High Schools in 1973 and the Five-Year Technical School Promotion Plan in 1976, vocational high schools were restructured and divided into four specialized categories: (1) machinery technical high schools (*kigye konggo*), (2) experimental technical high schools (*sibŏm konggo*), (3) specialized technical high schools (*t'uksŏnghwa konggo*), and (4) general/regular technical high schools (*ilban konggo*).[8] These technical high schools, especially the first three types (which were considered to be "elite"), were intended to produce a massive number of skilled male workers to meet the rapidly rising demand from the large HCI firms. They were also heavily funded by the government: in 1977, the public education spending per high school student in a technical high school was ₩182,158, which was higher than for students in a commercial high school (₩128,300) and general high school (₩128,173) (J.-H. Lee and Hong 2014, 78).

This investment is evident in the sheer number of schools built during Park's rule, including 19 machinery technical high schools, 12 specialized technical high schools, 11 experimental technical high schools, and 55 regular technical high schools (Y. Kim 2002, 109). The total number of technical high schools increased from 72 in 1975 to 197 in 1980 (Pak 2003, 43), and a total of 391,870 technical high school graduates were produced during the years under the Third and Fourth FYED Plans (1972–81) (H.-A. Kim 2020, 34). More than any other educational institution, technical high schools provided skilled workers needed for the country's industrialization (J.-H. Lee and Hong 2014, 19). These technical high schools and the aforementioned vocational training (both public and in-plant) were the two main channels that the government relied on to produce and train elite skilled workers in the 1970s—and they delivered, producing approximately two million skilled workers between 1972 and 1987 (H.-A. Kim 2020).

This rapid growth did not extend to higher education for quite some time. Although universities and colleges were initially developed in the 1960s, Park Chung Hee strictly controlled the quota for higher education institutions to match the supply and demand for labor (i.e., to prevent an oversupply of graduates and rising unemployment rates). Any expansion that did occur was only in fields that the government deemed necessary to provide human resources for industrial development; these fields included science and engineering education, which were crucial in meeting the demand of the heavy chemical industry in the 1970s. It was not until the 1980s, under Chun Doo Hwan's rule, that the higher education sector expanded significantly, and that brought other changes as well.

From Vocational Education and Training to Higher Education

When Chun Doo Hwan came to power through a military coup in 1980, following the assassination of Park Chung Hee in 1979, he faced myriad economic and political problems. Domestically, he was confronted right away with demonstrations against his coup-born military regime, and this "Spring of Seoul" ended with his brutal suppression of demonstrations by students and citizens in the Kwangju Massacre of mid-May 1980. Additionally, the world economy was in a depression due to the second oil shock (in 1979), which led to a surge in global trade protectionism. This context resulted in a reduction of South Korean exports and a widening deficit in the current account (11% of gross domestic product in 1980), and by 1980, the economy was in its worst period since the Korean War (1950–53). A negative growth rate was recorded for the first time since 1962, and inflation soared.

To control inflation and achieve socioeconomic stability, Chun's government adopted conservative monetary policy and tight fiscal measures, such as implementing a government spending freeze, raising interest rates, and reducing credit. The government also reduced its intervention in the economy (which had defined Park's export-oriented industrialization policy), and it liberalized policies on imports and foreign investments to promote competition. These policies helped the Korean economy get back on track, and it resumed its rapid growth by achieving an average of 9.2% real growth between 1982 and 1987 and 12.5% between 1986 and 1988 (Savada and Shaw 1990, 138). In that process, the Chun government also committed to promoting social (and not just economic) development by addressing the economic inequities and social problems that had arisen during Korea's industrialization; these issues were at the root of much popular discontent at that time (Graham 2003, 56). To reflect the government's commitment to overall social development, the name of the Fifth FYED Plan (1982–86) was changed to Five-Year Economic and *Social* Development.

These economic reforms and the increased emphasis on social development drove changes in the underlying principles of education policy as well. First, the government's perception of the role of vocational education changed. Whereas the prior regime had invested in technical high schools and vocational training institutes to meet the needs of short-term workforce supply, the Chun government emphasized long-term workforce supply by fostering technicians with multiple skills and with the ability to adapt to rapid technological changes. To that end, the government emphasized basic science education, increased the number of universities focused on science and engineering, and established science high schools to provide a specialized curriculum for students gifted in mathematics. Correspondingly, the government abolished the Specialization Initiatives at Technical High Schools and reduced its budget share for vocational education by approximately half—from 6% in the 1970s (comparable to the budget share for higher education at that time, which was 5.5%–7%) to 3.5%–3.8% in the 1980s (J.-H. Lee and Hong 2014, 58). As a result of these changes, the number of vocational high schools and their enrolled students decreased as well: the percentage of vocational high school graduates (out of total high school graduates), which had increased from 40.8% in 1965 to 59.6% in 1973, decreased to 36% in 1990 (J.-H. Lee and Hong 2014, 28).

In addition to changing the educational policy, Chun's government played less of an active role in promoting in-plant vocational training. Since the introduction of the Basic Vocational Training Act in 1976, more companies (with 300 workers or more as opposed to 500 workers or more) were obligated to provide in-plant training, and companies were given the option to pay a vocational training levy (0.5% of total payrolls) in lieu of providing in-plant training. However, in response to the slowdown in economic growth caused by the 1979 oil shock, the obligation to provide in-plant vocational training was now imposed only on large companies (Ra and Kang 2012, 34). As the standard training levy was far lower than the actual costs of providing in-plant training at that time, many of the companies opted to pay the levy and simply did not provide in-plant training. By 1986, about two-thirds of the companies took this approach (K.-W. Lee 2005, 58). The number of in-plant training institutes, which had exceeded 500 when the 1974 Vocational Training Special Measure Act imposed a compulsory in-plant training system on enterprises, declined to 137 in 1987. The number of in-plant trainees likewise declined, from 337,000 during the Fourth FYED Plan period (1977–81) to 115,000 during the Fifth FYED Plan period (K.-W. Lee 2005, 59). As a result, even though the government maintained the number of trainees at *public* training institutes, the *total* number of trainees (public and in-plant trainees combined) decreased from 495,739 to 273,151 during that period (K.-W. Lee 2005, 59).

Even as vocational education and training declined under the Chun government, higher education was greatly expanded following the enactment of the 7.30 Educational Reform Measure (hereafter "7.30 Education Reform") on July 30, 1980, also known as the "Measures for Educational Normalization and Elimination of Excessive Private Tutoring." This reform was enacted to restore the stability of the academy, reorganize the educational climate, and eliminate the problem of overheated (or, as the act refers to it, "excessive") private tutoring (*kwawoe*), which persisted despite the standardization of middle and high school education in the 1960s and 1970s.[9] High private tutoring costs and excessive competition for college admission were the most pressing social-cum-educational concerns of the Korean people at the time (H. J. Choi and Park 2013). Hence, Chun attempted to enhance his political stature by announcing an education reform that addressed these problems. The 7.30 Education Reform banned private tutoring, abolished individual college entrance exams and replaced them with a standardized national exam, accredited more private tertiary institutions, and increased college admission quotas. To this end, Chun's educational policy—unlike Park's, which focused on the technical role of education for economic development—sought to promote social development by solving problems in education and educational development.

Although the 7.30 Education Reform mainly aimed to tackle the chronic problem of overheated private tutoring through these actions, its main outcome was the quantitative expansion of the higher education sector. College and university enrollment increased more than threefold, from 891,328 students in the 1970s to 2,933,683 students in the 1980s. As shown in figure 4.1, while the number of tertiary education institutions increased steadily over time, student enrollment increased dramati-

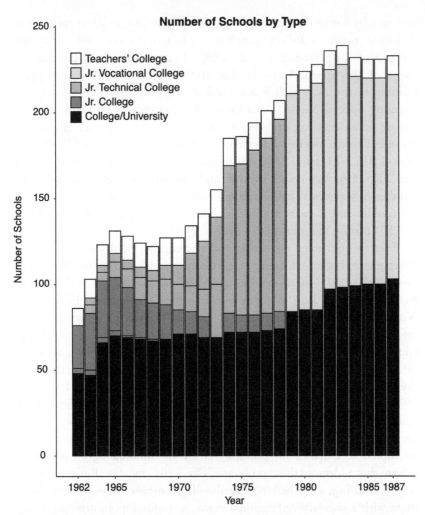

Fig 4.1. Number of schools (*above*) and levels of student enrollment by school type (*facing page*), 1962–87. Statistics are from Korea Statistical Yearbook, 1963–1988.

cally, especially in the 1980s. The difference in the slopes (i.e., the rates of change) between the number of schools and student enrollment is even more remarkable when focusing on the colleges and universities (shaded in black). From 1961 to 1987, the number of four-year colleges and universities increased from 48 to 103, at a rate of about two colleges per year. As for the matriculation rates, student enrollment increased by an average of 82,395 students per year from 1980 (the beginning of Chun Doo Hwan's rule) to 1987 (when Korea transitioned to democracy).

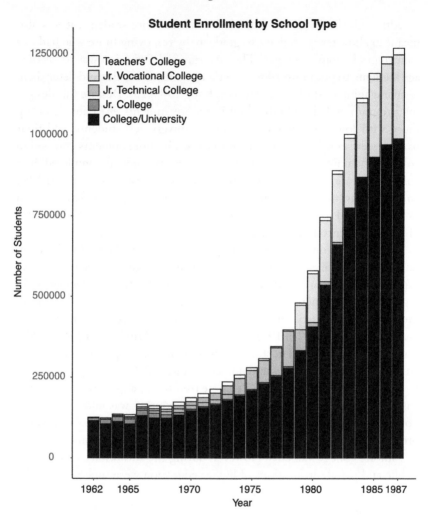

This dramatic increase in student enrollment was driven by a single element of the 7.30 Education Reform, the Graduation Quota Program (GQP; Chorŏp chŏngwŏnje), which increased the number of students admitted to universities by more than 30% in 1981 and the subsequent years. That is, with the implementation of the GQP, the government required all colleges and universities to admit 130% of each school's present admission level in March 1981 (the first month of the 1981 academic year in Korea). Universities followed the government's new order and lowered required admission scores to allow more students to be admitted.

Although the GQP was intended to admit more students, it was also meant to allow fewer students to graduate by removing those who had low college grade point averages. The government's intention was to encourage students to put more effort into their academic studies and deter them from engaging in student activism (S. Kang 1988, 28). Despite this design, the program ended up both admitting more students *and* failing to drop those with low grade point averages, as universities, students, and their parents were consistently against it. As a result, more students enrolled in colleges and universities in a given year, and more students completed their college education as well. The expansion rate increased to 150% in 1982 and each year until 1985, when the government granted greater discretion to colleges and universities in enrollment size (between 100% and 130% of their 1979 enrollment levels).

As one may wonder whether there were noticeable differences between public and private educational institutions in the course of the educational expansion, it is worth noting that as the overall rate of participation in higher education increased, the private sector occupied a greater share of the education industry: the proportion of private colleges and universities increased from 68.8% in 1965 to 79.9% in 1987 (Mun'gyobu 1965, 1987). A similar trend is found in student enrollment: the proportion of students enrolled in private colleges and universities was 72.3% in 1965 and 77.3% in 1987 (Mun'gyobu 1965, 1987). These trends may appear to illustrate the basic tenets of modernization theory: as the country was undergoing economic development, the population had more access to formal education, providing more independent critical thinking and socialization opportunities among college students. However, during the authoritarian period, all public and private institutions of higher education were supervised by the central government (i.e., the Ministry of Education), and university establishment and student population policies were especially important means of government control (J. Kim and Kim 2013). In particular, private universities were under the control of the Private School Law, and it was not until the 1990s (i.e., after democratization) that the government started to deregulate the education sector and grant more autonomy to private educational institutions (J.-E. Chae and Hong 2009).

Vocational Education and Training and Regime Stability

Through the expansion of vocational education and training in the 1960s and 1970s, the regime successfully mobilized about two million skilled workers to enter the HCI sector. However, unlike the light manufacturing workers, who were engaged in the democratic union movement throughout the 1970s and 1980s, HCI workers remained docile and were largely absent from the labor movement until the Great Workers' Struggle in 1987. Hyung-A Kim (2020) argues that the collective acquiescence of these workers was not merely the result of the labor policies of the Park and Chun regimes, but rather was the result of a "social contract" formed between the state and the HCI workers: their state-sponsored vocational education and skills training essentially put them in the state's debt. Thus, the expansion of vocational education and training had a doubly stabilizing effect on the regime: first because it produced skilled workers, who drove the economic growth that helped legitimize the regime, and second because it generated state dependence among those who received that education and training. However, as demonstrated in chapters 2 and 3, the development of industrial complexes to house these and other workers facilitated the development of the labor movement, which had a destabilizing effect on the regime in the long term. Additionally, as this section of the chapter will show, the government ultimately helped eliminate some of the constraints that had prevented labor activism from emerging and developing by not continuing to provide vocational education and training in the longer term.

This trajectory follows a particular observed pattern in authoritarian regimes. Because such rulers face threats from the masses and from the elites with whom they rule (Acemoglu and Robinson 2006; Boix 2003; Svolik 2012), they often seek ways to enhance their regimes' durability. Albertus, Fenner, and Slater (2018) argue that they can do so by providing broad public services (such as housing, education, basic services, jobs, and land) to undermine the position of preexisting elites (e.g., rival service providers) and enmesh the citizens in relationships of dependence, which compromises their ability to individually defy or collectively mobilize against the regime. The authors refer to such comprehensive distributive programs under authoritarian conditions as "coercive distribution."

Although other kinds of authoritarian distribution exist, coercive distribution is distinct in that it is both comprehensive and (as the name suggests) coercive (Albertus, Fenner, and Slater 2018). It is comprehensive because, unlike clientelism, in which goods or services are exchanged for political support, it reaches both supporters *and* opponents. And, unlike pure public goods that are nonexcludable (i.e., one person cannot reasonably prevent another from consuming the good) and nonrival (i.e., one person's consumption of the good does not affect another's),[10] coercive distribution allows the regime to credibly threaten severe sanctions (through retraction of goods and services) against those who fail to comply with its terms. This form of distribution usually occurs in three major phases: displacement of rival elites, enmeshment of citizens in relations of dependence, and upkeep—or lack thereof.

This first phase, displacement of elites, usually happens at the outset of a new authoritarian regime, and though it did occur in South Korea, it was less extensive than it sometimes is because historical circumstances meant that there were lower levels of threat from the domestic elites. During the early years of authoritarian rule under Park Chung Hee, South Korea faced an existentially high external threat from North Korea,[11] which made any threat from domestic elites and the masses seem lesser in comparison (Greitens 2016).[12] And the threat truly *was* smaller—the landed elites, which are traditionally understood to be the "obstructers" of democracy (Moore 1966), had already been dissolved through the land reform in the 1940s and 1950s. Furthermore, the clientelistic relations that existed between the industrial bourgeoisie (*chaebŏl*) and the state during the Rhee regime (1948–61) created "a politically weak and dependent bourgeoisie" (H. B. Im 1986, 246).[13] Soon after his regime's onset, Park solidified this relationship by granting amnesty to the local bourgeoisie, who in the postliberation period had amassed fortunes through illegal activities in exchange for collaboration with the government's plans for export-led development (H. B. Im 1986; E. M. Kim and Park 2011).

Still, there was a certain amount of elite displacement. The state provided low-interest loans, tax cuts, and foreign capital to big businesses with a proven track record of risk-taking, managerial capability, and high performance, and it let failing business groups flounder (E. M. Kim and Park 2011). Park also nationalized all commercial banks in 1961, which allowed the state to control sources of capital and discipline the big businesses. Most importantly, as stated by Eun Mee Kim and Gil-Sung Park (2011, 269), "Park made it clear to the businesses that his support for their industrial ventures came on the condition that they did not seek political power for themselves." This relationship between the state and big businesses more or less continued under the subsequent Chun regime.

Whereas the first phase was less extensive than it is under some authoritarian regimes, the second phase—enmeshment of citizens in relationships of dependence—was robust. The Park government deployed vocational education and training programs to make its citizens (and, more specifically, the youth and workers) rely on the state if they wished to achieve social mobility and economic security. Through its implementation of the

Specialization Initiatives at Technical High Schools in 1973 and the High School Equalization Policy in 1974, the government produced a large number of vocational high school graduates and trainees who otherwise would have pursued nonvocational education.[14] In this way, the equalization policy measures deprived youth (including the bright students from rural areas) of access to other "elites" in society (i.e., intellectuals in Seoul), who could have influenced them to participate in antigovernment activities.

This deprivation was intentional. As further elaborated later in this chapter, colleges and universities in Korea were the breeding ground for antigovernment activities during the authoritarian era. College students were the vanguard of Korea's democracy movement, and the elite universities in Seoul dominated the student movement. These universities drew youth from around the country—before the high school equalization policy was implemented in 1974, many young students from small cities or rural areas moved to Seoul to pursue elite secondary education and, they hoped, increase their chances of being accepted to Seoul National University (SNU) or other elite universities. This pattern is reflected in the SNU annual survey of the entering class from the 1960s and 1970s, which shows that before the government implemented the equalization policy, most SNU students were from cities, primarily Seoul. After the policy was implemented, the proportion of students from Seoul at SNU decreased steadily, from 54% in 1974 to around 40% through the 1980s. According to *Seoul National University since 1946*, this decrease is most likely due to the increased number of students attending high schools in their hometowns instead of moving to Seoul to enroll at elite high schools and attend SNU (Sŏul Taehakkyo 60-yŏnsa P'yŏnch'an Wiwŏnhoe 2006). In this way, the regime's policy worked as intended.

During this enmeshment stage, vocational education and training also functioned as a form of coercive distribution (and not as a pure method of clientelism) because of the *universality* of the programs offered. A significant segment of the population was provided with the opportunity to enter (and receive the benefits of) technical high schools or vocational training centers, including in-plant training.[15] Additionally, these programs and their attendant benefits were accessible to citizens *before* they demonstrated loyalty to the regime, which meant the programs were not clientelistic in nature.

Once entered into the vocational education and training programs, students and trainees were instilled with a sense of pride in becoming "skilled workers for our homeland's modernization"—even if they had no such pride or loyalty when they joined. Park Chung Hee himself frequently visited factories, technology and research centers, and construction sites to show his active involvement in designing and implementing major economic development policies and programs (S. Moon 2009). In demonstrating his prioritization of vocational education, Park also visited technical high schools and ordered these schools to cultivate elite technicians who would become the "flag bearers of the modernization of the fatherland" (*choguk kŭndaehwa ŭi kisu*).[16]

In addition to the national recognition they received, these elite technical high schools and students received various compelling financial and material benefits from the government.[17] A large proportion of the students—including more than half of those enrolled in the machinery technical high schools—received tuition discounts and loans for living costs (H.-A. Kim 2020, 32). Students of Kŭmo Technical High School, a specialized technical high school founded by Park Chung Hee in 1973, received almost everything, including payment of school fees, skills training costs, textbooks, uniforms, and other study-related materials, as well as meals and accommodations, and the guarantee of employment after graduation (H.-A. Kim 2020, 23). Moreover, students who acquired precision (Class II) licenses received ₩100,000 per year as a scholarship directly from the president (J.-H. Lee and Hong 2014, 75). The Class II craftsmen qualification—obtained by attending the elite technical high schools or the vocational training program—guaranteed employment and symbolized social mobility, which was especially attractive for those who belonged to the lower-middle class (typically from the rural areas) and could not afford to send their children (or could send only their eldest son) to college. Given these powerful incentives, the regime succeeded in recruiting bright students to these vocational high schools and away from colleges and universities.

Among the most enticing benefits for graduates of such institutions was the ability to find immediate employment at defense industry firms and to serve as "worker soldiers" (*t'ŭngnyebyŏng*; "special soldiers") for five years in lieu of the three-year compulsory military service.[18] This path was appealing to young male graduates and trainees because it offered economic security. As worker soldiers, they had paid jobs at promising companies *and* they were able to fulfill their mandatory military service. These years also counted toward their years of work experience, which directly impacted their future pay and promotion. As stated by Hyung-A Kim (2020, 40), HCI workers were "eager to seize this unprecedented educational opportunity not only for their country's modernization but also for their own goal of a better life with a secure job and better upward social mobility."

Despite the fact that access to these programs was universal (i.e., it was neither given as a reward nor withheld as a punishment) and notwithstanding the distinct benefits they offered, participation in them came at a cost: participants who were noncompliant with the government's agenda were punished on the back end. As documented by Hyung-A Kim (2013, 581; 2015, 61), in return for these financial and material benefits, "those who entered technical high schools or vocational training centers, or even in-plant training, had to abide by the state's terms and conditions that demanded 'no free-riding' and strictly performance-based resource allocation." Students who failed at their required tasks—whether academic or nonacademic—had their financial subsidies and other privileges withdrawn (H.-A. Kim 2020, 30). And even for those who completed the programs and became worker soldiers in the defense industry, the associated privileged status was fragile. Those who failed to meet the company's requirements were dismissed and immediately conscripted into military service. And because the labor law prohibited workers in the defense industry from engaging in collective bargaining due to national security concerns, those who participated in the anti-FKTU democratic union movement (which was antigovernment in nature, as discussed in chapter 2) were also arrested or fired. In these ways, the government ensured economic productivity *and* political loyalty from the workers it mobilized through vocational education and training programs.

These first two phases of coercive distribution achieved the regime's goals, but like many (or even most) such programs, South Korea's failed at the third stage: the upkeep stage. As discussed earlier in this chapter, in stabilizing the economy in the early 1980s, the Chun government changed not only the country's economic development strategy but also its vocational education and training policies. The Specialization Initiatives at Technical High Schools was abolished, and the obligation to provide in-plant vocational training (or pay the standard training levy) was now imposed only on large enterprises. Additionally, although student enrollment in vocational schools had increased significantly under Park's rule, the youth still preferred to attend academic high schools—even in 1980 there were only 764,000 students enrolled in vocational high schools, compared to 932,000 attending academic schools (Seth 2002, 128). This combination of the policy change and the preexisting preference for academic education resulted in a significant reduction in the number of vocational schools, students, and trainees.

As the government's investment in vocational education and training programs dwindled in the 1980s, fewer workers were produced by the technical high schools and vocational training institutions, which meant

106   Seeds of Mobilization

that fewer workers received material benefits from the state and remained vulnerable to their retraction. Concurrently, the expansion of higher education led to the quantitative expansion of the student movement, which was politicized and included students' involvement in the labor movement as students-turned-workers (chapter 3). In this context, an uprising by the formerly enmeshed HCI workers became much more thinkable and feasible.

And, as demonstrated in chapter 3, the ecological conditions surrounding the industrial complexes played a critical role in facilitating the labor movement's gradual growth and in building its underlying strength. Through their shared living arrangements and ecology-nurtured leisure activities surrounding the government-built industrial complexes, male HCI workers in Ulsan, Masan, and Ch'angwŏn were also able to develop workers' consciousness, form unions, and organize strikes during the 1987 Great Workers' Struggle. As pointed out in *My Love, Trade Union Confederation in Masan-Ch'angwŏn*, the technical high school alumni associations and vocational training center alumni associations that organized these gatherings played a critical role in mobilizing the workers in Masan and Ch'angwon during the struggle (H. Kim and Mach'ang Noryŏnsa Palgan Wiwŏnhoe 1999). Thus, these social gatherings—which were utilized to protest against the regime—were themselves the by-products of the state-subsidized vocational education and training programs.

University Higher Education and Regime Instability

It is perhaps understandable that in a society that has historically valued scholarly pursuits,[19] college students would come to play a significant role in the development of modern Korea (P. Y. Chang 2015a; N. Lee 2007; M. Park 2008; C. Yi 2011). Following liberation from Japanese colonial rule in 1945, students were the primary agents of some of the most important political transitions in the country. Their ability to play this central role was based not only on Confucian cultural values, which taught that they had a moral mandate to evaluate political leaders, but also on the material expansion of tertiary education and the resulting increase in matriculated students in colleges and universities. As discussed earlier in this chapter, the government intended all levels of education to provide a continual flow of skilled labor to a rapidly growing economy, but their impact didn't stop there. Rather, institutions of higher education brought together social movement actors who had ready access to social, cultural, and human capital and who facilitated the emergence of large-scale antigovernment protests throughout the authoritarian period. In this section, I show that the expansion of higher education had a destabilizing effect on the regime because it led to the creation of a nationwide student movement. And students within this movement ultimately played a critical role in forming alliances with workers (chapter 3) and opposition politicians (chapter 5) to successfully mobilize against the authoritarian regime in the 1980s.

Popularization of the Student Movement

The 1980s popularization (*taejunghwa*) of the Korean student movement was a process in which student activism (i.e., student involvement in protests, including pro-democracy protests) became widespread and familiar to the public. In Korea, it was in the 1980s when student activism became an accepted and expected part of student life and culture. The most significant change in university culture at that time was the rapid spread of "activist culture" (*undongkwŏn munhwa*). "Literally meaning 'those who are in the [democratization] movement sphere,' the term *undongkwŏn* applied both to individual activists and to the democratization movement as a whole, whose articulated goal was to bring democracy, justice, and reunification to Korea" (N. Lee 2005, 911). Additionally, whether they identified with the label or not, college students in the 1980s were highly exposed to and influenced by *undongkwŏn* culture on college campuses (Sŏul Taehakkyo 60-yŏnsa P'yŏnch'an Wiwŏnhoe 2006, 754).

Due to the rise of this activist culture, on-campus protests and street demonstrations became quite prevalent among college students. According to a survey conducted by the Seoul National University Center for Campus Life and Culture in 1987, nearly half of the SNU student population (46.6%) participated in protests in 1986 (Sŏul Taehakkyo 60-yŏnsa P'yŏnch'an Wiwŏnhoe 2006, 753). This participation rate was found to be similar to those of Yonsei and Korea Universities, the two comparable elite universities in Korea (Sŏul Taehakkyo 60-yŏnsa P'yŏnch'an Wiwŏnhoe 2006, 753). Furthermore, as pointed out by Namhee Lee (2007), the student movement was ultimately popularized to the extent that it was no longer dominated by these three elite schools in Seoul and by "movement-prone" universities such as Chonnam National University in South Chŏlla Province—it extended well beyond those institutions. As will become clear in this section, students' own agency and their movement ideologies certainly played a significant role in popularizing the movement, but it was the government's expansion of higher education that provided favorable

108   Seeds of Mobilization

ecological conditions for creating a nationwide student movement that
made student protests widespread and familiar to the public.

The Drivers of the Movement's Growth

As mentioned earlier, higher education expanded considerably when the
Chun regime implemented the Graduation Quota Program. For the student movement, the significance of the dramatic increase in student enrollment was that it created a larger pool of potential activists, enlarging the
student population that could access material and cultural resources to
engage in student activism. As noted by Paul Chang, "The power of the
student movement was predicated upon students' ability to disrupt society
through large public demonstrations. This power was a function of the
stark growth in university enrollment . . . Universities often provided the
material (a place to gather) and cultural (exposure to political theory and
ideology) resources for mobilizing large numbers of people" (P. Y. Chang
2015a, 50–51).

The government's expansion of higher education, and the resulting
geospatial concentration of university students, also provided more students with the mobilizing structures to engage in collective action. Defined
as "collective vehicles, informal as well as formal, through which people
mobilize and engage in collective action" (McAdam, McCarthy, and Zald
1996), mobilizing structures allow dense social relationships to develop
and provide solidarity, leadership, communication networks, movement
recruitment, and collective action frames (Clemens 1996; McAdam 1982;
Snow, Zurcher, and Ekland-Olson 1980). In the Korean case, student councils (*haksaenghoe*) and department student organizations (*hakhoe*) served as
such structures, and students used them to organize protests in the 1980s.

In addition to this expansion of higher education, policy changes
around campus autonomy also facilitated the growth of the student movement. Starting in 1975, autonomous student organizations such as student
councils and department student organizations had been inaccessible due
to Park Chung Hee's promulgation of Emergency Decree No. 9, which
had rendered illegal all forms of government criticism. The Park government had also reestablished the state-controlled National Defense Student
Corps (Hakto Hoguktan),[20] dissolved the existing autonomous student
organizations, revised student regulations (making it difficult to reinstate
dismissed students), legalized the presence of security agents and the military on college campuses, extended students' military training, and curtailed various extracurricular activities. The Chun government, too, had

Learning to Dissent 109

been severely repressive from 1980 to 1983. Then, on December 21, 1983, Chun Doo Hwan's "campus autonomy" measures (Hagwŏn Chayurhwa Choch'i) lifted these restrictions. State security agents were withdrawn from college campuses, dismissed students and professors were reinstated, and the National Defense Student Corps was dissolved.[21]

These campus autonomy measures were a part of a series of liberalizing policies intended to bring about "national unity" and "grand reconciliation." According to Sunhyuk Kim, "the political liberalization was due to the misperceptions of the regime and international pressure" (S. Kim 2000, 98). Specifically, Chun perceived its regime to have entered a relatively stable period and relaxed its repressive policies in response. The regime also needed to generate favorable public opinion (both domestic and international) given the upcoming National Assembly election (scheduled to be held in February 1985) and the two international sporting events that Korea was hosting: the 1986 Asian Games and the 1988 Summer Olympics.

Regardless of the government's intentions, though, the changes meant that student activists no longer had to resort to underground networks to recruit members and organize their activities, as they had done during and after Park's repressive Yusin regime and the Chun regime's Kwangju Massacre (N. Lee 2007). Additionally, the more open environment on college campuses made it possible for student activists to rebuild student councils and strengthen the student movement.[22] As stated in the *History of Korea's Democratization Movement*, students' efforts to rebuild student councils were widespread:

> [Following Chun's liberalization policy,] forming a self-governing student council was an irreversible trend on university campuses. The rapid spread of self-governing student councils in 1984 was especially noticeable in the provincial areas [i.e., areas outside of the capital city, Seoul]. There were efforts to build democratic student councils even at small universities, where student activism was relatively weak. By 1985–1986, almost all universities could reestablish their student councils, allowing universities to become a strong base and a driving force for the democratization movement. (Minjuhwa Undong Kinyŏm Saophoe 2010, 224–25)

With the revival of student councils on university campuses across the country, student groups evolved from small, disconnected units to national organizations, and collaboration among universities on a national scale

110 Seeds of Mobilization

resulted in more coordinated activities among student groups in the 1980s (H. Choi 1991, 186). In this way, the government's expansion of higher education created the ecological conditions for them to organize on-campus and intercampus student organizations and protests, just like how industrial complexes created the conditions for workers to organize and engage in collective action within and across firms (chapter 3).

National Federation of Student Associations

On April 17, 1985, around 2,000 students from 23 universities across the country gathered at Korea University and formed the Chŏn'guk Haksaeng Ch'ong Yŏnhap (Chŏnhangnyŏn; National Federation of Student Associations, NFSA), with SNU Student Council president Kim Minsŏk as the chairperson (*wiwŏnjang*) and the student council presidents of Sungkyunkwan University (Seoul and Suwon campuses), Pusan National University, and Chonnam National University as the four vice-chairpersons (*puwiwŏnjang*; Chosun Ilbo 1985; Minjuhwa Undong Kinyŏm Saophoe 2006, 434–35). This amalgamation of student councils (or student governments, *haksaenghoe*) from universities across the country played a significant role in mobilizing students across regions and levels of prestige. It also established the Committee of the Three *Min* Struggle (Sammint'u) as the vanguard organization within the NFSA (with Korea University Student Council president Hŏ Inhoe as the chairperson).[23] This committee led most of the student movement in 1985, including the occupation of the Seoul U.S. Information Service building in May 1985 (Minjuhwa Undong Kinyŏm Saophoe 2006, 435).[24]

Although the NFSA was the most extensive and inclusive nationwide student coalition to date, it was not the first. Nearly 15 years earlier, in 1971, a national student organization called the National Alliance of Youth and Students for the Protection of Democracy (Minju Suho Chŏn'guk Ch'ŏngnyŏn Haksaeng Ch'ongyŏnmaeng; known as the Students' Alliance) was formed by 200 students from five elite schools in Seoul (Seoul National, Korea, Yonsei, Sogang, and Sungkyunkwan Universities) and two major provincial schools (Kyungpook National and Chonnam National Universities). This organization was immediately dissolved by the Park government. In response, students recommitted to the strategy of establishing a nationwide network to coordinate diverse student groups across different universities and, in 1973, formed (what later became known as) the National Democratic Youth and Student Alliance (Chŏn'guk Minju Ch'ŏngnyŏn Haksaeng Ch'ongyŏnmaeng). Although the government again immediately repressed this effort, the alliance left behind an important structure: the "3-3-3" structure.

This structure consisted of three core groups of students at each of the three major institutional and geographic levels (P. Y. Chang 2015a, 69). The student leaders at SNU's Liberal Arts College, Law College, and Department of Business Administration made up the "SNU core," which coordinated the national network. It first contacted students at other SNU colleges and then contacted the Yonsei and Korea Universities' central student leaders. The students at these three universities became the "Seoul city core," and they were responsible for contacting other universities in the city. SNU students were also responsible for contacting students at two key regional universities—Chonnam National University (in Chŏlla Province) and Kyungpook National University (in Kyŏngsang Province)—who then contacted students at other schools in their respective provinces.

The National Democratic Youth and Student Alliance's nationwide structure was an important innovation, but it reflected a key limiting characteristic of the 1970s student movement: student activism was located only at elite universities in Seoul (such as Seoul National, Korea, and Yonsei Universities) and some of the major provincial (or regional) universities, such as Chonnam National University. The NFSA, in contrast, exceeded that 3-3-3 structure and extended throughout the country. As shown in figure 4.2, its regional council was made up of *four* regional branches (one for each major region of the country): Seoul, Chungbu (Kyŏnggi, Kangwon, North Ch'ungch'ŏng, and South Ch'ungch'ŏng Provinces), Honam (North Chŏlla and South Chŏlla Provinces), and Yŏngnam (North Kyŏngsang and South Kyŏngsang Provinces).[25] The Seoul branch was further divided into four sub-branches: southern, northern, western, and eastern.[26] Additionally, the Central Executive Committee consisted of the student council presidents of various universities throughout the country—beyond those that were previously involved in the National Democratic Youth and Student Alliance—including Seoul National, Korea, Yonsei, Sungkyunkwan (Seoul and Suwon campuses), Sogang, Chonnam National, and Pusan National Universities. Its broader network also included provincial universities that were not "movement-prone" and universities in Seoul that did not have a long-standing tradition of student activism, including women's universities.

Utilizing this extensive organizational structure, the student movement became more organized. It developed protest repertoires, which increased the overall size and frequency of student protests, including coalitional protests and rallies (*yonhap siwi*; *yonhap chiphoe*) by multiple student groups.

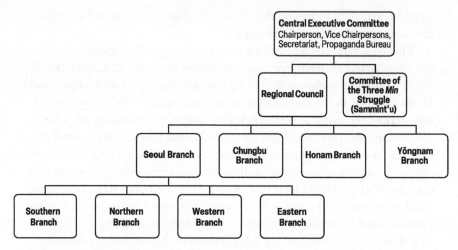

Fig 4.2. Organizational chart of the National Federation of Student Associations.
Source: *Chosun Ilbo* (July 19, 1985).

It was through the NFSA network that major coalitional protests were organized.

The first significant example occurred when students held on-campus events to commemorate the April 19 Student Revolution of 1960, which brought down the first authoritarian regime in South Korea by successfully pressuring President Syngman Rhee to resign. At 4:00 p.m. on April 19, 1985, 7,000 students from 26 universities across the country gathered at the 4.19 National Cemetery (located in Suyu district in Seoul) to attend the 4.19 memorial ceremony, organized by the NFSA (Minjuhwa Undong Kinyŏm Saophoe 2010, 237). Following the memorial ceremony, each school, divided by region, held street demonstrations until later in the evening. At 6:30 p.m., about 500 students demonstrated in the Samyang district. At 7:00 p.m., Sogang University and Ewha Women's University students protested in front of the Namgajwa train station. At 7:20 p.m., Seoul National University students protested at the Pangsan Market entrance, and at 8:35 p.m., about 300 students protested at the Kangnam Terminal (Seoul Express Bus Terminal). In the subsequent years, the 4.19 Struggle continued to be organized in similar ways: (1) students first held commemorative demonstrations on their respective campuses, (2) students from different schools congregated at the 4.19 National Cemetery in Seoul to hold a joint ceremony, and (3) students held street demonstrations in various locations around the city (Minjuhwa Undong Kinyŏm Saophoe 2010, 237).

Similarly, the annual May Struggle, during which protests memorialize the 1980 Kwangju Uprising, began following an event organized by the NFSA. On May 6, 1985, the NFSA announced the May Struggle Declaration at its second conference, for which approximately 700 students from 16 universities across the country were gathered at Korea University. At its third conference, held on May 14 at Yonsei University and attended by students from 26 universities, the organization warned that if the Chun regime continued to evade responsibility for the Kwangju Massacre, it would launch an all-out struggle against the regime. Two days later, on May 16, approximately 8,000 students from 14 universities in Seoul and 7,000 students from 25 provincial universities participated in protests demanding official recognition of the truth of the Kwangju Uprising and punishment for those responsible. And on the following day (May 17), approximately 40,000 students from 80 universities followed suit. As with the 4.19 Struggle, students in subsequent years developed the following routine for the May Struggle: students (1) organized on-campus protests during the annual college festival (*taehak ch'ukche*) in May, (2) held street demonstrations, (3) battled with police, and (4) held sit-ins on campus (Minjuhwa Undong Kinyŏm Saophoe 2010, 238).

In sum, the revival of autonomous student organizations at newly expanded colleges and universities all over the country led to the formation of the NFSA, which turned student activism into a mass movement by building an extensive and inclusive network structure and developing new protest repertoires. The individual student organizations on each campus and the NFSA itself (the amalgamation of these student councils) served as the mobilizing structures in creating a nationwide student movement and ultimately popularizing the Korean student movement in the 1980s.

Geographic Distribution of Student Protests

With the availability of mobilization structures, especially starting in 1984, the student movement meaningfully expanded beyond the elite universities in Seoul and other so-called movement-prone universities. Figure 4.3 displays the number and breakdown of student protests in Seoul versus the provincial areas (i.e., the areas outside of Seoul) from 1980 to 1987.[27] The dip in the number of protests between 1980 and 1984 reflects the severity of the Chun regime's repression following the Spring of Seoul and the Kwangju Uprising in 1980, but the number of student protests did increase overall. Importantly, this overall increase in student protests, especially between 1985 and 1987, was driven by student protests outside

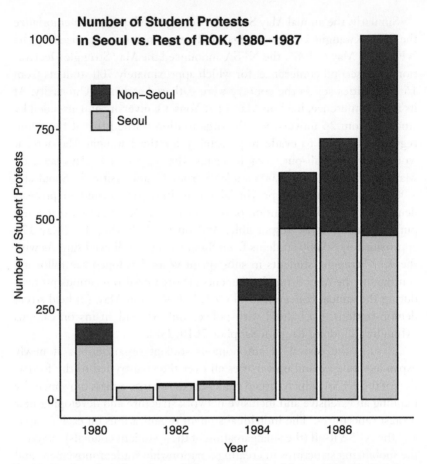

Fig 4.3. Number of student protests in Seoul vs. outside of Seoul, 1980–87. Statistics are from the author's dataset.

of Seoul: whereas the number of protests in Seoul remained relatively stable from 1985 to 1987, the number of protests increased dramatically in the provincial areas. Thus, from 1984 to 1987, the proportion of protests that occurred in Seoul decreased each year—from 83% to 75% to 64% to 45%, respectively.

This shift in proportion from Seoul to provincial areas is also reflected in table 4.2, which lists the schools that hosted joint on-campus events and protests in the 1980s. As discussed earlier, coalitional protests by students from different schools became more prevalent after the reinstatement of student councils in 1984 and then the formation of the NFSA in 1985. As the table shows, starting in 1985, these protests were hosted by more schools in

Learning to Dissent 115

TABLE 4.2. Location of Joint On-Campus Protests in the 1980s

	Schools in Seoul	Schools in Provincial Areas
1980	Ewha Women's Univ	
1984	SNU, Korea Univ, Yonsei Univ, Sungkyunkwan Univ, Ewha Women's Univ, Hankuk Univ of Foreign Studies, Chungang Univ, Kyunghee Univ	
1985	SNU, Korea Univ, Yonsei Univ, Sungkyunkwan Univ, Ewha Women's Univ, Hankuk Univ of Foreign Studies, Chungang Univ, Kyunghee Univ, Konkuk Univ, Kukmin Univ, Dongguk Univ	Chonnam National Univ (Chŏlla), Chungnam National Univ (Ch'ungch'ŏng), Mokwon Univ (Ch'ungch'ŏng)
1986	SNU, Korea Univ, Yonsei Univ, Sungkyunkwan Univ, Sogang Univ, Hankuk Univ of Foreign Studies, Chungang Univ, Kyunghee Univ, Hanyang Univ, Konkuk Univ, Kukmin Univ	Chonnam National Univ (Chŏlla), Pusan National Univ (Kyŏngsang)
1987	SNU, Korea Univ, Yonsei Univ, Hankuk Univ of Foreign Studies, Danguk Univ, Konkuk Univ, Methodist Theological Univ	Chonnam National Univ (Chŏlla), Kyungpook National Univ (Kyŏngsang), Chosun Univ (Chŏlla), Pusan National Univ (Kyŏngsang), Yonsei Univ Wonju Campus (Kangwon), Chungnam National Univ (Ch'ungch'ŏng), Gyeonggi College of Science and Technology (Kyŏnggi)

Source: Author's dataset.

Seoul, by those in the provincial areas, and, most importantly, by those that did not have a long-standing history of student activism (i.e., schools other than Seoul National, Korea, Yonsei, Chŏnnam National, and Kyungpook National Universities). The frequency and originating location of coalitional protests reflected not only the increased strength of the student movement in the mid-1980s but also the enhanced mobilizational capacity and solidarity within the student movement (across schools and regions).

Alongside this shift in which universities were hosting coalitional protests, there was also a shift in where other major events for the movement were happening. Two thousand students from 23 universities had gathered at Korea University to form the NFSA in 1985, but only two years later, more than 4,000 students from 95 schools across the country gathered at Chungnam National University (in South Ch'ungch'ŏng Province, located in the central region of South Korea) and formed the National Council

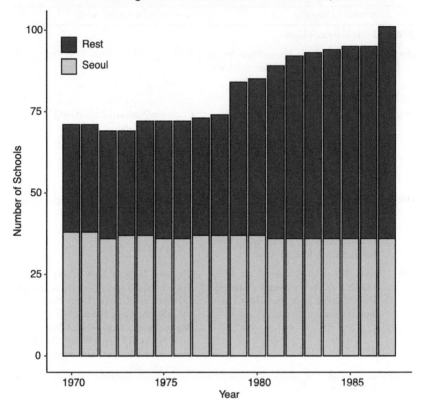

Fig 4.4. Number of colleges/universities (*above*) and students in Seoul vs. non-Seoul areas (*facing page*) in South Korea, 1970–87. Statistics are from the Korea Statistical Yearbook, 1971–88.

of Student Representatives (Chŏnguk Taehaksaeng Taep'yoja Hyŏbŭihoe; Chŏndaehyŏp) (Minjuhwa Undong Kinyŏm Saophoe 2006, 486). It is noteworthy that such an important national event for the student movement was held at a nonmajor provincial school, further attesting that student activism became more prevalent and widespread in the 1980s—and that the elite schools in Seoul no longer dominated the movement.

The trend of increasing student protests (including the organization and frequency of coalitional protests), especially in the provincial areas, resulted from the expansion of higher education under Chun's regime—and, specifically, from the GQP. The change in quotas was significant because of how restrictive they had been in the preceding decades. In the 1960s and 1970s, Korea's rapid industrialization had accompanied rapid

Number of College Students in Seoul vs. Rest of ROK, 1970–1987

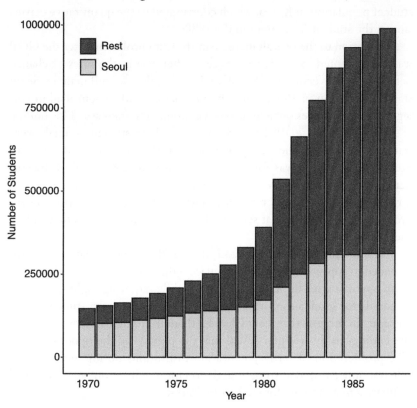

urbanization and population concentration in the Seoul metropolitan area, and the government had wanted to limit the population growth in the metropolitan area. To do so, it had reduced the quota for student enrollment at colleges and universities in the Seoul metropolitan area but increased the quota at regional colleges and universities. This change had led to a higher proportion of schools located outside of Seoul, from 34% to 69% between 1970 and 1987. As a result, when Chun's education reform and the accompanying increase in quotas were implemented in the 1980s, the dramatic increase in student enrollment was even more pronounced for regional schools. This pattern is displayed in figure 4.4, which illustrates that the proportion of college students who enrolled in schools located outside of Seoul rose from 33% to 68% at that time. It also shows that the increase in the overall number of tertiary education institutions and the number of students enrolled in them was driven by institutions in regions outside of

Seoul. These patterns suggest that it was Chun's GQP that increased the student population in Korea, which contributed to the quantitative expansion of the student movement in the 1980s.

In addition to the overall increase in student enrollment after the GQP was implemented in 1981, we notice a difference in the rates of change between Seoul versus non-Seoul regions. Student enrollment in Seoul started to plateau in 1984, while the number of students enrolled in colleges and universities outside of Seoul continued to increase. This finding is significant because 1984 was the year in which student councils were reinstated, and the following year was when the National Federation of Student Associations was formed. The quantitative expansion of the student population—which was more evenly spread out across the country as a result of these different rates of change—helps to explain why student protests began to happen at schools all over the country when they did: in the mid-to-late 1980s.

Chun's education reform (and the GQP in particular) had been intended to appease the Korean populace—the regime intended to provide more opportunities for higher education while requiring higher academic standards for graduation, which would discourage college students from engaging in protests that would distract them from their studies. However, the findings in this chapter reveal that the policy had the opposite effect. The proliferation of tertiary education institutions during authoritarian rule not only ensured a strong foundation for mobilization but also helped facilitate a new strategy for student mobilization.

Conclusion

The authoritarian governments in Korea instigated the expansion of vocational and higher education to bolster and complement the country's industrial development. Their emphasis on technical and vocational training, as well as on developing the skills necessary in an evolving export-oriented global economy, helped produce a well-educated labor force that contributed to rapid economic growth. As this chapter has shown, through the implementation of the 1973 Specialization Initiatives at Technical High Schools and the 1974 High School Equalization Policy, the government produced a large number of vocational high school graduates and trainees who would otherwise have pursued nonvocational education. In doing so, the regime deprived these youth of access to other elites, who could have encouraged them to participate in antigovernment activities.

When they entered into this enmeshed relationship with the authoritarian state, these students and trainees were transformed into HCI workers, who ensured economic productivity and political loyalty to the regime. However, like many programs of coercive distribution, the vocational education and training programs failed at the upkeep stage. And failing to maintain these programs made it possible for the formerly enmeshed HCI workers to consider and pursue an uprising.

The expansion of tertiary education in the 1970s and especially in the 1980s generated a large population of college students. As shown in this chapter, the Graduation Quota Program, in particular, contributed to the creation of a nationwide student movement by creating a larger population of students in *all* regions of the country, with mobilizing structures available to them to facilitate collective action. In this way, the students who were expected to participate in the country's industrial drive instead became the vanguard of the democracy movement.

As the next chapter will show, these student organizations served as mobilizing structures for the 1987 June Democratic Uprising, which resulted in the regime's capitulation to the public demand for democratic reforms. As stated in *Seoul National University since 1946*, students' widespread involvement in the June Democratic Uprising could not have been orchestrated by a few activist organizations—student councils were the only organizations with the potential to orchestrate large-scale mobilization at that time (Sŏul Taehakkyo 60-yŏnsa P'yŏnch'an Wiwŏnhoe 2006, 873). And, indeed, many students gathered under the banner of the student council to engage in mass public demonstrations during the June Democratic Uprising. The next chapter will focus on the alliance formed between opposition politicians and college students during the 1985 National Assembly election, and it will examine whether and how the student organizations linked the electoral activities to pro-democracy protests during the June Democratic Uprising.

FIVE

From College Campuses to Ballot Boxes

Mobilizing for Democratic Reforms

The preceding chapters of this book demonstrated that the geospatial concentration of workers and students—resulting from the autocrats' industrial and educational policies—translated into an increased capacity for those groups to organize and engage in collective action. In that process, interfirm and intercampus networks were created, and the student movement formed alliances with workers and opposition politicians. Unlike the worker-student alliance, which is widely considered to have been significant in the development of the labor movement, the alliance formed between the political opposition and college students in the 1980s has not garnered much attention for its impact on South Korea's democratization. This difference may be partly due to the fact that the political opposition did not play any significant role in the student-led April 19 Revolution against Syngman Rhee's rule in 1960 that previously brought down the country's first authoritarian regime. Additionally, throughout much of the authoritarian period, the cooperation and alignment between the political opposition and civil society existed only through individual connections and commitments, and not through institutional channels of joint organizations (S. Kim 2000, 73). Nevertheless, the political opposition ended up playing a key role in the second such breakdown: it was able to successfully pressure the Chun Doo Hwan regime (1980–88) to make democratic concessions in 1987, and it did so by forming a grand pro-democracy coalition with civil society organizations.

The turning point in the relationship between civil society, including students, and the political opposition was the 12th National Assembly election in 1985. For the first time under Chun's rule, *genuine* opposition parties (i.e., parties that were not created or sponsored by the incumbent regime)—including the newly formed New Korea Democratic Party (NKDP; Shinhan Minjudang)—were allowed to contest against the ruling party. It was also the first time that university students, who had not identified with a political party since the 1960s, aligned themselves with the political opposition (S. Kim 2000, 85). These two groups rallied around their demand for constitutional revision, including the reinstatement of direct presidential elections. Two years later, a nationwide pro-democracy movement for free, democratic elections—known as the June Democratic Uprising—emerged. These mass demonstrations successfully forced the authoritarian incumbent to allow democratic reforms, including direct presidential elections, and led to the establishment of the Sixth Republic of Korea, the present-day democratic government of South Korea.

This chapter explores whether and how the alliance formed between the opposition politicians and college students during the political liberalization period in the 1980s under Chun Doo Hwan's rule—specifically, the 1985 National Assembly election—affected the pro-democracy protests during the 1987 June Democratic Uprising. In examining this relationship, I situate the Korean case within existing debates in the electoral authoritarianism and social movement literatures regarding the impact of elections on protests in autocracies. In doing so, I highlight the moderating role that mobilizing structures play in that relationship. Specifically, regarding the case of Korea, I show that student organizations served as mobilizing structures and played a critical role in linking electoral activities to antigovernment protests—indeed, without these organizations, this link did not materialize. As the chapter's empirical analysis will demonstrate, the areas that were more supportive of the NKDP during the 12th National Assembly election engaged in more protests during the 1987 June Democratic Uprising *only* in areas with a high proportion of college students. Student organizations and networks were denser in these areas and served as mobilizing structures for the uprising. This finding substantiates the impact that the alliance between the political opposition and college students had on the democracy movement, thus inviting further research on this relationship. It also underscores the structural basis of mobilization under authoritarian regimes more generally.

Elections and Protests in Authoritarian Regimes

An enduring debate within the comparative politics literature on *authoritarian durability* concerns whether multiparty elections stabilize authoritarian regimes or contribute to their democratization. Many political scientists have argued that authoritarian leaders can strategically use elections and electoral institutions to ensure regime survival (Blaydes 2011; Boix and Svolik 2013; Brownlee 2007; Bueno de Mesquita et al. 2004; Gandhi 2008; Gandhi and Przeworski 2007; Greene 2007; Magaloni 2006; Magaloni 2010; Magaloni and Kricheli 2010; Simpser 2013; Slater 2010; Svolik 2012; J. Wright 2011; J. Wright and Escribà-Folch 2012), and the fact that "competitive authoritarian regimes" have thrived in the post–Cold War era (Levitsky and Way 2010) supports this argument. In such regimes, "formal democratic institutions [such as elections] exist and are widely viewed as the primary means of gaining power, but . . . incumbents' abuse of the state places them at a significant advantage vis-à-vis their opponents" (Levitsky and Way 2010, 5–7). That is, autocrats can often hold multiparty elections while still engaging in serious democratic abuses, which creates an uneven playing field and helps to consolidate their power. They can use such elections to prevent or solve intra-elite conflict, such as by spreading the spoils of office to the domestic political elite or as a focal point for patronage distribution to the citizenry (through vote-buying) (Blaydes 2011; Gandhi 2008; Gandhi and Przeworski 2007; Geddes 2005; Lust 2006). Additionally, by holding and winning elections by huge margins, autocrats can signal regime stability while simultaneously obtaining information about the regime's supporters and opponents (Simpser 2013). Such election-induced legitimacy also contributes to regime durability by providing international benefits such as foreign aid and international legitimacy from outside actors (Beaulieu and Hyde 2009; van de Walle 2002). In these and other ways, regimes can use elections as a tool to further entrench their own power.

Other scholars, however, have found that elections can actually undermine authoritarian regimes (Bunce and Wolchik 2006; 2011; Donno 2013; Edgell et al. 2018; Hadenius and Teorell 2007; Lindberg 2006a, 2006b; Philipp and Thompson 2009; Tucker 2007). They argue that opposition leaders and citizens often use elections and electoral protests to challenge authoritarian incumbents (Beaulieu 2014; Beissinger 2002; Bunce and Wolchik 2011) and show that regularly held elections can facilitate democratization (Hadenius and Teorell 2007; Roessler and Howard 2006) by instilling democratic values (Lindberg 2006a, 2006b). Additionally, electoral fraud committed by incumbents can backfire, sparking mass antiregime protests and thereby destabilizing authoritarian rule (Eisenstadt 2007; Hafner-Burton, Hyde, and Jablonski 2014; Knutsen et al. 2019; Lehoucq and Molina 2002; Philipp and Thompson 2009; Schedler 2006; Tucker 2007).

Several studies have presented more nuanced arguments to clarify this enduring debate regarding the impacts of authoritarian elections on dictatorships. Bernhard, Edgell, and Lindberg (2020) find that the regime's survival is dependent on the regime's ability to reduce electoral uncertainty through the institutionalization of multiparty elections. Morgenbesser and Pepinsky's (2019) study on Southeast Asia underscores the importance of conceptually distinguishing elections as causes of democracy versus as features of democracy to properly assess the causal effect of elections on democracy. Knutsen, Nygård, and Wig (2017) argue that we need to distinguish the short-term and long-term effects of elections and find that elections are more likely to destabilize the regime in the short term but not in the long term. By focusing on the overall relationship between authoritarian elections and regime change (breakdown or democratization, or both), these studies help elucidate some of the conditions under which elections have stabilizing versus destabilizing effects on authoritarian regimes. However, by considering all protests, popular revolutions, and coups d'état that occur in the aftermath of elections, these studies assume—and do not problematize—the mobilizing effect of elections.

As a matter of fact, the literature is divided over the impact of elections on *social movements*. According to Doug McAdam and Sidney Tarrow (2010), elections can serve as political opportunities that can empower such movements. For example, as research shows, elections increase the cost of repression and are witnessed by an international audience (Blaydes 2011; J. Wright 2011). Elections also provide opportunities for social movement groups to partner with new institutional allies, such as opposition parties, to advance their claims (Trejo 2014). In turn, by collaborating with civil society groups during their campaigns, opposition parties can portray themselves as a mass movement and signal their capacity to engage in a postelection mobilization when necessary (Bunce and Wolchik 2011).

Despite the potential benefits for social movements, some studies suggest that the political opportunities provided by elections can have the opposite effect—they can demobilize the social movement during the process of building a large formal organization (Piven and Cloward 1979) or even reduce citizens' popular involvement in politics (Blee and Currier 2006; Hirschman 1979). An election can also serve as a "safety valve," regulating social discontent by allowing citizens to privately and safely address their grievances with the regime at the ballot box (Brownlee 2012; Buehler 2013; Lust-Okar and Jamal 2002) instead of doing so publicly and in a way that directly demands regime change. By providing them with an alternative, nonviolent channel through which opposition groups can release political energy that might otherwise drive more visible protest, autocratic regimes can harness elections as a tool to direct, contain, and weaken political discontent (Buehler 2013).

These studies imply that elections can affect authoritarian durability through their impact on mass social protest. Yet by focusing on the "average effect" of elections, they offer conflicting evidence and empirical implications regarding the relationship between elections and protest under authoritarian regimes. The next section will explore one way that this debate can be reconciled.

Elections, Protest, and Mobilizing Structures in the Authoritarian Context

One way to make sense of these conflicting findings is to simultaneously consider the mobilization and demobilization of antiregime protests as plausible outcomes of introducing multiparty elections. That is, perhaps elections have different effects *within* autocratic societies across social segments or geographic areas.

Here I theorize that the trade-off between protesting and voting posed by the introduction of multiparty elections in authoritarian regimes is moderated by the availability of mobilizing structures—that is, the effect of elections depends on the extent to which mobilizing structures are available in a given area. This argument proceeds in three steps. First, the introduction of multiparty elections creates an opening in the political opportunity structure. Under authoritarian regimes, participation in protest is incredibly costly for citizens, given the low chances of success and the severity of state repression. Multiparty elections provide citizens with a state-sanctioned (and therefore safer) method of addressing their grievances: they can cast votes for opposition party candidates. Although rallies and campaigns during election cycles provide such candidates with opportunities to mobilize voters, being able to vote for these candidates can alter an individual's decision regarding whether to get involved in protests. In other words, because voting for an opposition candidate is a safer means of voicing one's discontent in an authoritarian regime, it can then *substitute* for one's engagement in antiregime protests.

Second, the extent to which voting for the opposition party does, in fact, substitute for protest depends on the availability of mobilizing structures. Defined as "collective vehicles through which people initially mobilize and begin to engage in sustained collective action" (McAdam 2017, 194), mobilizing structures are found to be important for the emergence (McAdam 1982), sustenance (Rupp and Taylor 1987), and impact of social movements (Andrews 1997, 2004). Specifically, mobilizing structures help build dense networks of social relationships and thus provide solidarity, leadership, a communication network, movement recruitment, and collective action frames (Clemens 1996; McAdam 1982; Snow, Zurcher, and Ekland-Olson 1980). Such networks include kinship and friendship networks, information networks among activists, movement communities, and more formal organizations (e.g., colleges and churches) where mobilization may be generated, even if that is not their primary aim. Many social movement scholars would restrict the term "mobilizing structures" to grassroots organizations and informal networks that are essentially free from elite control (McAdam 2017, 198). The informal and grassroots aspects of mobilizing structures are especially critical for movement emergence in authoritarian societies where people lack the ability and freedom to establish and utilize formal organizations to advance their interests.

Lastly, mobilizing structures and framing help transform objective opportunities (arising from elections) into de facto opportunities for mobilization. Framing is a process in which social movements are "actively engaged as agents in a struggle over the production of mobilizing and counter-mobilizing ideas and meanings" (Benford and Snow 2000, 613). According to the social movement literature, collective action frames, derived from *perceived* opportunities, serve as action-oriented sets of beliefs and meanings that inspire and legitimate the activities of social movement groups (Benford and Snow 2000; Gamson and Meyer 1996; Klandermans 1997; Kurzman 1996; Voss 1993). Political openings remain as potential (rather than actual) opportunities until collective action frames are engaged—that is, until they are perceived and defined as opportunities by a group of actors sufficiently well organized to leverage them (McAdam, McCarthy, and Zald 1996; D. Suh 2001). Elections can provide such opportunities for opposition candidates and social movement forces to mobilize around a common goal: electoral victory. Further, elections generate a clear outcome—electoral performance—which shapes the "cognitive opportunity" of movement participants and the general public by providing information on the likelihood of successful collective action (Choe and Kim 2012).

126 Seeds of Mobilization

In sum, *I hypothesize that the effects of elections on protest are moderated by the availability of mobilizing structures*; this effect is especially pronounced under authoritarian regimes, where formal (i.e., noncorporatist) organizations are either nonexistent or difficult to observe. The empirical implication is that *the electoral mobilization (generated during election cycles) is more likely to be linked to further street mobilization during and after the elections only when mobilizing structures are available to be leveraged by antiregime activists in the first place. In the absence of, or with limited availability of, such mobilizing structures, citizens are more likely to be demobilized* due to the existence of a "safer" institutional channel (i.e., voting) that they can use to address their grievances.

From the 1985 National Assembly Election to the 1987 June Democratic Uprising

Following the assassination of President Park Chung Hee on October 26, 1979, General Chun Doo Hwan seized political power through a military coup, and his neomilitary force formed the Democratic Justice Party (DJP; Minjŏngdang) as the ruling party. They also created and sponsored the Democratic Korea Party (Minhandang) and the Korean Nationalist Party (Kungmindang) as "opposition parties" (*kwanje yadang*) that were "unable and unwilling to question and challenge the political legitimacy of the regime" (S. Kim 2000, 84). The newly installed constitution for Chun's Fifth Republic of Korea stipulated a single seven-year presidential term, which reflected greater constraint on the executive than was written into the 1972 Yusin Constitution for the Fourth Republic of Korea (1972–80)—that constitution had guaranteed a six-year term with no limits on reelection for the president. Even under this new constitution, however, the president was elected indirectly through a rubber-stamp national electoral college called the National Council for Reunification (T'ongil Chuch'e Kungmin Hoeŭi), which had been formed under the Yusin constitution. Because this national electoral college gathered in a large gymnasium (i.e., Janchung Arena in Seoul) to "elect" a president who ran unopposed, the Korean populace often referred to the new presidential elections as the "gymnasium elections" (*ch'eyukkwan sŏn'gŏ*).

The first few years under this regime were characterized by severe state repression of political and civil society. Following its violent suppression of a popular uprising in Kwangju city (in South Chŏlla Province) in May 1980, the regime carried out a series of large-scale coercive campaigns to "cleanse" or "purify" (*chŏnghwa*) both political and civil society. It dissolved the existing National Assembly, which had been South Korea's unicameral legislature, and replaced it with the Legislative Council for National Security (Kukka Powi Ippŏp Hoeŭi). This legislature pro tempore not only institutionalized but also further intensified state repression (S. Kim 2000, 79). On November 3, it passed the Political Climate Renovation Law, which banned anyone "responsible for causing political and social corruption of fomenting confusion" from formal political activities. This law set up the Political Renovation Committee, which issued blacklists disqualifying 567 politicians and intellectuals from engaging in politics. In addition, the bills controlling assembly and demonstration and the Basic Press Law (press censorship) were passed on November 29 and December 26, respectively. On March 25, 1981, which fell during this period of severe political repression, the 11th National Assembly election was held but included no *genuine* opposition party—that is, a party that was neither created nor supported by the regime. Chun had already forcibly dissolved the New Democratic Party (Sinmindang), which had been the main opposition party during the Park regime, and no other such party had taken its place.

Starting in 1983, however, Chun's government began to loosen its tight control over society (see chapter 4 for more details). During this period of limited political liberalization, Chun allowed a genuine opposition party to compete in the 12th National Assembly election in 1985. This move was not intended to make the elections more truly democratic; instead, it represented a deliberate effort by the incumbent government to divide opposition groups by allowing them to form their own political parties (S.-C. Kim 2016, 30). Despite this intention, as of January 18, formerly ousted opposition politicians formed and united under the New Korea Democratic Party. On February 12, with constitutional reform as their main platform, the political opposition participated in elections for the first time under Chun's rule.

Because they now had the option to cast votes for a genuine opposition party, Korean citizens showed great interest in the 12th National Assembly election. Compared to the 11th National Assembly election held in 1981, the 1985 election experienced a 36% increase in rally attendance and an unprecedented turnout rate of almost 85%—the highest voter turnout since 1961 (H.-G. Chung, Kim, and Chung 2004). The significance of voting in these elections is described as follows in the August issue of the monthly magazine *Shin Tonga*:

> [Under the Fifth Republic of Korea], the people (*minjung*) could neither speak nor hear as citizens because the National Assembly

128   Seeds of Mobilization

didn't represent them and the press wasn't able to properly inform them. It was finally through the act of voting during the [1985 National Assembly] election that people were able to express their frustrations and rebellious sentiments. (G. Yi 1987, 186)

Similarly, political scientist Jang-Jip Choi described participation in the 1985 election as a "peaceful revolution" carried out through the act of voting against the authoritarian incumbents (J.-J. Choi 2002, 216).

Despite the fact that the ruling DJP's candidates had access to the state's political machinery and sizeable election campaign funds, the NKDP became the leading opposition in the National Assembly, winning 29% of the total national votes (compared to 35% for the DJP). In Seoul alone, the NKDP garnered 42.7% of the votes, which was 15% more than what the DJP received (27%). The NKDP's victory in 1985, described as the "new party tornado" (*sindang tolp'ung*), was a complete surprise to the ruling DJP—the prominent opposition leaders (Kim Young Sam and Kim Dae Jung) were still banned from participating in politics, and the election had been held in the winter so as to decrease voter turnout (Sŏng et al. 2017, 85).

Alliance Formation between Students and the NKDP

The NKDP's electoral success relied heavily on the support of civil society groups, especially student groups. As explained in chapter 4, the 1980s was when the student activism became more prevalent and widespread across the country. Although some radical student groups attempted to boycott the National Assembly election altogether, most of the people's movement (*minjung undong*) groups, including student groups, decided to participate in the 1985 election (S. Kim 2000, 85).[1] The Youth Coalition for Democracy Movement (Minch'ŏngnyŏn) was the first to declare that the student movement should take advantage of the electoral space to advance their causes (Sŏng et al. 2017, 86).[2] Subsequently, in early January 1985, the National Alliance of Student Associations Election Planning Committee (Ch'onguk Taehaksaeng Yŏnhap Sŏn'go Taech'aek Wiwŏnhoe) was formed, and the first and second reporting rallies (*pogo daehoe*)[3] of the Student Alliance for Democratic Elections (Minju Ch'ongsŏn Haksaeng Yŏnhap) were held at Seoul National University on January 14 and at Yonsei University on January 29. Immediately following these rallies, students campaigned and demonstrated both on- and off-campus, urging people to engage in the electoral struggle (*ch'ongsŏn t'ujaeng*) against the ruling party in the upcoming election (Sŏng et al. 2017, 86). In addition to the Youth Coalition for Democracy Movement's public backing of the NKDP, students campaigned for the NKDP candidates, disseminated leaflets, and protested in the street, shouting slogans such as "Do not vote for the DJP!" and "We oppose one-party dictatorship by the DJP!" (DongA Ilbo 1985; Kyŏnghyang Sinmun 1985). Some even shouted antigovernment slogans at the incumbent party candidate's campaign rally (Minjuhwa Undong Kinyŏm Saophoe 2006, 430).

The opposition NKDP also demonstrated its alliance with the student movement by nominating a formerly imprisoned student activist Yi Ch'ŏl as the NKDP candidate for the Sŏngbuk district—a college town—in Seoul. Yi Ch'ŏl was one of the main organizers of the National League for Democratic Youth and Students (Chŏn'guk Minju Ch'ŏngnyŏn Haksaeng Yŏnmaeng)—a national network for the anti-Yusin student movement— that was banned in 1974 as an antistate organization planning to overthrow the government (see chapter 4).[4] Yi's election slogan—"Death row prisoner Yi Ch'ŏl has returned to Sŏngbuk"—and campaign pledges, including his fight for academic freedom, found on his campaign poster signaled his student activist identity. Yi's participation in the National Assembly election as an NKDP candidate stimulated student engagement in campaign activities and his victory solidified the student–political opposition alliance during the 1985 National Assembly election.

As a result of this alliance, the 1985 election marked the first time since the early 1960s that university students publicly supported a particular political party (S. Kim 2000, 85). Furthermore, the alliance formed between the opposition NKDP and civil society groups subsequently developed into the National Coalition for Democracy Movement (Minjuhwarŭl Wihan Kungmin Yŏllakkigu or Min'gugnyŏn), a grand pro-democracy coalition against the authoritarian regime.

Constitutional Reform as a Master Frame for Postelection Mobilization

Following the forging of these alliances and the NKDP's electoral success, the issue of constitutional reform—which had first been introduced as the NKDP's campaign pledge during the 1985 election—became a "master frame" in the 1980s democracy movement (Han'guk Minjujuŭi Yŏn'guso 2016). Master frames, common to a cluster of movements or "cycle of protest" (Tarrow 1998), are "sufficiently elastic, inclusive, and flexible enough [compared to collective action frames that are context specific] so that any number of other social movements can successfully adopt and deploy it in their campaigns" (Benford 2013, 1). As pointed out in P. Y. Chang and Lee's (2021, 14) study on the protest networks of South Korea's democracy movement, democratic reforms and state repression were systemic issues that were relevant to multiple social groups and were "fundamental goals associated with Korean democracy." The issue of constitutional reform, as a master frame, was linked to group-specific (or local) issues (e.g., labor rights for workers, media censorship for journalists, and academic freedom for students) and contributed to the movement's solidarity in the 1980s. And this particular master frame was developed through the alliance that civil society groups—including student groups—formed with the political opposition during and after the 1985 National Assembly election.

In February 1986, a year after the election, the NKDP and the People's Movement Coalition for Democracy and Reunification (PMCDR; Minju T'ongil Minjung Undong Yŏnhap or Mint'ongnyŏn) launched a campaign to collect ten million signatures in support of revising the constitution.[5] Together, the NKDP and PMCDR also formed the National Coalition for Democracy Movement and, in major cities around the country, organized mass rallies demanding constitutional reform. This coalition temporarily broke down in May 1986, when the NKDP decided to participate in the Special Committee on Constitutional Revision in the National Assembly and compromised in ways that were unacceptable to many in the coalition, including the two de facto leaders (Kim Young Sam and Kim Dae Jung) and hardliners of the NKDP. The grand pro-democracy coalition between the PMCDR and the political opposition (now the Reunification Democratic Party; Tongil Minjudang) was soon restored in May 1987 as the National Movement Headquarters for Democratic Constitution (NMHDC; Minju Hŏnpŏp Chaengch'wi Kungmin Undong Ponbu or Kungmin Undong Ponbu).[6] Such a restoration of the coalition was possible due to their agreement on the importance of achieving direct presidential elections through constitutional reform.

June Democratic Uprising and the Authoritarian Breakdown

Just before the NMHDC was formed, on April 13, 1987, President Chun Doo Hwan announced in his "April 13 Defense of the Constitution" speech that he would no longer tolerate "wasteful" discussions on constitutional reform. Furthermore, on May 18, 1987, the Catholic Priests' Association for Justice (Ch'ŏnjugyo Chŏngŭi Kuhyŏn Chŏn'guk Sajedan) revealed that a Seoul National University student named Pak Chongch'ol had been tortured to death by the police. Chun's speech and

Pak's death sparked a strong mobilization against the regime. This mobilization erupted into the historic protest cycle that came to be known as the June Democratic Uprising.

Approximately one million people, including opposition politicians, students, workers, and middle-class citizens, participated in these pro-democracy protests. On June 10, under the leadership of the newly formed NMHDC, approximately 400,000 people in 22 cities staged mass anti-regime demonstrations across the country. These demonstrations were known as the Uprising Rally to Defeat the April 13 Decision and to End Dictatorship. The NMHDC also orchestrated the National Rally for Banishment of Tear Gas Grenades on June 18 and the Great National March of Peace on June 26. As reflected in the slogans used by protestors— "Constitutional reform!" (*hohŏn ch'ŏlp'ye*) and "Down with the dictatorship!" (*tokchae t'ado*)—the main objective of the uprising was democratic constitutional reform.

This intense struggle ended when Chun's handpicked successor, Roh Tae Woo, made the June 29 Declaration. In it, the incumbent party promised to (1) amend the constitution to provide direct presidential elections; (2) revise the Presidential Election Law to ensure free and competitive elections; (3) grant amnesty to political prisoners, including Kim Dae Jung; (4) respect human dignity and extend the right of habeas corpus; (5) abolish the 1980 Basic Press Law and promote freedom of the press; (6) strengthen local and educational autonomy; (7) create a political climate conducive to dialogue and compromise; and (8) carry out social reforms to build a clean and honest society. The unprecedented nationwide mass protests in 1987 significantly increased the costs of repression and made it more likely for the incumbent regime to concede democracy.

The June Democratic Uprising that led to these changes was driven largely by college students, who formed the major portion of the protestors (C. Chung 2011, 174) and staged street demonstrations almost every single day from June 10 to June 26 despite schools still in session (Sŏ 2011, 596). Moreover, student organizations, such as the Association of Student Representatives in Seoul (Sŏdaehyŏp), the Association of Student Representatives in Pusan (Puch'onghyŏp), and the Association of Student Representatives in Taegu (Taedaehyŏp), were the main organizational force behind the two national rallies that bookended that period (6.10 *kungmin taehoe* and 6.26 *p'yŏnghwa tae haengjin*, respectively). The active involvement of students during this successful uprising was rooted in the historical tradition of student activism. As pointed out in chapter 4, students had been key actors during critical moments in South

132 Seeds of Mobilization

Korea's democracy movement, including the 1960 April Revolution (which demonstrated the "first massive and bottom-up expression of the desire and willingness to fight for democracy") and the 1980 Kwangju Uprising (which "radicalized" the democracy movement) (N. Lee 2007). The central role of college students in these events has been explained by the fact that they were "the only social group with the resources (time and knowledge) and preexistent mobilizing structures (student councils and societies) that enabled them to challenge the power holders" (M. Park 2012, 140). These resources made all the difference—the "nexus of senior and junior (*sŏnbae-hubae*) ties" among students and student activists (N. Lee 2007), circulation of texts, "circles" (*ssŏk'ŭl*; extracurricular clubs, from the English word "circle"), and seminars (or reading groups) were vital in sustaining the student movement throughout the authoritarian period, especially when the student movement was forced to operate underground during Park Chung Hee's "Emergency Decree Era" (1974–79) (P. Y. Chang 2015a; N. Lee 2007). Once student councils (*haksaeng-hoe*) were revived in 1984 after Chun's liberalization policy, they served as mobilizing structures that facilitated collaboration among universities on a nationwide scale, including the orchestration of protests that occurred during the June Democratic Uprising.

Empirical Analysis

The traditional narrative implies that the constitutional reform movement (1985–87) created continuity between the 12th National Assembly election and the June Democratic Uprising, but a direct link between them—and what moderates that link—has not been empirically explored before. In this section, I empirically examine whether and how the expanding political opportunities in the 1985 election—that is, having the option to express antiregime sentiment by being able to vote for a genuine opposition party (NKDP)—impacted people's participation in the subsequent nationwide antiregime protests during the 1987 June Democratic Uprising.

Data and Methods

I utilize an original dataset of 1,194 events that occurred during the June Democratic Uprising, between Chun's April 13 Statement (April 13, 1987) and the June 29 Declaration (June 29, 1987). This dataset includes all events during this period that are recorded as protest events in two primary sources: *The Great June Uprising for Democratization*, published by the Christian Institute for the Study of Justice and Development (Han'guk Kidokkyo Sahoe Munje Yŏn'guwŏn 1987a), and the Korea Democracy Foundation sourcebooks (introduced in chapter 1; see the appendix for the detailed data description). By utilizing these publications, which are compiled from a variety of primary sources, I avoid the data limitations of relying solely on national newspaper reports (which many such datasets do)—such reports are typically incomplete, especially given the Basic Press Law (and, thus, the high degree of press censorship) under Chun's rule. This original dataset supplements the existing dataset on South Korea's democracy movement by the Stanford Korea Democracy Project,[7] which is heavily biased toward events that occurred in the capital city, Seoul. To my knowledge, no other dataset contains comprehensive information on events that occurred in other regions of the country.

The unit of analysis is the county (*si, gun, gu*). The outcome (or dependent) variable is the intensity of protest in a given county during the June Democratic Uprising. Specifically, this variable measures the total number of protest events observed in each county from April 13, 1987, to June 29, 1987.[8] Figure 5.1 displays all protest sites during the June Uprising with circles, and it displays the share of votes the NKDP received in each county in shades of gray (with darker shades indicating a greater vote share for the NKDP). Table 5.1 reports the regional variation in the number of protest events at the provincial level.

The main explanatory variable, *NKDP Vote Share*, measures the amount of support that the opposition NKDP received during the 1985 National Assembly election. This data comes from the National Election Commission.[9] For ease of interpretation of the marginal effect of the NKDP vote share in a nonlinear model, the NKDP vote share is coded as a dummy variable to distinguish between counties with low versus high levels of electoral support for the NKDP. Specifically, I code districts with values higher than the third quartile (32%) as high and those with values lower than 32% as low. I use the third quartile because it is the median of the upper half of the data. I also use a continuous measure and another dummy variable with 62.5 percentile cut-off point (i.e., the median of the first and third quartiles of the distribution, 24%) and find similar results.[10]

In order to ensure that this measure effectively captures electoral support for the political opposition, I use the Ordinary Least Square (OLS) regression method to regress the 1985 NKDP vote share on the combined vote shares of the opposition candidates—Kim Young Sam and Kim Dae Jung—in the first direct presidential election in December 1987. The

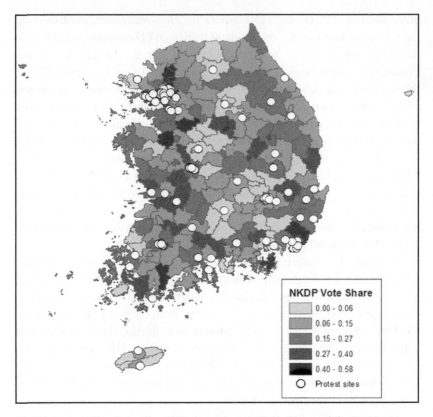

Fig 5.1. Protest sites during the 1987 June Democratic Uprising and the NKDP vote share in 1985. Election data are from the National Election Commission of the Republic of Korea and the protest data are from the author's dataset.

results (with and without the inclusion of control variables in Models 1 and 2, respectively), as reported in table 5.2, show that there is a statistically significant and positive relationship between the two. The coefficient of the *1985 NKDP Vote Share* (in Model 2) indicates that, holding everything else constant, a 1% increase in the opposition NKDP vote share is associated with a 14% increase in the combined vote shares of the two prominent opposition candidates during the 1987 presidential election.

In the empirical analysis, I separately consider the main effect of the NKDP vote share on protest intensity and the effect of the NKDP vote share conditional on the availability of mobilizing structures by including an interaction term: *Proportion of College Students* × *NKDP Vote Share*. The *Proportion of College Students* variable is constructed by dividing the col-

TABLE 5.1. Number of Districts and Events (per 100,000 People) for Each Province during the 1987 June Democratic Uprising

Province	Number of Districts	Events (per 100,000 people)
Seoul	17	1.74
Pusan	10	3.98
Taegu	6	5.71
Inch'ŏn	4	5.77
Kyŏnggi	27	3.25
Kangwŏn	21	3.52
Ch'ungbuk	13	2.01
Ch'ungnam	18	3.57
Chŏnbuk	18	4.90
Chŏnnam	29	4.91
Kyŏngbuk	31	1.59
Kyŏngnam	27	1.25
Cheju	4	2.87

Source: Author's dataset.

TABLE 5.2. 1985 NKDP Vote Share and Combined Vote Shares of the Opposition Candidates in the 1987 Presidential Election

	Dependent Variable: Opposition Vote Share (1987)	
	Model 1	Model 2
1985 NKDP Vote Share	35.219***	14.111***
	(10.341)	(6.090)
Population Density		7.059***
		(1.542)
(Log) College Student Population		1.832***
		(0.625)
Honam Region		47.488***
		(1.857)
Yŏngnam Region		–0.376
		(1.768)
Constant	43.205***	22.041***
	(2.752)	(4.116)
Observations	211	211
R^2	0.053	0.796
Adjusted R^2	0.048	0.792

Note: Standard errors are in parentheses.
*$p < 0.1$, **$p < 0.05$, ***$p < 0.01$

lege student population by the total population of a given county using data from the *1985 Population and Housing Census* published by Kyŏngje Kihoegwŏn (Economic Planning Board). This measure captures the degree of density of student networks and their related organizational capacity in a given county. As discussed earlier, college students—the dominant social group within the democracy movement—had ample access to resources and preexistent mobilizing structures (M. Park 2012). Arguably, they also represented the population most likely to protest given that, unlike other social groups, they were free from personal constraints imposed by full-time employment and family commitments that might otherwise deter them from participating in protest events (McAdam 1988; Snow, Zurcher, and Ekland-Olson 1980).

Given the expectation that student organizations and networks will be denser in areas where the proportion of college students is higher, the *Proportion of College Students* represents the finest data available at the subnational level. For certain time periods, the *Korean University Yearbook* series provides information on student associations at junior colleges and universities in Korea, but there are no publications containing such data for years in question (1985–87). Moreover, it is impossible to obtain complete data on student groups and their activities because severe control of dissident activities on- and off-campus during the authoritarian period led many such groups to operate primarily underground until the mid-1980s. Still, the data that *does* exist on the number of student associations in 1983 shows that this number is strongly and positively correlated ($r = 0.93$) with the student population in 1985 (as shown in fig. A5.1 in the online appendix).[11] For these reasons, despite its limitations, the variable *Proportion of College Students* serves as a reliable proxy for the availability of mobilizing structures.

Several control variables are included in the empirical analysis. Electoral competitiveness, which may affect NKDP vote share, is measured by the total number of candidates competing in each electoral district using data from the National Election Commission.[12] To control for previous levels of support for the opposition, I use a district's abstention rate from the 1981 National Assembly election, in which no genuine opposition party was allowed to participate. One can arguably assume that those who abstained from participating in the previous election are more likely to have been dissatisfied with the ruling party and supportive of the opposition (Birch 2010; Lijphart 1997). Population size, industrialization (population employed in the industrial sector), urbanization (population density), and unemployment (population unemployed) are also included to control for

From College Campuses to Ballot Boxes

the structural factors highlighted by modernization theory (e.g., Lerner 1958; Lipset 1959) and grievance-based theories of social movement (e.g., Davies 1962; Gurr 1970; Kornhauser 1959; Muller 1985). These variables are constructed using data from the *1985 Population and Housing Census*.

Although state repression is likely to have impacted levels of protest, there is no county-level data on repression prior to the onset of protests. Therefore, I include dummy variables for counties with a prior history of pro-democracy protests, as these areas were more likely to experience state repression or surveillance. The pro-democracy protests in question include the 1979 Pusan-Masan Uprising, 1980 Kwangju Uprising, and 1986 Inch'ŏn May 3 Uprising. I also include province fixed effect to account for any underlying regional pattern or trend that is not captured by the control variables. (See table A5.1 in the online appendix for summary statistics of all variables.)

In addition, to ensure that the values of the dependent and main independent variables used in the statistical analysis are consistent for each observational unit—that is, people voting and protesting in their respective counties—I also use as a robustness check a subset of observations that is limited to protest events on days when the NMHDC organized national rallies during the June Democratic Uprising. Such events are more likely to have included mass participation by citizens in their own electoral districts—they were much larger in scale than the protest events that occurred on other days, and citizens were more likely to join large-scale protests happening in their own districts than to join smaller protest events in distant districts (where participation would be both costlier and riskier). As shown in figure 5.2, in my dataset on the June Democratic Uprising, four days in particular—June 10, June 18, June 21, and June 26—exhibited the highest number of mass events with more than 10,000 participants, and the NMHDC was involved in three of them. The results (which are reported in table A5.5 in the online appendix) do not substantively differ from the results using all observations.[13]

Because the dependent variable of interest is a nonnegative count of protest events with excessive zeroes (i.e., counties with no protest events), the statistical model that I use to analyze the data is a zero-inflated negative binomial model.[14] Protests are rare events by nature, so the aggregation of such events is often "inflated" with structural zeroes in datasets on subnational protest events. These structural zeroes represent cases that have zero probability of ever experiencing protests. Treating these cases as protest-free observations within a model can lead to biased inferences, but eliminating them from the sample not only excludes a significant portion

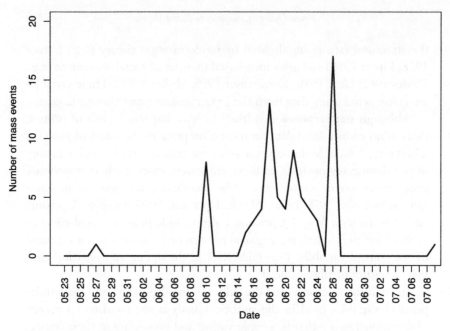

Fig 5.2. Number of mass events during the 1987 June Democratic Uprising. Mass events are events with more than 10,000 participants. Statistics are from the author's dataset.

TABLE 5.3. Predictors of Protest Intensity during the 1987 June Democratic Uprising

	(1)		(2)	
Protest Events Equation (negative binomial with log link)	Coefficients	IRR	Coefficients	IRR
NKDP Vote Share × Proportion of College Students			0.543*** (0.191)	1.722
NKDP Vote Share	−1.033*** (0.380)	0.356	−3.302*** (−0.876)	0.037
Proportion of College Students	0.708*** (0.104)	2.030	0.555*** (0.105)	1.741
Controls	✓		✓	
Province FE	✓		✓	
Inflate Equation (binomial with logit link)				
NKDP Vote Share × Proportion of College Students			0.787 (1.318)	
NKDP Vote Share	33.631 (27.751)		2.348 (3.789)	
Proportion of College Students	−6.396 (4.322)		−1.269 (0.957)	
Controls	✓		✓	
Log Likelihood	−290.382		−286.135	
Number of Observations	210		210	
Nonzero Observations	76		76	

Note: Standard error in parentheses. IRR = incidence rate ratio.
*p < 0.1, **p < 0.05, ***p < 0.01

of relevant protest observations but also produces selection bias (Clark and Regan 2003; Lemke and Reed 2001; Xiang 2010). In the case in question, the districts could have zero counts for various reasons: (1) there were attempts to organize protest events, but they were either insignificant or unrecorded or (2) protests just never took place. Hence, the expected count is expressed as a combination of these two processes:

$$E(n_{events} = k) = P(no\ mobilization)^*0 + P(mobilization)^*E(y = k \mid mobilization)$$

Results and Discussion

The regression results from the zero-inflated negative binomial model are presented in table 5.3. The lower half of the table reports the inflate equation of the model, which is the extent to which there are more zeroes in the data than are implied by the negative binomial distribution. A negative estimate means that an increase in the explanatory variable increases the probability of observing at least one event. The upper half of the table reports the coefficients corresponding to the count (protest events) equation of the model. Given the difficulty of directly interpreting the results from a nonlinear regression model, the coefficients obtained from the count portion of the model are transformed into incidence rate ratios (IRR) to facilitate substantive interpretation.

Column 1 of table 5.3 presents the results of a model specification that does not include the interaction term, and column 2 presents the results that include the interaction term—*NKDP Vote Share* × *Proportion of College Students*. Both columns 1 and 2 include all control variables and province fixed effects.[15] As expected, the protest events equation in column 2 shows that the main effect of the *Proportion of College Students* on protest intensity is statistically significant and positive. The IRR suggests that a one-unit increase in the proportion of college students (i.e., the percentage of the total population being college students) in a given county is associated with a 72% increase in the number of protests. The main effect of *NKDP Vote Share* is also statistically significant but negative. Holding all other variables at constant, districts with high opposition vote share (i.e., vote share higher than 32%) exhibited fewer protests (96.3% lower in these districts). These findings suggest that voting for a genuine opposition party candidate functioned as a safety valve, allowing citizens to let off steam, rather than as a focal point generating proactive electoral mobilization.

The coefficient of the interaction term, *NKDP Vote Share* × *Proportion of*

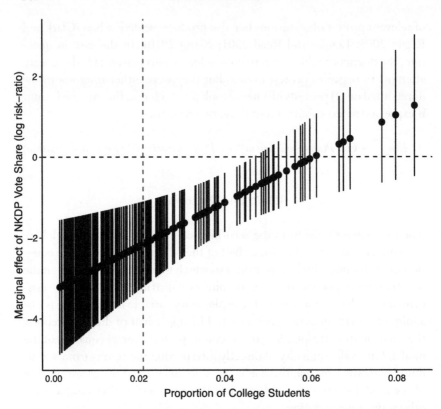

Fig 5.3. The relationship between NKDP vote share and protest intensity at different levels of proportion of college students, with 95% confidence intervals.

College Students, is also statistically significant, suggesting that there is a difference in the effect of *NKDP Vote Share* across different values of the moderating variable, *Proportion of College Students*. The coefficient is positive because the effect increases as the proportion of college students increases, but the main effect is negative, as indicated by the negative coefficient of the *NKDP Vote Share* variable. To substantively interpret the interaction term to discuss the conditional effect of *NKDP Vote Share*, I follow Hilbe (2011) in calculating the IRR of the marginal effects of *NKDP Vote Share* on protest intensity at different levels of *Proportion of College Students*.[16] Figure 5.3 plots the log-risk ratio (logged IRR) of *NKDP Vote Share* on the *y*-axis and the proportion of college students in a given county on the *x*-axis for ease of interpretation and visualization of the relationship. The average effect of NKDP vote share on the June Democratic Uprising protests is indicated by the dashed vertical line.

As the figure shows, the negative effect of NKDP vote share on protest intensity is significant and stronger in districts with a lower proportion of the college student population. The effect of *NKDP Vote Share* is negative in districts where there are smaller proportions of college students, but that effect dissipates in districts with larger proportions of college students. This result suggests that the dampening effect of elections on protest is mitigated by the availability of mobilizing structures.

Several reports produced by people's movement groups on the 1985 National Assembly election animate the above empirical results. They show that the diverging effects of voting for the opposition NKDP on levels of protest during the June Democratic Uprising depended on student activism surrounding the elections. Although these publications focus on collective action during the 1985 National Assembly election, they provide insights into how people's electoral experiences, such as campaign rallies, may have impacted their subsequent involvement in pro-democracy protests.

These documents suggest that the election functioned as a safety valve for dissatisfied citizens and highlight the role of campaign rallies by the NKDP, in which students were actively involved. As an example, according to the March 1985 issue of the *Road to Democratization* (*Minjuhwa ŭi kil*; published by the Youth Coalition for Democracy Movement),

> the election functioned as an outlet for [the middle class], who were dissatisfied with the incumbent regime but had to suppress their hope for liberal democracy. [During the election], their hope [for such democracy] was expressed in the form of public opinion formation at campaign rallies and electoral support for the new party [NKDP]. (KDF Open Archives No. 00208314, 11)

Similarly, a report produced by the Chŏnnam Democratic Youth Association (Chŏnnam Minju Ch'ŏngnyŏn Hyŏbŭihoe), entitled "An Analysis of the 12th National Assembly Election Results and Its Prospects," explained people's increased interest during the 12th National Assembly election as a way to express their feelings about the regime:

> There was no practical way for people to express their dissatisfaction with the current political system. The increased voter turnout can be explained by people's willingness to express their support for the new party [NKDP], which was the smallest possible mark of transformation that people could make to the current system. (KDF Open Archives No. 00121827, 7)

142   Seeds of Mobilization

The same report also stated that the NKDP campaign rallies naturally developed into mass street demonstrations, in which participants shouted slogans such as "Down with military dictatorship!" and "Reveal the truth of the May 18 Kwangju Uprising!" (KDF 00121827, 6). These slogans had been used in antigovernment, pro-democracy protests throughout the 1980s, and they reappeared during the June Democratic Uprising.

Despite the size of these demonstrations, there was variation in people's exposure to political rallies during the short campaign period, as pointed out in the abovementioned Youth Coalition for Democracy Movement publication:

> Seoul is the epicenter of enthusiasm for democratization. During the [12th National Assembly] election, "campaign fever" in Seoul brought about electoral victory for the new party by defeating the ruling party. However, while political rallies were well attended by white-collar workers, students, and citizens in Seoul, they did not reach the poor and laborers in the outskirts. (KDF Open Archives No. 00208314, 12)

This varying exposure to campaign rallies during the 12th National Assembly election may explain the diverging effects of elections on people's subsequent participation (or lack thereof) in pro-democracy protests.

An evaluation report of the 12th National Assembly election by the Inch'ŏn Region Social Movement Association (Inch'ŏn Chiyŏk Sahoe Undong Yŏnhap) further suggests that people's varying exposure to campaign rallies was shaped by activist strategies. In the report, the Inch'ŏn activists acknowledge that the Korean people's desire for democratization was manifested in their rally attendance and the electoral victory of the NKDP. Moreover, they admit that they underestimated the people's desire for democratization and regret neglecting the use of street tactics at campaign rallies to channel that desire into antigovernment protests. As stated in its "An Analysis of the General Election,"

> many of the democracy movement activists at the campaign rallies were disseminating leaflets or passively shouting slogans with the rest of the crowd as if they were dancing at someone else's party. There was lack of enthusiasm at the campaign rallies happening in Inch'ŏn, and at these rallies, the activists could not even successfully disseminate the leaflets. (KDF Open Archives No. 00153296, 19)

This assessment by the Inch'ŏn Region Social Movement Association is consistent with the empirical result: the proportion of college students in counties in Inch'ŏn ranged from 2% to 3% (average 2.59%) and, as figure 5.4 shows, the relationship between *NKDP Vote Share* and *Protest Intensity* is negative for values between 2% and 3% (0.02–0.03). Not surprisingly, in the Chogno and Chung districts of Seoul, where the largest NKDP campaign rallies were held (with more than 100,000 attendees; KDF Open Archives No. 00153296, 19), the proportion of college students is higher (5.25% and 4.29%, respectively); as seen in the graph, the dampening effect of elections is substantively reduced where there is a greater proportion of college students.

To summarize, I find that voting for the opposition party had a demobilizing effect on protest. However, when including an interaction term to empirically examine the conditional effect that elections had on protest behavior, I find that the dampening effect was weaker in areas where the proportion of college students is high. And, as this section has shown, the importance of dense student networks—exhibited in student involvement in campaign rallies for the political opposition—is underscored in the primary documents produced by social movement actors at that time.

Conclusion

Existing studies of authoritarian elections offer conflicting findings and suggest contradictory empirical expectations regarding the impact of elections on social movements. Using new subnational-level data, this chapter has shown that holding more competitive elections where genuine opposition parties are allowed to contest against the dominant ruling party can co-opt the opposition energy by providing a nondisruptive way for citizens to let off steam (i.e., by voting for the opposition party). However, the dampening effect that such elections can have on pro-democracy protests is mitigated by the availability of mobilizing structures such as student organizations and networks. The findings suggest that elections can have both positive and negative effects on authoritarian regimes by simultaneously decreasing and increasing antiregime protests in different geographic regions or social segments. Moreover, when protesting on the streets and voting for the opposition party are considered as different forms of protest, the findings suggest that multiparty elections in authoritarian regimes could dampen one form of protest while amplifying another.

The findings of this chapter also recast the traditional understanding of South Korea's democratization by highlighting the critical enabling factor—mobilizing structures—that mitigated the dampening effect of elections on protest during the democratic transition period. While previous studies on Korea's democratization largely overlooked the role of elections in authoritarian Korea by characterizing them as unstable political institutions corrupted by irregularities and fraud (e.g., S. Im 2010), this study has shown that in the absence of mobilizing structures, elections may have further stabilized the dictatorship.

In the case of authoritarian Korea, student organizations and networks served as such structures. College students possessed the resources and networks that not only sustained the student movement throughout the authoritarian period but also helped the opposition NKDP break into the fight for constitutional reform, both within and outside the legislature.

The chapter also revealed that the alliance formed between college students and opposition politicians outlived the electoral achievements of the NKDP in 1985 and led to the development of constitutionalism (constitutional revision for direct presidential elections) as a master frame, which mobilized the public to fight for democratic reforms in 1987. It was the grand coalition formed by these two and other social movement groups representing the different segments of Korean society that successfully pressured the authoritarian regime to make democratic reforms. This pressure from civil society was effective partly because it existed in combination with U.S. pressure on the Chun government not to repeat the 1980 Kwangju Massacre and because the ruling party was confident that it would gain control over and win the subsequent democratic elections (Slater and Wong 2013, 2022). Nevertheless, the "mesomobilization" (or movement integration) observed in the June Democratic Uprising was unprecedented and essential for democratization (C. Chung 2011).

This grand coalition, which brought together civil and political society and was deemed "the greatest and strongest in the history of Korea" (S. Kim 2000, 104), was able to rally behind the slogan of "constitutional revision for direct presidential elections" to achieve democratization, but it was unable to sustain itself in the immediate post-transition period. This dissolution occurred both because Korea transitioned to democracy during a noncrisis situation that generally allows authoritarian leaders to enjoy wider support, fewer protests, and fewer internal divisions (Haggard and Kaufman 1995, 1997) and because each group had its own understanding of the meaning and goals of democracy (Choi 1993). Whereas the political opposition and the urban middle class were most concerned with the procedural conceptions of liberal democracy (such as direct presidential elections), students and workers focused on a substantive conception of democracy that included socioeconomic equalities. This divide became evident when workers continued to demand socioeconomic change during the Great Workers' Struggle, but middle-class citizens "did not rush back into the streets to help the working class achieve [effective political representation]" (Cumings 1997, 393). Additionally, as the next chapter will show, the political ideologies formed during the authoritarian period among different *political generations* persisted into the democratic period and affected their beliefs about how society should function.

SIX

Beyond the Democratic Transition

Democratization and Generational Divides

Whereas previous chapters of this book examined how economic growth impacted South Korea's democratic transition in the late 1980s, this chapter explores the enduring effects of that process in the democratic period. Chapters 2 through 5 collectively demonstrated that Korea democratized as a result of authoritarian state-led development, though in a nonlinear fashion. The chapters also showed that the industrial and education policies of the authoritarian era resulted in geospatial concentration of workers and students that not only increased their capacity to organize and engage in collective action but ultimately helped spread the antiregime protests throughout the country. These protests exerted significant pressure on the incumbent regime to democratize by reinstalling direct presidential elections. The organizational capacity of the social forces that brought about this change, including their capacity to form horizontal linkages with one another and with the political opposition, was built over the course of decades. We would expect that these decades-long processes that resulted in democratic transition not to simply end with the transition; rather, it would also have lingering effects in the post-transition period.

Moreover, as I have argued and demonstrated in this book, modernization and economic development, at different time scales, had opposite effects on the authoritarian regimes that created them. Initially, the industrial and education policies—along with the economic growth they generated—provided the autocrats with opportunities to co-opt the masses and increase regime support. However, in the long term, those same modernization policies contributed to the nationalization of antiregime protests that ultimately brought down the authoritarian regime. The time-varying, contradictory effects that modernization and economic development had on regime durability reveal that Koreans in different eras had wildly different experiences of economic growth, authoritarianism, and democracy—that is, their different responses to these multifaceted social, economic, and political phenomena reveal their different relationships to those phenomena. In summary, then, the nonlinear and nonmonotonic process by which economic development led to democracy may have effects that not only endure well beyond the moment of democratization but also vary across political generations, which have divergent experiences of economic growth and authoritarianism.

In this chapter, using Korean General Social Survey (KGSS) data from 2003 to 2013, I empirically investigate whether generational differences exist in political attitudes and behavior in democratic Korea. I first provide evidence in support of the hypothesis that a salient generation gap exists in the democratic period. I then investigate what explains the generational differences. I argue that the answer lies in each generation's relative prioritization of economic development versus democracy, which is heavily shaped by their varying formative experiences (or lack thereof) of economic growth and authoritarian rule. The findings of this chapter suggest that not only did economic development have a democratizing effect on the regime through generational replacement in civil society (given that democratization became more likely as the previously co-opted generation, which tolerated and even supported the authoritarian rule, was gradually replaced by those who opposed authoritarian rule), but it also has continuous impacts on people's political attitudes and behavior in the post-authoritarian period.

Political Generations and Generational Effects in South Korea

As first described in Karl Mannheim's (1952, 290) classic essay "The Problem of Generations," generational (or cohort) effects are the results of the fact that "individuals who belong to the same generation, who share the same year of birth, are endowed, to that extent, with a common location in the historical dimensions of the social processes." Scholars have explored how such effects contribute to various social and political outcomes, including political participation (e.g., W. Miller 1992; W. Miller and Shanks

1996), civic engagement (e.g., Putnam 1995), social movements (e.g., Jennings 1987), and democratization (e.g., Haddad 2012). Although similar in some regards, generational effects are distinct from life cycle or age effects (i.e., the differences attributable to people's respective positions in the life cycle) and period effects (which affect all people who live through a given era, regardless of their age).[1]

A key argument of the theory of generations is that a generation (or cohort) is strongly influenced by major historical or political events that occur during their formative years (ages 17–25), establishing a set of attitudes and worldviews that guide and shape their political behavior through the rest of their lives (Mannheim 1952). Studies on political socialization also emphasize the importance of the impressionable years in explaining how people's political preferences and political action are shaped through socialization agents such as family, school, peers, (conventional and social) media, and political context (Neundorf and Smets 2017). Indeed, according to M. Kent Jennings, "individuals coming of age during periods of pronounced stress and drama, epochal events, or rapid socio-economic change are often said to be uniquely identified in a political scene" (Jennings 1987, 368). For instance, research shows that in the U.S., the generation born between 1910 and 1940—especially those who attended grade school during the Great Depression and spent World War II in high school—have been exceptionally civically engaged: they vote more, join more civil associations, read newspapers more, and trust others more than do members of the younger generations (Putnam 1995, 2000). Research also shows that, while the baby boomers became more politically conservative as they aged, one portion of these baby boomers—specifically those who were involved in the anti–Vietnam War protests and the civil rights movement of the 1960s—formed a "protest generation" that remained distinctive with respect to issues and objects associated with their political baptism (Jennings 1987).

In Korea, the so-called 386 generation has been described as a distinct generation because of the ways in which its members impacted national politics. The term "386 generation" (*sampallyuk sedae*) was coined in the early 1990s, in reference to what was then the latest computer model—Intel's 386. It refers to Koreans who at the time were in their thirties (hence "3"), who had entered colleges and universities in the 1980s (hence "8"), and who had been born in the 1960s (hence "6").[2] Unlike most members of other generations, its members actively participated in the pro-democracy movement against right-wing authoritarian rule and brought about democratization through their protest efforts. As shown in chapters 4 and 5, the members of this generation created a nationwide student movement in the 1980s and formed an alliance with the political opposition to exert popular pressure on the incumbent regime to democratize. And, as showcased in chapter 3, student activists of this generation utilized ecology-dependent strategies of labor mobilization by becoming disguised workers and creating the worker-student alliance that brought labor power to the forefront of the democracy movement in the 1980s. Because of the unique political context in which they developed their sociopolitical identities, 386ers are understood to have carried the legacy of the democracy movement in the post-transition period—that is, they have maintained their left-leaning ideological orientation as both voters and politicians.

Despite its unique place in history, the 386 generation is not the only one that has shaped and been distinctively shaped by Korea's tumultuous political history. In fact, Korean society is composed of multiple generations that were shaped by drastically different political contexts (see table 6.1). Because members of each generation experienced the nation's economic progress and democratization at different stages in their own lives, they developed remarkably different views of and approaches to the opportunities and challenges presented by the modern era.

Koreans who are older than the 386 generation ("pre-386 generations") were born during tumultuous times, when the majority of the population was affected by absolute poverty. The first of these, known as the "Korean War generation," includes all those who were born before 1942. Members of this generation experienced Japanese colonial rule (1910–45), national independence in 1945, and the Korean War (1950–53). The next generation, known as the "postwar industrialization generation" (1942–51), experienced political turmoil such as the 1960 April Revolution and the 1961 May 16 Coup. The "Yusin generation" (1952–59) includes those who were in their twenties during Park Chung Hee's repressive Yusin regime (1972–79). On the heels of this generation followed the aforementioned "386

TABLE 6.1. South Korea's Political Generations

Birth Years	Political Generations
1988–1993	Candlelight Generation
1979–1987	World Cup Generation
1970–1978	IMF Generation
1960–1969	386 Generation
1952–1959	Yusin Generation
1942–1951	Postwar Industrialization Generation
Before 1942	Korean War Generation

Source: Noh, Song, and Kang (2013a, 125).

150 Seeds of Mobilization

generation," members of which were born in the 1960s (1960–69), when industrialization began under Park Chung Hee's authoritarian rule.

Unlike the pre-386 generations and the 386 generation itself, the younger generations ("post-386 generations") were born during a period of economic prosperity. Born in the 1970s (specifically 1970–78), the first of these generations is known as the "IMF generation" because its members experienced the 1997–98 Asian Financial Crisis (commonly referred to as the "IMF Crisis" in Korea). The "World Cup generation" (1979–87) was born during Chun Doo Hwan's authoritarian rule. In their late teens or in their early to mid-twenties, they experienced the 2002 Korea/Japan FIFA World Cup, during which millions of Koreans wearing red T-shirts gathered in the streets to cheer for their national soccer team. Members of this generation were first able to exercise their voting rights during the progressive administrations of Kim Dae Jung (1998–2003) and Roh Moo-hyun (2003–8). Finally, the youngest political generation, called the "Candlelight generation" (birth years 1988–93), experienced the 2008 candlelight protest against U.S. beef imports in their late teens and early twenties.[3] They became eligible to vote at a time of rapid changes in the political environment, such as the activation of online fan clubs for politicians and the spread of unconventional forms of political participation offered by digital media technologies.

The particular life experiences of each generation inevitably shaped their knowledge of the major events, issues, and relevant actors in Korean political history, including those associated with the Korean War, inter-Korean relations, the U.S.–Republic of Korea alliance, authoritarianism, and democracy. The pre-386 generations that directly experienced the Korean War tended to perceive the U.S. as their savior, their liberator from North Korean aggression, and an indispensable ally.[4] They focused their efforts on lifting the country out of poverty while also confronting North Korea and the greater communist threat by strengthening South Korea's alliance with the United States. In addition, they were strongly influenced by Park Chung Hee's economy-first ideology—this hegemonic ideology, which meshed developmentalism, anticommunism, and nationalism, was used to justify the authoritarian government's suppression of political rights and civil liberties (see chapter 2 for details). In this context, the "left = communist" frame emerged and became embedded in the older generation, which continues to equate "communism" with "left" (Korea Exposé 2017).

In contrast, the 386 generation's formative experiences led them to adopt a divergent stance toward U.S.–Republic of Korea and inter-Korean relations.[5] Arguably "the most vocal, active, and self-conscious generation in contemporary Asia" (Pyle 2008, 10), the 386 generation is also distinguished by its leading role in the 1980s pro-democracy movement against U.S.-supported right-wing authoritarian rule. As college students in the 1980s, the 386ers also pioneered protests that were directed almost as much at the U.S. as they were at authoritarian ruler Chun Doo Hwan—they even carried out violent attacks on the U.S. cultural centers and other American facilities.[6] According to most observers, this anti-Americanism was a reaction to the 1980 Kwangju Uprising (or Kwangju Massacre), during which the U.S. was allegedly complicit in the Chun government's brutal crackdown on thousands of protestors (Brazinsky 2009; Shin and Hwang 2003). The incident provoked anger and a sense of betrayal among student activists, who had previously considered the U.S. to be an ally in the struggle for democracy. As they experienced or learned about the massacre, many came to believe that the U.S. was responsible for perpetuating military dictatorship in Korea (Brazinsky 2009).

As the student movement was radicalized, members of it grew skeptical of the South Korean regime's anti–North Korea propaganda, which tied the "bad," "evil," and "threatening" image of North Korea with the "good" and "benevolent" image of the United States throughout the 1960s, 1970s, and 1980s (Jung 2010, 951–52). The National Liberation (Minjok Haebang), one of the two main factions of the student movement in the 1980s, espoused anti-imperialism (which was treated as synonymous with anti-Americanism) and believed that various problems in South Korean society resulted from the U.S.-influenced division of Korea.[7] The Chuch'e Sasangpa (Chusapa), a pro-North Korean group within the National Liberation, was also formed in the 1980s and this subgroup supported the Chuch'e ideology, the North Korean political ideology developed by Kim Il Sung.[8]

The post-386 generations were born during a time of rapid economic growth, spent their childhood in a prosperous and democratic environment, and then experienced the 1997–98 Asian Financial Crisis. Thus, whereas the 386 generation enjoyed a booming economy with plenty of jobs available, the younger generation struggled with unemployment and fierce competition, which was created by the financial crisis and the neoliberal economic reforms implemented during that time.[9] According to a study on these younger generations, unlike their elders, they demonstrate ideological pragmatism and do not show a consistent tendency toward progressivism or conservatism (S.-Y. Park 2007). The same study points out that, despite having experienced or participated in anti-American candle-

152 Seeds of Mobilization

light vigils in the 2000s, this generation exhibits "practical nationalism"—that is, they become nationalistic only when it suits their interests. According to Sun-Young Park (2007, 2), they "would go to McDonald's for hamburgers after burning the U.S. flag at a candlelight vigil in a protest against America. They do not think it is contradictory to accept the American culture on one hand, while claiming to condemn a U.S. action." This version of nationalism is distinct from that of the older generations, which exhibit anti-Japanese and anti-American sentiments associated with Japanese colonial rule and the Kwangju Massacre, respectively. Moreover, having experienced a confrontational period of inter-Korean relations during their young adulthood (e.g., the sinking of the South Korean Navy ship *Chŏnan* in March 2010 and shelling of Yŏnpyŏng Island in November 2010), they are more likely to view North Korea as an enemy rather than as a land of "fellow brethren" (J. Kim et al. 2015, 18).

In sum, although the 386 generation has long been regarded as unique in its political influence in Korean society, this section has shown that there are other political generations—those that came before and after the 386 generation—that are also important in their own ways. Just as the 386 generation was shaped by their experiences with fighting against U.S.-supported right-wing authoritarian rule in the 1980s, prior generations were uniquely impacted by the ways that autocrats co-opted them during the "Miracle on the Han River." Likewise, the generations that followed are exceptional in that they had no direct experience of authoritarianism or the pro-democracy movement, so their political attitudes and behaviors—unlike those of their elders—were not directly shaped by those phenomena. Perhaps economic growth had time-varying, contradictory effects on authoritarian durability (as demonstrated in the earlier chapters of this book) in part as a result of these generational differences.

Is There a Generational Gap in Post-Transition South Korea?

Generational politics began to receive increased attention among scholars and the general Korean public starting in 2002, when Roh Moo-hyun, a former pro-democracy activist and the presidential candidate of the progressive Millennium Democratic Party (Saech'ŏnnyŏn Minjudang), won the 16th presidential election with overwhelming support from the younger generations in the country.[10] Roh received 58.8% and 61.2% of the votes from the 386 generation and younger voters, respectively (W.-T. Kang 2009, 83). For the first time, the electoral results suggested that the impact of regional voting—which had dominated Korean electoral politics since democratization in 1987—might be weakening, and the generational divide in political ideology could be emerging as a new political cleavage in Korea (Cheng and Kim 1994, 82). However, the conservative party's subsequent victories in the 2007 and 2012 presidential elections suggested that the 386 generation was becoming more conservative, and therefore that the cohort effect of the progressive 386 generation might be disappearing. Then a generational voting pattern reappeared during the snap presidential election in 2017, which immediately followed the impeachment of Park Geun-hye (G.-W. Shin and Moon 2017). Those aged 20–59 tended to vote for progressive candidate Moon Jae-in (Minjoo Party; Tŏburŏ Minjudang), whereas those 60 and older tended to vote for conservative candidate Hong Joon-pyo (then Liberty Korea Party; Chayu Han'guktang). These electoral trends that indicate the ebb and flow of the generation effect led to a new line of research on whether the cohort effect of the 386 generation exists among Korean electorates and political elites.

Previous studies on generational effects on political attitudes and behavior among the Korean *electorate* (as opposed to studies focused on political elites) have focused on analyzing the cohort effect of the 386 generation on vote choices—and because this generation is seen as the progressive one in Korea, many scholars have used it as the reference group when analyzing the effects of generational differences on political outcomes. As a result, the current literature on such effects explores whether the generational effects of the progressive 386 generation are found in electoral behavior beyond the 2002 presidential election. The results of these studies are divided. Those that analyzed the voting patterns of the 2007 presidential and 2008 legislative elections, in which the conservatives won, concluded that the generation effects of the 386 generation have disappeared and that aging effects have prevailed (e.g., W.-T. Kang 2009; C. W. Park 2008; M.-H. Park 2009; W.-H. Park 2012, 2013; Yoon 2009). In contrast, studies that focused individually on the 2007 presidential, 2010 local, and 2012 presidential elections found evidence to support the claim that generational effects—including those of the 386 generation—on vote choice continue to exist (e.g., Chung 2012; N.-Y. Lee 2008; N.-Y. Lee 2010; Noh, Song, and Kang 2013b).

Similarly, studies using (mostly) cross-sectional data on presidential elections yield mixed and thus inconclusive results. Jaehoo Park (2011) examined generational changes in voting choice and ideology from the 1992 to the 2007 presidential elections and did not find evidence of a cohort effect of the 386 generation. Ah-Ran Hwang (2009) investigated the generational differences in ideological orientation across the 1997, 2002, and 2007 presidential elections and showed that the cohort effects of the "democratization realization generation" (birth years 1967–71, including members of the 386 generation) were evident in 1997 and 2002, but that *both* cohort and period effects were at play during the 2007 presidential election. Noh, Song, and Kang (2013a) analyzed the presidential elections between 1997 and 2012 and showed that the 386 generation's level of support for progressive candidates, progressiveness, and identification with the progressive party remained similar across the four elections, thus demonstrating the existence of the cohort effect of the 386 generation. Saejae Oh (2015) analyzed ideological orientation and candidate choice in the five presidential and six legislative elections between 1992 and 2012 and found cohort effects of the 386 generation in the 2002 and 2012 presidential elections and the 2004 and 2012 legislative elections only. This author explained that the cohort effect is conditional on the extent to which political parties mobilize voters based on ideological issues in a given election (S. Oh 2015; S. Oh and Lee 2014). These varied findings suggest that the cohort effect of the 386 generation as well as the conditionality of the effect may vary across elections and types of elections, but the continued focus on the generational effect by scholars of Korean politics indicates its importance for electoral politics in the post-transition period.

There are also a few existing studies on *political elites*—again, focusing on the 386 generation—that suggest that generational effects also matter for policymaking. The 386 generation was the dominant generation represented in the progressive incumbencies of Kim Dae Jung (1998–2003) and Roh Moo-hyun (2003–8). In the Roh administration, approximately 70% of Blue House[11] staff belonged to the 386 generation (Ryu 2013, 132), and roughly 33% of both the 16th (2000–2004) and 17th (2004–8) National Assemblies consisted of former pro-democracy movement activists from the 386 generation (S. Kim, Chang, and Shin 2013, 245). The studies that provided these statistics find that the political ideologies forged through the historical experience of the democracy movement (including anti-Americanism) continued to impact the political actions and foreign policy preferences of these policymakers. Specifically, using the 2005 East Asia Institute elite survey, Yongwook Ryu (2013) finds that the political elite belonging to the 386 generation held more favorable sentiments toward North Korea and less favorable sentiments toward the U.S. He further shows that their distinctive emotions, perceptions, and policy preferences toward North Korea and the U.S. contributed to South Korea's foreign policy changes (i.e., greater engagement with North Korea) under the

Roh administration. Similarly, by analyzing roll call data on South Korea's participation in the Iraq War, S. Kim, Chang, and Shin (2013) find that legislators with greater involvement in the democracy movement were significantly more likely to vote against sending Korean troops to support the U.S. war in Iraq.

These studies on generations and their political effects in South Korea suggest that there is a reasonable amount of evidence that, even after the democratic transition, members of the 386 generation maintained their ideological orientations (whether their progressiveness or their views toward other countries) as shaped by their formative experiences in the 1980s pro-democracy movement. The findings also suggest that age or period effect, or both, may diminish the cohort effect of the 386 generation, but it is unclear whether that effect has diminished to the point that it has disappeared. Furthermore, the exclusive focus on the 386 generation did not generate enough information for us to fully understand the generational effects of the other political generations in the post-transition period. The subsequent analysis aims to fill this gap.

Empirical Analysis

Data and Methods

Building on previous studies, I investigate whether there are generational differences in political attitudes and behavior in the democratic period; however, I do not limit my investigation to the cohort effect of the 386 generation. I also expand my analysis beyond election years and people's vote choices. To do so, I utilize responses to the Korean General Social Survey[12] from 2003 to 2012.[13] In this survey, approximately 2,000 individual respondents per year are drawn from a national sample of adults (age 18 or older) who live in South Korea. That dataset for all survey years combined includes 14,889 total observations (see table A6.1 in the online appendix for summary statistics of all variables).

Generation is the independent variable and the generations of the respondents in the KGSS are categorized according to the delineation of Noh, Song, and Kang (2013a), and they are named based on the most significant historical event they experienced during their formative years: Korean War (pre-1942), Postwar Industrialization (1942–51), Yusin (1952–59), 386 (1960–69), IMF (1970–78), World Cup (1979–87), and Candlelight (1988–93). I combine and sort these generations into three groups:

pre-386 generation, 386 generation, and post-386 generation. The War, Industrial, and Yusin generations are coded as the "pre-386 generation," and the IMF, World Cup, and Candlelight generations are coded as the "post-386 generation." Although I acknowledge that variations exist within each generation group (based on individual or regional-level factors), this categorization allows me to distinguish between those who were largely co-opted by the authoritarian rulers who provided economic growth and upward mobility (i.e., the pre-386 generation), those who resisted authoritarian rule (i.e., the 386 generation), and those who had no direct experience of authoritarianism (i.e., the post-386 generation).

I use the logistic regression and ordinal logistic regression models to analyze the effect of the generation variable on political behavior (i.e., voter participation), political attitude (i.e., political ideology and attitudes toward North Korea and the U.S.), and civic engagement (e.g., signing a petition, boycotting products for political reasons, participating in a demonstration, attending a political meeting, attempting to contact politicians, raising political funds, and using media and the internet to express one's views). The KGSS data on voter participation and political attitudes are available for all survey years, whereas data on civic engagement are only available for 2004 and 2009.

The age variable is included to control for the effect that age may have on a person's political attitudes and behavior, regardless of belonging to a particular political generation. Regionalism (i.e., province of residence being Chŏlla or Kyŏngsang),[14] gender, college education, and household income are also included as control variables, as these factors are likely to be correlated with political attitudes and behavior. I also control for the survey year to ensure that the results are not driven by any political event that occurred in that particular year.

Hypotheses

Based on the findings from existing studies and descriptive information on the Korean political generations and generational effects, I first hypothesize that there exist generational (or cohort) effects (i.e., not just age and period effects) in political behavior, political attitude, and civic engagement. I also hypothesize that the 386 and post-386 generations are more likely to hold progressive political ideologies compared with the pre-386 generation, not only due to the age effect (in which we would expect people to become more conservative as they age) but also due to the cohort effect based on their experiences from the authoritarian period. That is, given the time-varying, contradictory effects that economic growth had on support for authoritarian rule, the pre-386 generation contains a higher proportion of the Korean populace that was co-opted by the right-wing (anticommunist) authoritarian regime. Therefore, they are more likely to hold a conservative ideology even in the post-transition period.

Relatedly, because the pre-386 and 386 generations were exposed to anticommunist propaganda and radical leftist ideologies during the ideologically charged authoritarian era, they are more likely than the post-386 generation to be partisans. And given that partisans are more likely to vote than nonpartisans in Korea (J. Lee 2004; J. Lee and Hwang 2012), we would expect the pre-386 and 386 generations to exhibit a higher turnout rate than the post-386 generation. Specifically, with regard to people's views toward the U.S. and North Korea, I hypothesize that the 386 generation (compared to the pre-386 and post-386 generations) is more likely to have an unfavorable view toward the U.S. and a favorable view toward North Korea given their active participation or exposure, or both, to the radicalized (leftist) student movement in the 1980s, which espoused anti-American and pro-reunification rhetoric.

I also hypothesize that the 386 generation is overall more likely to be civically engaged than either the pre-386 or post-386 generations. This hypothesis is derived from the fact that the 386ers were able to successfully bring about democratization through collective action. We can expect those experiences in the pro-democracy movement to have a lasting impact even in the post-transition period, as "one major outcome of mobilization is the formation of a political generation, a cohort of activists who are committed to the cause in enduring ways" (Whittier 2004, 540). And as discussed in other chapters of this book, students and youth (today's 386 generation) were the dominant social groups in the pro-democracy movement in the 1980s. Because rallies and demonstrations were the most popular tactics they used throughout the 1970s and 1980s (with the most heavy use occurring in the 1980s) (G.-W. Shin et al. 2011), we would expect the 386ers to be more likely to engage in those noninstitutional forms of political participation.

The analysis, then, tests the following hypotheses:

H_1: There are generational differences in political behavior, political attitude, and civic engagement.

H_2: The pre-386 and 386 generations are more likely to turn out to vote than the post-386 generation.

H_3: The 386 and post-386 generations are more likely to be progressive than the pre-386 generation.

H_4: Compared to the pre-386 and post-386 generations, the 386

158 Seeds of Mobilization

generation is more likely to have an unfavorable view of the U.S. and a favorable view of North Korea.

H_{5a}: Compared to the pre-386 and post-386 generations, the 386 generation is overall more likely to be civically engaged.

H_{5b}: Compared to the pre-386 and post-386 generations, the 386 generation is more likely to sign petitions and participate in demonstrations (which were the dominant strategies used by the pro-democracy movement in the 1980s).

Results

To examine whether there are generational differences in *voter participation*, I use the dependent variable VOTELAST, found in the KGSS dataset. I recode the values of the variable as 1 if the respondent answered "voted" to the survey question asking whether the respondent voted in the previous election, and 0 otherwise. Figure 6.1 shows the results from the logistic regression analysis using the 386 generation (GEN386) as the reference group. Providing support to the H_2 hypothesis (the pre-386 and 386 generations are more likely to turn out to vote than the post-386 generation), the figure shows that the post-386 generation is significantly less likely to turn out to vote, holding everything else constant.[15] The odds of the post-386 generation turning out to vote is 36% lower than the odds of the 386 generation doing so. The result also shows that the pre-386 generation is more likely to vote than the 386 generation, but the difference is not statistically significant.

The generational effect on *political ideology* is examined by using the PARTYLR variable in the KGSS dataset as the dependent variable. The respondents were asked, "To what degree do you think yourself politically liberal or conservative?" The responses are coded as (1) very liberal (*chinbojŏk*), (2) somewhat liberal, (3) neither liberal nor conservative (*posujŏk*), (4) somewhat conservative, and (5) very conservative.[16] Figure 6.2 presents the result using the ordered logit model, and the overall results provide support for the H_3 hypothesis (that the pre-386 generation is more politically conservative than the younger generations).[17] Ceteris paribus, belonging to the pre-386 generation (versus the 386 generation) is associated with an increasing conservatism of one's political ideology. Additionally, belonging to the post-386 generation is associated with being less conservative (i.e., more progressive), but the difference between the 386 generation and post-386 generation is not found to be statistically significant. These findings are consistent with the H_3 hypothesis (the 386 and

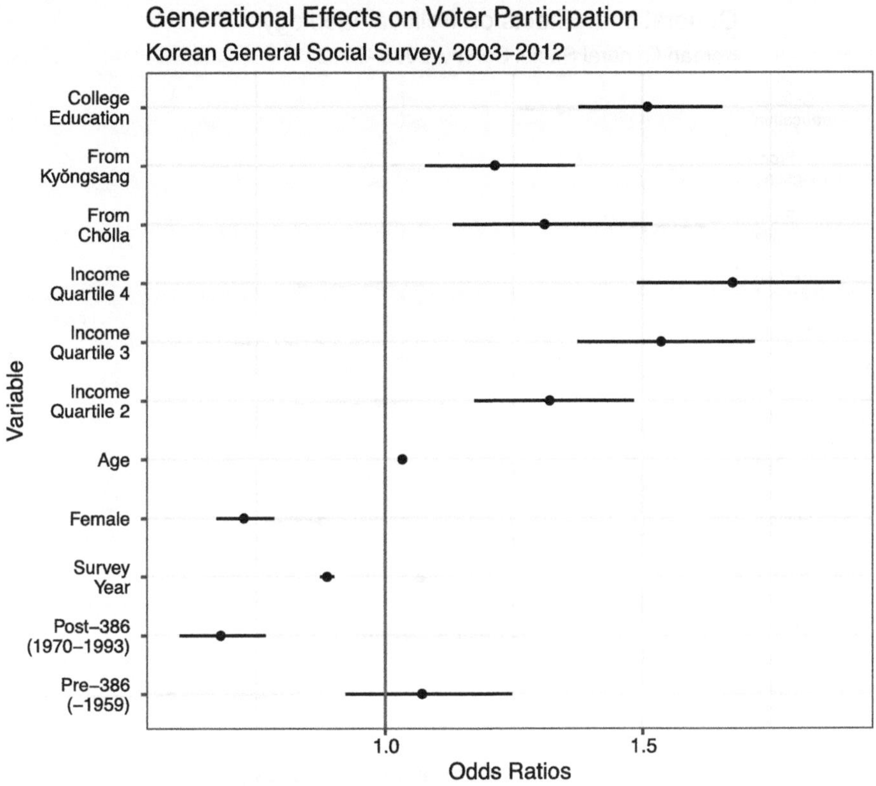

Generational Effects on Voter Participation
Korean General Social Survey, 2003–2012

Fig 6.1. Voter participation. Baseline: 386 Generation.

post-386 generations are more likely to be progressive than the pre-386 generation) and Sun-Young Park's (2007) claim that Koreans belonging to the post-386 generation are free from ideological or political bias and are mostly apathetic to politics.

Figures 6.3 and 6.4 display the percentage of voters for each generation and the percentage of liberals in each generation across the survey years. These figures show that the results in figures 6.1 and 6.2 (displaying the average effects from 2003 to 2012) are not driven by the life cycle effect. When a life cycle effect *is* at play, differences between younger and older people are largely due to their respective positions in the life cycle. For example, as people age, they are expected to become more conservative over time and vote at higher rates, remain relatively stable throughout middle age, and gradually decline as physical infirmity sets in. If the life cycle effect—as opposed to the generation (or cohort) effect—were at play

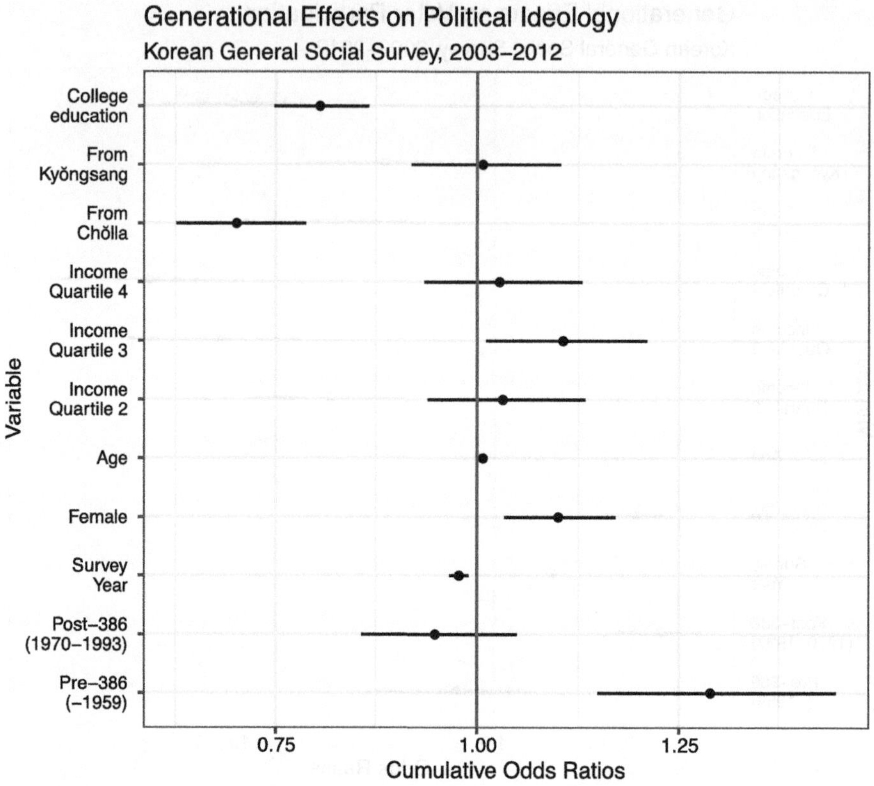

Generational Effects on Political Ideology
Korean General Social Survey, 2003–2012

Fig 6.2. Political ideology. Baseline: 386 Generation.

here, we would expect the percentage of those who voted (in fig. 6.3) to increase across the survey years among the post-386 generation, remain relatively stable for the 386 generation, and decline for the pre-386 generation. We would also expect the percentage of liberals (in fig. 6.4) to decline across the survey years for all three generation groups. Yet we do not observe such changes in figures 6.3 and 6.4, which suggests that the results in figures 6.1 and 6.2 are capturing the generational effects.

To examine South Koreans' *attitudes toward North Korea and the U.S.,* I first use the NORTHWHO variable from the KGSS data to investigate whether there is a generational difference in people's attitudes toward North Korea. The KGSS survey asks, "What do you think North Korea is to us? Please choose only one. (1) a country to support, (2) a country to cooperate with, (3) a country to guard against, and (4) a country to fight against." Figure 6.5 displays the results using the ordered logistic logit

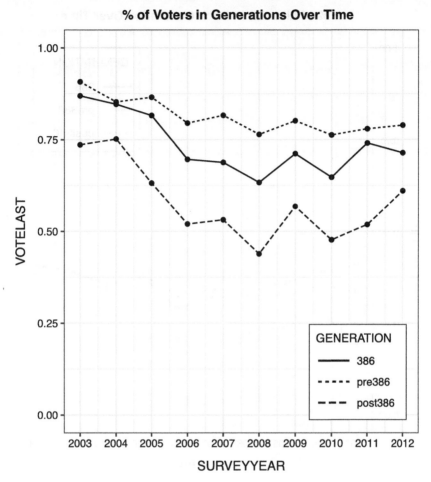

Fig 6.3. Voter turnout by generation group, 2003–12.

model.[18] Consistent with the H_4 hypothesis (which posits that the 386 generation is more likely to be sympathetic toward North Korea), both the pre-386 generation and post-386 generation are found to be more hostile toward North Korea than the 386 generation. The result also reveals that the pre-386 generation is most hostile toward North Korea.

Additionally, I examine the responses to the KGSS survey question corresponding to the SEDISTAN variable: "Which countries do you feel closest to among the following countries: USA, Japan, North Korea, China, or Russia?" The responses (summarized in table 6.2) show that, out

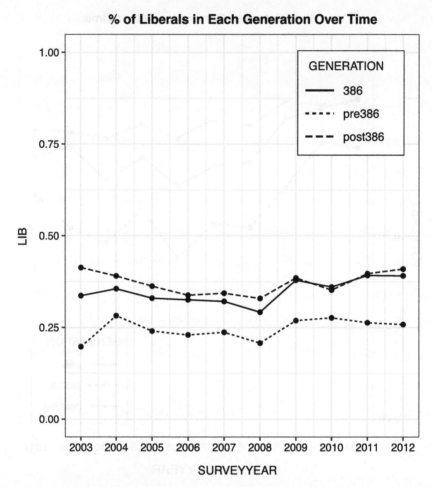

Fig 6.4. Political ideology by generation group, 2003–12.

of all political generations, the 386 generation and the IMF generation feel least close to the U.S. and feel closest to North Korea, whereas the War and Industrial generations feel closest to the U.S. and least close to North Korea.

When examining the generational differences in people's views toward North Korea and the U.S. across the survey years, it is clear that the pre-386 generation has been consistently least favorable toward North Korea (fig. 6.6) and most favorable toward the U.S. (fig. 6.7). At the same time, figures 6.6 and 6.7 demonstrate that people's closeness to North Korea decreases

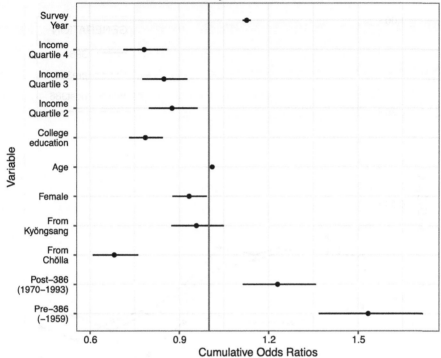

Fig 6.5. Attitude toward North Korea. Baseline: 386 Generation.

TABLE 6.2. Attitudes toward the United States, Japan, North Korea, China, and Russia

	United States	Japan	North Korea	China	Russia
Korean War (–1941)	**79%**	6%	**11%**	4%	1%
Postwar Industrialization (1942–51)	**75%**	5%	**13%**	6%	1%
Yusin (1952–59)	66%	5%	19%	9%	1%
386 (1960–79)	**51%**	8%	**29%**	11%	1%
IMF (1970–79)	**48%**	11%	**30%**	10%	2%
World Cup (1980–87)	51%	15%	24%	9%	1%
Candlelight (1988–93)	62%	15%	15%	6%	2%

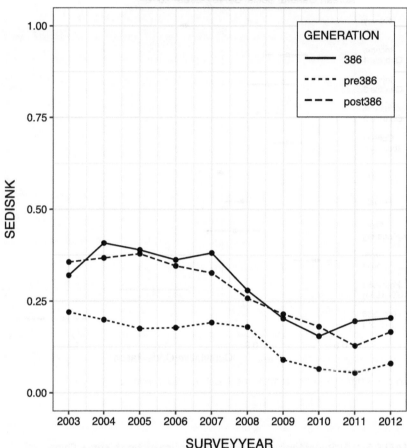

Fig 6.6. Attitude toward North Korea by generation group, 2003–12.

over time across all generations, and closeness to the U.S. increased across all generations starting around 2008, when Lee Myung-bak became president. Under his conservative government (2008–13) and the conservative government of Park Geun-hye (2013–17), hardline approaches toward North Korea were reciprocated in the form of provocative acts by North Korea, resulting in high tensions on the peninsula. This experience of hostility may have contributed to the changes in people's closeness with North Korea and the U.S. Moreover, figures 6.6 and 6.7 show that although the gap between the pre-386 generation and the other generations (386 and

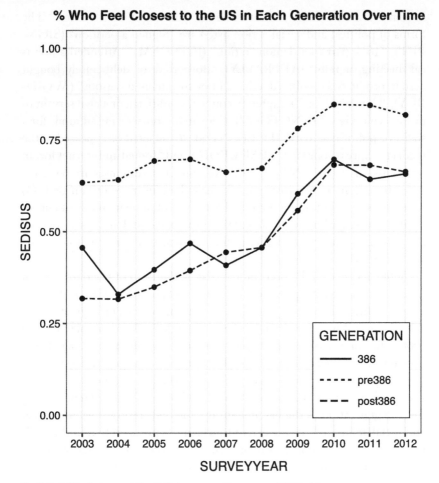

Fig 6.7. Attitude toward the U.S. by generation group, 2003–12.

post-386) persists over time, people's attitudes toward North Korea and the U.S. are changing regardless of age. Collectively, these findings suggest that there may exist both period and generational effects on people's attitude toward North Korea and the U.S.

Finally, to examine whether there are generational differences in *civic engagement* in the post-transition period, I use the KGSS data from the years 2004 and 2009 (the only two years for which data on civic engagement is available). The survey item reads, "Here are some different forms of political and social action that people can take. Please indicate, for each one, whether you have done any of these things in the past year. If you

166 Seeds of Mobilization

have not done it, please indicate whether you might do it or not." The forms of political and social action listed are "Signed a petition" (SIGN-PET), "Took part in a demonstration" (JOINDEM), "Attended a political meeting or rally" (ATTRALLY), "Boycotted, or deliberately bought certain products for political, ethical or environmental reasons" (AVOID-BUY), "Contacted, or attempted to contact, a politician or a civil servant to express your views" (CNCTGOV), "Donated money or raised funds for a social or political activity" (POLFUNDS), "Contacted or appeared in the media to express your view" (USEMEDIA), and "Joined an Internet forum or discussion group" (INTERPOL). Respondents' responses are recorded as (1) have done in the past year, (2) have done in more distant past, (3) have not done it but might do it, and (4) have not done it and would never do it. I created a binary variable, taking the value of 1 if the respondent engaged in the activity (whether in the past year or the more distant past) and 0 otherwise.

Table 6.3 reports the odds ratio—that is, the ratio of the odds that an individual engages in a given form of social and political action to the odds that an individual does not engage in the action. An odds ratio greater than 1 indicates that increases in the value of the independent variable raise the probability of a person engaging in the action; for ratios less than 1, the probability is reduced. The independent variable is the generation variable indicating whether an individual belongs to the pre-386 generation (1 if yes, 0 otherwise), 386 generation, or post-386 generation. Hence, using the 386 generation as the baseline group, the odds ratio for each political and social action tells us the extent to which the probability of individuals belonging to one group versus the other (e.g., pre-386 generation versus 386 generation; 386 generation versus post-386 generation) increases or decreases.

The results reported in table 6.3 provide evidence to support hypotheses H_{5a} and H_{5b} by demonstrating that the 386 generation has been more civically engaged during the democratic period, especially regarding participation in demonstrations and signing petitions. Columns 1 and 2 show that the 386 generation engages in these actions more than both the pre-386 and post-386 generations. Belonging to the pre-386 generation—as opposed to the 386 generation—reduces the odds of signing a petition by approximately 36%; likewise, belonging to the post-386 generation (as opposed to the 386 generation) reduces the odds by 24%. Moreover, compared to the pre-386 generation, the 386 generation is more likely to boycott products for political reasons and attend political meetings or rallies (columns 3 and 4). The 386 generation is also more likely to contact

TABLE 6.3. Odds Ratios for Logistic Regression Analysis of the Generational Difference in Civic Engagement in 2004 and 2009

	Dependent Variables (Political and Social Actions)							
	SIGNPET	JOINDEM	ATTRALLY	AVOIDBUY	POLFUNDS	CNTCTGOV	USEMEDIA	INTPOL
Pre-386 Generation	0.637***	0.431***	0.632*	0.587***	1.043	0.936	0.657	0.731
Post-386 Generation	0.756**	0.631***	0.852	0.939	0.840	0.545***	0.643	0.771
Age	0.987**	1.000	1.013	0.987*	0.991	1.010	1.005	0.971*
Gender	1.168*	0.468***	0.481***	1.347***	1.023	0.644***	0.496***	0.505***
College Education	1.597***	2.390***	1.989***	2.012***	1.372***	1.505**	1.460*	2.193***
Income	1.051***	1.037***	1.053***	1.028**	1.036***	1.032**	1.043**	1.012
Chŏlla	1.005	1.520**	1.977***	1.177	1.297*	1.001	0.744	1.408
Kyŏngsang	0.923	0.876	1.126	1.082	0.782*	0.982	1.299	1.262
Survey year	0.869***	0.900***	0.935**	0.858***	1.009	0.926***	0.963	0.969
Observations	2,745	2,741	2,727	2,742	2,725	2,727	2,723	2,723

*Note: *$p < 0.1$, **$p < 0.05$, ***$p < 0.01$

government officials and politicians than the post-386 generation (column 6). For the remaining forms of social and political action (POLFUNDS, USEMEDIA, INTPOL), there's no statistical difference between the 386 generation and the other two generation groups.

With regard to the control variables, as one would expect, those with higher education and income levels are more likely to engage in forms of political and social action. Additionally, respondents from the Chŏlla Provinces are more likely to have participated in demonstrations or attended political meetings and rallies. This finding could be explained by the aforementioned Kwangju Uprising, which occurred in South Chŏlla Province during Chun's rule in May 1980 and may have activated people's interest in social and political action. Moreover, the results also reveal that women are more likely to sign petitions and attend political meetings and rallies, whereas men are more likely to join demonstrations, contact government officials, and use the media or internet to express their views.

The results reported in this section collectively provide evidence to support hypothesis H_1—that there are generational differences in voter participation, political attitudes, and patterns of civic engagement in democratic Korea. This generational effect appears not only during election cycles but also on an everyday basis.

What Explains the Generational Differences in the Democratic Period?

Given that I have found evidence for generational effects on political attitudes and behavior in the democratic period, the logical next step is to ask what explains these generational differences. In this section, I argue that each generation's relative prioritization of economic development and democracy—as shaped by their formative experiences of economic growth and authoritarianism (or lack thereof)—contributes to its unique political attitudes and behavior in the democratic era.

My argument builds on Ronald Inglehart's argument that economic development promotes intergenerational value change, which has implications for political development. More specifically, he argues that as countries industrialize, there is an intergenerational cultural shift from an emphasis on economic and physical security (materialist or survival values) toward an emphasis on self-expression, subjective well-being, and quality of life (postmaterialist or self-expression values) (Inglehart 1990, 1997; Inglehart and Welzel 2005, 2009). This cultural shift emerges among cohorts that have grown up under conditions in which survival is taken for granted.

Beyond the Democratic Transition   169

As stated by Kenneth Pyle, "Industrialization—especially rapid catch-up industrialization—brings with it social dislocations caused by the movement of people from the country to city, by the psychological strain caused by the undermining of old values and the disturbance of vested interests by economic change, and by widening differences between generations" (Pyle 2008, 6). Therefore, experiencing rapid industrialization and economic security at a formative age is more likely to impart self-expression values that prioritize free choice and motivate political action (Inglehart and Welzel 2009, 38). This theory of intergenerational value change can be applied to the Korean case to understand how rapid and compressed modernization played a role in producing the generational divide during and after the authoritarian period.

As alluded to earlier in this chapter, among the generations that spent their impressionable years under authoritarianism, the 386 generation was the youngest, and its members were the first generation to grow up free from poverty. Although some 386ers (born in the early 1960s) experienced poverty in their childhood, they do not share the profound sense of economic and national insecurity that their parents did during parts of Japanese colonial rule and the Korean War. When rapid industrialization began under Park Chung Hee, the 386 generation was able to take advantage of the increased opportunities for socialization created by urbanization and the expansion of education and mass media. Between 1960 and 1990, the urban population grew from 28.3% to 79.9% of the total population. The mass media (television, newspapers, and radio) also developed rapidly, reaching almost every household by 1979 (J.-J. Choi 1989, 71). As shown in chapter 4, with the government's expansion of higher education, college and university enrollment also increased dramatically, especially in the 1980s, thereby providing more opportunities for independent, critical thinking and socialization among college students. In contrast, those born between 1955 and 1959—the generation immediately preceding the 386 generation—were in their formative period of political socialization in the 1970s, when state-led industrialization and the oppressive rule of the authoritarian regime coexisted. They lived "a life of petty citizens" who were "too busy making a living" (Ma and Kim 2015, 91–92). They experienced economic growth, but they could not take much interest in political issues or actively participate in the pro-democracy movement (Ma and Kim 2015).

As a result, despite being separated by only a single generation, the 386 generation and their parents formed differing views regarding authoritarianism. The older generation was willing to accept a dictatorship as long as it delivered economic growth. "[They were] proud to move from bicycles to motorbikes, and then to cars, and they were happy when it became affordable to vacation in Jeju Island and then even sometimes overseas" (Lankov 2008). In contrast, to the 386ers, the war is only a distant memory, recalled largely through their parents' stories and the dictatorship's official anticommunist propaganda. "They were not ready to accept the tacit deal military dictators made with [the previous generations]: authoritarianism in exchange for economic growth. The 386ers wanted complete democracy" (Lankov 2008).

These differences in the 386 and pre-386 generations' views toward the authoritarian past are also revealed through how they remember former dictator Park Chung Hee and his economic achievements. According to Ma and Kim (2015), the collective memories of industrialization and dictatorship shared by the former period Korean baby boomers (born between 1955 and 1959; belonging to the Yusin generation) included nostalgia for strong leaders, values that prioritize economic growth over political freedom and democratization, resistance to groups critical of the dictatorship (including both the earlier pro-democracy movement and contemporary progressive civic organizations), and anticommunist ideology. Woojin Kang (2016a) similarly finds that the older the citizen, the more likely they are to demonstrate political nostalgia for Park Chung Hee, such as by identifying Park's government as the best since the 1960s. The study also shows that those who believe in prioritizing economic development over democracy are more likely to show political support for Park's government. According to Seungsook Moon (2009, 4), the differing memories of Park Chung Hee—especially the sharp contrast between glorifying and demonizing him—are based on one's "relative priority of economic development and democracy for the advancement of the Korean nation and the Korean people." The glorifying, nostalgic memories of Park reveal people's desire for a strong leader who can deliver economic growth and security (even at the expense of democracy), whereas the demonizing memories reveal the idea that individual rights and the practices of democratic procedures are important, and that repressive dictatorship is not an inevitable condition for economic growth (S. Moon 2009, 9).

To empirically investigate the idea that people's relative prioritization of economic development and democracy—shaped by their experiences of the authoritarian past—can account for the generational differences in the post-transition period, I utilize data from the Asian Barometer Survey from 2003 to 2015. This survey asked how respondents in Korea perceived economic development vis-à-vis democracy and whether one was more impor-

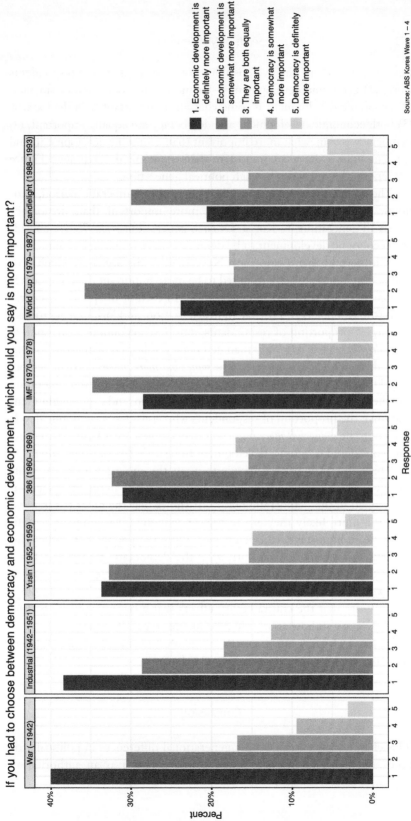

Fig 6.8. Preference for economic development vs. democracy by political generation, 2003–15.

tant than the other. The five possible choices available to the respondents were: (1) economic development is far more important than democracy, (2) economic development is somewhat more important than democracy, (3) both economic development and democracy are equally important, (4) democracy is somewhat more important than economic development, and (5) democracy is far more important than economic development. Figure 6.8 reports the responses by each political generation.

The figure shows that, overall, even in the democratic period, economic development was considered more important than democracy across all generations in Korea. Of each generation, 50%–70.6% considered economic development to be definitely more important or somewhat more important than democracy. Nevertheless, the *degree* to which economic development was considered to be more important than democracy changes starting with the 386 generation. In each of the pre-386 generations (the Korean War, Postwar Industrialization, and Yusin Generations), the largest proportion of respondents considered economic development to be *definitely more important* than democracy, followed by those who considered economic development to be *somewhat more important* than democracy. However, the pattern is reversed when looking at the 386 generation and the post-386 generations (the IMF, World Cup, and Candlelight Generations): the proportion of respondents who considered economic development to be *somewhat more important* than democracy is larger than those who considered economic development to be *definitely more important*.

This observed pattern suggests that the intergenerational value change—which helped drive Korea's democratization in the first place—is maintained in the democratic period. It shows that the older the generation, the more likely they are to regard economic development as definitely more important than democracy. Only the youngest (Candlelight) generation—the first to be born *after* the democratic transition—has a distinctly higher proportion of respondents who consider democracy to be *somewhat more important* than economic development. These findings demonstrate that the contradictory effects that economic growth had on South Korea's authoritarian rule continue to impact Korean society as an authoritarian legacy, and these effects manifest in the generational differences in people's political attitudes and behaviors.

Conclusion

This chapter conceptualized the generational differences in political attitudes and behavior in post-transition South Korea as an authoritarian legacy reflecting the time-varying, contradictory effects that economic growth had on the authoritarian regimes. Using the KGSS data from 2003 to 2012, I examined whether generational differences exist in voter turnout, political ideology, attitudes toward North Korea and the U.S., and patterns of civic engagement in the democratic period. The results demonstrated that there indeed is a generational divide in democratic Korea: the pre-386 generation is more conservative, the 386 generation is more civically engaged, and the post-386 generation is less engaged in politics. The oldest pre-386 generation is also the most favorable toward the U.S. and the most hostile toward North Korea.

The chapter also revealed that the intergenerational differences in political attitudes and behavior in the democratic period are driven by their members' relative prioritization of economic development and security (i.e., holding *survival* values) versus democracy (i.e., embracing *self-expression* values). The generations' differing relative prioritization of economic development versus democracy has been shaped by their varying formative experiences (or lack thereof) of economic growth and authoritarianism. The 386 generation was the first generation to consider economic development to be somewhat more important than democracy, and the youngest (Candlelight) generation was the only generation—born and raised in a democratic Korea—that responded that democracy is somewhat more important than economic development. This pattern of intergenerational change is consistent with Inglehart and Welzel's (2005) revised theory of modernization, which says that only when physical and economic security is taken for granted can self-expression values shape people's political behavior and attitudes. Moreover, it suggests that a generational shift in the relative prioritization of economic development versus democracy may drive not only democratization but also democratic consolidation. As demonstrated in other parts of this book, social changes resulting from modernization and economic development give rise to a new "democratizing generation" that gradually replaces the previously co-opted generation of the authoritarian period. Therefore, in the post-transition period, as this new generation becomes a majority of the electorate, of civil society organizations, of legislature(s), and of businesses, we observe the visible transformation of politics and "real democracy" taking root in the country (Haddad 2012).

Lastly, this final empirical chapter provided evidence to support the view that political ideologies formed during a historical period may persist—rather than change—over time. As will be discussed in more detail in the concluding chapter, increased political polarization has become one of the main threats to Korea's democracy. The generational divide in Korean

174 Seeds of Mobilization

politics was clearly manifested during the 2016–17 Candlelight Revolution, when more than 16 million Korean citizens cumulatively participated in weekly candlelight protests from November 2016 to March 2017 to call for the impeachment of Park Geun-hye (the daughter of dictator Park Chung Hee). Park was embroiled in a corruption scandal involving her confidant Choi Soon-sil's interventions in political affairs and bribes that she received in return for favors to businesses such as Samsung (South Korea's biggest conglomerate). In response, the older, conservative *taegeukgi* protestors (translated as the Korean national flag) launched a series of pro-Park rallies, demanding the arrest of candlelight protestors and calling them *jwapa ppalgaengi* ("pro–North Korean leftists"). They believed that they were preventing Korea's liberal democracy from collapsing under the influence of pro–North Korean (leftist) forces in the country (H. Lee 2018). The split between anti-Park and pro-Park protestors in 2016–17 revealed a serious generational gap in the country. However, as the findings of this chapter have shown, the generational divide and the anticommunist rhetoric espoused by the older *taegeukgi* protestors are not entirely new. As a matter of fact, generational differences in political attitudes and behavior have been observed throughout the post-transition period. The rising political polarization is therefore one concrete example of the ways in which the contradictory effects of economic growth from the authoritarian period matter beyond the democratic transition. Furthermore, it is manifested through the different generations with varying relationships (or lack thereof) with economic development and authoritarianism.

SEVEN

Conclusion

Development, Democracy, and Authoritarian Legacy

In the latter half of the 20th century, starting with a handful of countries in East Asia in the 1960s and 1970s, some of the world's poorest countries made the "fastest and biggest development gains in history" (Radelet 2015, 5). These changes were frequently accompanied by the fall of the dictatorship. However, the precise relationship between development and democracy remains a live question in debates among social scientists and policy practitioners, and its answer takes on new importance today, as such scholars and practitioners work to understand what has led to the decline of democracy even in established democracies around the world.

To help clarify that relationship, this book focused on the case of South Korea, a country that transitioned to democracy after having developed economically under authoritarian rule and that is often regarded as a "dream case of a modernization theorist" (Przeworski and Limongi 1997, 162). As explored in earlier chapters, the case requires a more nuanced interpretation than the "dream case" framing allows because development contributed not only to democratization (as predicted by the theory) but also to authoritarian durability. That is, before the predicted shift toward democratization, rapid industrialization initially served as a key pillar of regime legitimacy. It did create favorable structural conditions for the politicization and organization of workers, students, and other social groups—which over time coalesced into a nationwide pro-democracy movement that ended the country's authoritarian rule—but the path from development to democracy was not a direct one.

176   Seeds of Mobilization

As explained in detail in this book, these contradictory processes played out in two types of policy: industrial and education policies. Through an aggressive industrial policy, South Korean autocrats brought about rapid economic growth but also created a large working class in urban centers throughout the country. The construction of industrial complexes brought workers together in close proximity, inadvertently facilitating labor mobilization over several decades. The ecological conditions surrounding the industrial complexes (as described in chapters 2 and 3) not only fostered networks and solidarity among workers but also allowed for ecology-dependent movement strategies and protest tactics that generated interfirm, intrafirm, and cross-class mobilization. In these ways, industrial complexes became spaces for resistance, where workers and social activists came together to mobilize against the very regimes that created them.

Education policy had similarly contradictory effects. The government expanded education to buttress and complement the country's industrial development and to increase regime support, and, initially, they succeeded. The growing emphasis on vocational education and training, including the skills necessary in an evolving export-oriented global economy, helped produce a well-educated labor force that contributed to rapid economic growth and that was loyal to the regime, which had provided them with access to upward mobility in this way. However, the government eventually failed to keep up the training it provided, which undermined that loyalty. At the same time, the expansion of higher education contributed to the development of a nationwide student movement. The explosion in the number of students on university campuses in all regions of the country generated the ecological conditions for them to organize on-campus and intercampus student organizations and coalitional protests across the country. These student organizations served as mobilizing structures by enabling the students and opposition politicians to channel electoral activities into pro-democracy protests during the 1987 June Democratic Uprising, which triggered the democratic transition.

As this concluding chapter will show, the findings regarding South Korea's democratic transition have implications for the country's post-transition period as well as for democratization in other countries. The chapter introduces Taiwan as a reference case to help illustrate how the causal mechanism linking economic development and democracy differs in different transition paths. The comparison highlights the importance of examining not just the level of development but also the geospatial pattern of development in explaining when and how countries democratize in the

Conclusion

wake of economic growth. Lastly, the chapter addresses the economic and political legacies from the authoritarian period that continue to shape how democracy works in South Korea.

How Do the Findings from South Korea Help Clarify Modernization Theory?

This in-depth case study of South Korea demonstrated *how* economic development led to democracy, thereby answering a long-standing question and clarifying modernization theory by elucidating the theory's causal pathway. The Korean case reveals that the core causal variable connecting autocrat-led economic development with mass-initiated democratic transition is the organization of social forces. As we saw in earlier chapters, economic growth (that is, an increase in the country's *level* of economic development) initially benefited the autocrats by increasing support for the regime; however, the *geospatial pattern* of development created dense concentrations of workers and students across the country, which facilitated the development of a nationwide pro-democracy movement that successfully brought down the regime. And because the organization of social forces was a cumulative process, its effect on authoritarian durability was only observed over time.

Identifying the organization of social forces as the core causal variable over the entire trajectory of democratic transition (i.e., rather than just at the moment when the country democratized) thus allows us not only to explain the positive correlation between economic development and democracy at the endpoint but also to account for the nonmonotonic and curvilinear relationship between the two. Additionally, this understanding of the causal pathway in the Korean case clarifies that, although economic development that does not generate a geospatial concentration of social actors can result in democratic transition, whether and to what extent civil society and social movements play a role in that process may differ. Because social forces are less likely to organize in such contexts, any democratic transition that occurs will do so as a result of other causal mechanisms associated with economic development or external factors (such as international pressure), and it is less likely to be triggered by mass protests. To illustrate this point, we briefly compare the case of Korea to the case of Taiwan, a fellow "East Asian Tiger" that democratized around the same time but followed a rather different trajectory.

Korea and Taiwan Compared: Different Paths to Democratic Transition

Like Korea, Taiwan followed what appeared to be a straight path from poor autocracy to rich democracy. Figure 7.1 shows that its period of authoritarian economic growth (increase in real GDP/per capita purchasing power parity along the x-axis) was followed by reduced authoritarian government (increase in Polity score on the y-axis; –10 to –6 corresponding to autocracies, –5 to 5 corresponding to anocracies, and 6 to 10 to democracies), more economic growth, transition to democracy (reaching Polity score of 7), more economic growth, and further improvement of democracy.

Despite these similarities in economic development and the timing of democratization, however, Korea and Taiwan differed significantly in how the transition began and unfolded. Whereas Korea's democratic transition in 1987 was triggered by mass protests and was quite sudden, Taiwan's democratic transition in the late 1980s was led by elites—the ruling Kuomintang (Nationalist Party; KMT)—who carefully orchestrated a gradual process of political liberalization. In 1986, opposition forces called the *Tangwai* (translated as "outside the party"; i.e., non-KMT) established the Democratic Progressive Party (Minzhu jinbu dang), and the KMT regime did not suppress it. The country's formal democratization then began with the 1987 lifting of martial law, which had been in place on the island since the KMT's 1949 retreat there after losing the civil war. From 1989 through the 1990s, Taiwan gradually transitioned from a single-party authoritarian rule to a democratic, multiparty system.[1] Pro-democracy protests did occur in the early 1990s,[2] but they were limited to dissident intellectuals and college students in Taipei, the capital city of Taiwan (T. Wright 1999).

To explain why the transition processes were different in these two cases, existing studies refer to the different authoritarian regime types (single-party/party-based versus personalist regime) and their distinct approaches to containing political opposition. Taiwan was ruled by a single-party regime led by the KMT, a quasi-Leninist party state (T.-J. Cheng 1989) that penetrated all sectors of society.[3] Political participation at the national level was halted; however, local elections continued to incorporate the native Taiwanese elites. In contrast, Korea's military dictatorships were personalist regimes that focused on "consolidating power in the strongman's hands and prolong[ing] his political career indefinitely by any means" (Liu 2015, 66). These regimes employed a strategy of exclusion to contain both labor and political opposition (J.-J. Choi 1997; Y. Lee 2011). Additionally, opportunities for electoral participation were limited and sporadic, as there were no local elections, and presidential contestation

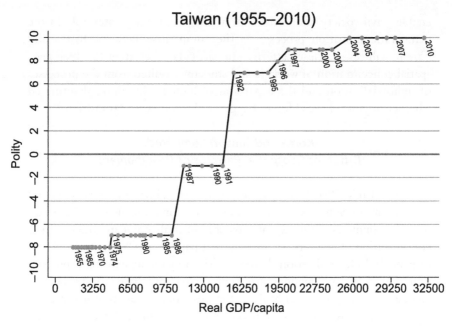

Fig 7.1. Development vs. democracy in Taiwan, 1955–2010. This figure comes from Goldstone and Kocronik-Mina (2013). The horizontal axis measures real GDP per capita using the Laspeyres Purchasing Power Parity measure from the Penn World Tables 6.1 (Heston, Summers, and Aten 2002). The vertical axis measures levels of democracy using the 21-point Polity IV scale (Marshall, Jaggers, and Gurr 2003).

dominated national elections if and when they were held. According to Yoonkyung Lee's (2011) comparative study of these two countries, Korea's authoritarian legacy of exclusion and repression fostered radicalism and militancy within the political opposition and the democratic labor movement. In Taiwan, however, the continued provision of electoral space at the local level led to the formation of the opposition Democratic Progressive Party as the "focal force for the democratization movement" (Y. Lee 2011, 63). Thus, when political space for electoral competition gradually opened up in Taiwan, elections became moments of significant democratization.

These institutional factors from the authoritarian era certainly help explain why social movements dominated the democratic transition in Korea but not in Taiwan; however, whether and how these factors connect to the democratizing effect of economic development has remained unclear. My main findings from Korea fill this gap: they suggest that differing *geospatial patterns of development* may explain why such development enables civil society and social movements to play a greater role in the democratic transition process. As the comparison between Korea and Taiwan will reveal, these patterns—in particular, the extent to which geospatial concentration of workers and students resulted from the processes of industrialization and the expansion of higher education—determined whether organized social forces triggered the democratic transition.

Korea and Taiwan Compared: Different Geospatial Patterns of Development

Hwa-Jen Liu's (2015) comparative study of labor and environmental movements in South Korea and Taiwan explores the first of these factors: the countries' differing patterns of industrialization and the resulting concentration of workers. In Taiwan, that pattern was "decentralized" (or dispersed). Industrialization there was driven by manufacturing exports of numerous small- and medium-sized enterprises, and these industrial establishments were spread evenly along the west coast, away from major cities and their suburbs. Taiwan's industrial employment in small factories in the rural areas "made it possible to transfer labor services from agricultural to non-agricultural activity without at the same time moving laborers from rural to urban areas" (Ho 1982, 984).[4] This employment pattern, as argued by Hill Gates (1979), produced a "part-time proletariat": that is, the industrial workers saw factory work as temporary and so did not consider themselves to be part of a working class (Gates 1979; Stites 1982).

In contrast, Korea's export-led growth was "centralized" (or geographically concentrated) and was dominated by large business conglomerates known as *chaebŏls*. As discussed in chapter 2, massive industrial complexes were constructed all over the country, but many were located in metropolitan areas.[5] This resulted in the spatial concentration of industrial workers and the gradual rise of densely populated working-class communities. According to Hwa-Jen Liu (2015), such large industrial establishments meant that labor disputes had the potential to involve more workers—and, indeed, the spatial distribution of industrial establishments in Korea and Taiwan roughly corresponded to the spatial distribution of their labor and environmental conflicts. These findings suggest that, despite the claims of earlier studies, workers' organizational capacity was impacted not only by the authoritarian regime's inclusion or exclusion of labor but also by such patterns in their industrialization.

The second of those factors—the promotion of higher education and the resulting concentration of students—also played important though different roles in each case. In Korea, higher education was expanded *prior* to the democratic transition, and students were the vanguard of the democracy movement. As shown in chapter 4, Chun Doo Hwan's 7.30 Education Reform, and the Graduation Quota Program in particular, dramatically increased student enrollment in institutions of higher education in the 1980s. Colleges and universities brought together social movement actors who had ready access to social, cultural, and human capital and who facilitated the emergence of large-scale antigovernment protests, including the 1987 June protests. In this way, the expansion of higher education destabilized the regime by popularizing the student movement in the 1980s, which in turn facilitated the mass-initiated democratic transition in 1987.

In contrast, Taiwan's expansion of education came as a *result* of the democratization process, and students there were not at the forefront of the democracy movement. According to Teresa Wright, "Although student protests have been influential, in general, when students have engaged in collective contention, they have done so in response to regime-initiated political liberalization" (T. Wright 2012, 101). Teresa Wright (1999, 2012) explains that not only did the KMT regime limit the growth of higher education institutions, but the party's extensive control over associations and expression at the campus level stifled the development of civil society on Taiwan's university campuses. And although higher education was expanded beginning in 1988 (after martial law was lifted in 1987), the massification of higher education was not accomplished until the 1990s (Tsai 1996; R. Wang 2003).[6] As William Lo (2014, 22–23) states, the rapid increase in the number of colleges during the democratization period resulted from the fact that the Taiwanese government was no longer able to only consider workforce development but also needed to consider the public voice when formulating its higher education policy. The differences between Taiwan's higher education expansion and that in Korea suggest that Taiwan's limited access to higher education—in addition to the imposed martial law and the KMT's extensive control over campuses—had stifling effects on student activism and its potential to develop into a pro-democracy force.

The comparison between these two countries sheds light on the mechanisms that drive different kinds of democratic transitions. It clarifies that differing geospatial patterns of industrialization (concentration versus dispersion) and the timing of higher education expansion (before or after democratization) contribute to the extent to which civil society groups have the organizational capacity to engage in collective action that could credibly threaten the incumbent regime. This has implications for

182 Seeds of Mobilization

modernization theory as a whole and our overall understanding of how democratization occurs.

Geospatial Patterns of Development and Democratization

My findings with regard to the Korean case of democratic transition, with references to the Taiwanese case in this chapter, support the main tenet of modernization theory: economic development does indeed lead to democracy. However, my study suggests that it is not merely the *level* of development but also the *geospatial pattern* of development that determines the *organizational capacity of the social forces*, which drives the democratic transition. As Rueschemeyer, Stephens, and Stephens (1992) have shown in their comparative case study of capitalist development and democracy, it is the transformation of class structure and changes to the balance of power between classes resulting from capitalist development (i.e., strengthening of the working and middle classes and weakening of the landed upper class) that make democracy more likely. My study on South Korea adds that the geospatial pattern of development can contribute to the changes in the balance of power between social classes and even between civil society and the authoritarian state, making democratization more likely.

In addition, the findings from the Korean case show that the *nationwideness* of this process by which economic development creates a geospatial concentration of social movement actors determines the likelihood of a *successful* democratic transition. In the 1970s (known as the "dark age for democracy" in Korea), there were pockets of students, workers, and other social activists (including Christians) who were engaged in antiregime protests (P. Y. Chang 2015a), but only a segment of these social actors in a few places in the country (mostly in Seoul) protested. The local-ness and relative isolation of these clusters made it easier for the regime to identify and repress them with force. In contrast, as shown in the empirical chapters of this book, the geospatial concentration of these actors as well as their increased organizational capacity (seen in the development of interfirm/campus events and the worker-student alliance) were observed more evenly across the country in the 1980s. It was in this context that large-scale nationwide protests erupted during the summer of 1987 and led to democratic reforms. Indeed, as noted by Dan Slater and Joseph Wong in their study on democratization in developmental Asia, it was the broad coalition of different classes found in Korea's antiauthoritarian movement that made it difficult for the regime to suppress it (Slater and Wong 2013, 725–26; 2022).

In summary, then, I used the South Korean case to clarify modernization theory by explaining how exactly economic development leads to democracy in a given country. I identified the organization of social forces as the core causal variable that links economic development and mass-initiated democratization. But it was the industrial and educational policies enacted by the autocrats "at the top" (specifically, the development of industrial complexes and the expansion of tertiary education) that contributed to the organization of social forces—and those forces facilitated the nationwide protests that ultimately brought about the democratic transition in 1987. In this way, my study revealed that it is not just the *level* of development but also the *geospatial pattern* of development that determines whether and to what extent social movements contribute to the democratization process. As the subsequent section will show, these findings also have implications for understanding the democracy that subsequently emerges.

The Legacy of the Authoritarian Era

Modernization theory has not only been used to explain democratic transition (i.e., the initial transition from an authoritarian or semiauthoritarian regime to a democracy) but also democratic consolidation (i.e., the process in which a new democracy matures and becomes unlikely to revert to authoritarianism). As stated by Seymour M. Lipset in *Some Social Requisites of Democracy: Economic Development and Political Legitimacy*, "The more well-to-do a nation, the greater the chances that it will sustain democracy" (Lipset 1959, 31). This claim was challenged in recent years when some G20 countries, including Brazil, India, Turkey, and the United States, experienced democratic weakening or temporarily turned into electoral autocracies (V-Dem Institute 2021).[7] And, according to Gi-Wook Shin, South Korea (also a member of the G20) was not an exception to this trend of democratic backsliding. He argued that, under the Moon Jae-in administration (2017–22), the country was showing signs of "democratic decay," symptoms of which included extreme political polarization, an erosion of the separation of powers, arbitrary changes to "the rules of game," the widespread use of double standards, and chauvinistic populism in foreign policy (G.-W. Shin 2020).

However, Gi-Wook Shin was not the first to declare a "crisis" in South Korean democracy. According to Sook-Jong Lee, democratization has created a society that is "more fragmented than ever before," with increased political polarization between progressive and conservative forces among both political elites and the masses (S.-J. Lee 2005). Additionally, scholars have long debated whether South Korean democracy is, in fact, consolidated because of its "imperial" presidency (as marked by strong presidential power vis-à-vis the legislature and the judiciary in the separation-of-powers system) and the weakness of its representative democracy (as marked by a weakly institutionalized party system and hyperactive civil society). These challenges or characteristics of Korean democracy could be better understood by considering the political and economic legacies from the authoritarian era.

Although Korea's authoritarian period is over, its legacies persist and contribute to political polarization in Korean society. Contradictions are inherent in a developmental dictatorship, and, as a result, the political legacy of Park Chung Hee remains divisive among citizens of Korea. Despite Park's record on human rights abuses, more than one-third (34.9%) of the respondents in the 2010 Korea Democracy Barometer survey identified his government as the best government since the 1960s (W. Kang 2016a, 52). The so-called Park Chung Hee nostalgia—defined by having "a large number of Koreans [who] reconstruct the social memory of the former authoritarian leader as a nationalist hero and are nostalgic of the time of his regime" (N. Lee 2009, 42)—is an authoritarian nostalgia that has been most pronounced among the conservative elements of society.

The tension between the progressive and conservative segments of Korean society was particularly evident following the 2012 election of Park Chung Hee's daughter, Park Geun-hye, as president. She had been the candidate of the conservative Saenuri Party, an "authoritarian successor party" (Loxton 2015) of Park Chung Hee's Democratic Republican Party, and she had explicitly aimed to rule as her father had: her campaign slogan, "Let's Try to Live Well, Again" (*dasi chal sara bose*), even directly referenced her father's own slogan from the New Village Movement (NVM) in the 1970s, "Let's Try to Live Well" (*chal sara bose*).[8] Then, as the end of Park Geun-hye's five-year term drew near in 2016–17, she became embroiled in a scandal involving corruption, bribery, and abuse of power, and millions of Korean citizens held candlelight vigils to call for her impeachment. In response, the older, conservative *taegukgi* (Korean national flag) protestors (mostly in their 60s and 70s) launched a series of *pro*-Park rallies, demanding the arrest of candlelight protestors and calling them *jwapa ppalgaengi* (pro-North Korean leftists).

This tension between the flag wavers and the candle holders revealed the chasm between older conservatives and younger progressives, who had differing memories and evaluations of Park Chung Hee's authoritarian rule. As shown in chapter 6, such differences can be explained by each generation's relative prioritization of economic development and democracy as shaped by their experiences of the authoritarian past (or lack thereof). In this context, we can understand why Park Geun-hye was such a polarizing force: to some, her 2012 presidential win represented the reemergence of conservative forces, and to others, it represented the authoritarian legacy.

This tension has contributed to a rapid rise of party polarization (i.e., increasing ideological distance between political parties) in the democratic period, when the 386 generation entered institutional politics en masse. As mentioned in chapter 6, this generation—members of which were born in the 1960s and attended university in the 1980s—is known to have spearheaded the pro-democracy movement, and they entered institutional politics as members of the National Assembly in the early 2000s. Nae-Young Lee's 2014 study on party polarization in Korean politics finds that the ideological distance between the two mainstream parties dramatically surged in 2004 and remained significant until 2012, in part as a result of this generation's involvement in politics:

> More than anything, newly formed parties and the existing both contributed to the significant increase of polarization in 2004. The two newly formed liberal parties entered the legislative arena during the 2004 election. Specifically, in November 2003, several young liberal legislators of the "386 generation" in the GNP [Grand National Party], MDP [Millennium Democratic Party], and KPPR [Korea People's Party for Reform] left their parties and created the Uri Party, which was to be held by the incumbent president Roh Moo Hyun. The newly formed liberal Uri Party dramatically shifted the ideological spectrum of the Korean party system by winning 38.3% of the votes during the 17th National Assembly elections in 2004. (N.-Y. Lee 2014, 14)

As Lee implies, Roh Moo-hyun certainly played a role in driving that change: he was a human rights lawyer and legislator who had defended student activists and had been critical of the Chun Doo Hwan regime in the 1980s. Approximately 70% of Roh's Blue House staff belonged to the 386 generation (Ryu 2013, 132), and roughly 33% of both the 16th (2000–2004) and 17th (2004–8) National Assemblies consisted of former pro-democracy movement activists from that generation (S. Kim, Chang, and Shin 2013, 245). This generation's entry into institutional politics thus contributed to the increase in political polarization in the 2000s.

It did so in later years as well: the 386 generation reemerged as the dominant force in institutional politics when President Moon Jae-in—a former pro-democracy activist who served as the chief of staff to former president Roh Moo-hyun—was elected in May 2017, following the 2016–17 Candlelight Revolution that led to the impeachment of Park Geun-hye. Moon's party, the Minjoo (Democratic) Party, had been the largest opposition party in the National Assembly since 2016 and 51.2% of its members belonged to the 386 generation (Joongang Ilbo 2019). When Moon was elected as the new president, he vowed to restore Korea's democracy by "eradicating deep-rooted evils perpetuated by those in authority" (J. Moon 2019). However, as pointed out by Gi-Wook Shin (2020, 102), the Moon government "demonized" the opposition, calling those with ties to the former conservative governments "great evil." Shin (2020, 103) argues that this all-out campaign by Moon's progressive government has further sharpened polarization, and such polarization among political elites threatens Korea's democracy because it undermines what Steven Levitsky and Daniel Ziblatt (2018) refer to as the "soft guardrails" of liberal democracy: mutual tolerance and forbearance, which prevent partisans from seeing their opponents as enemies and from "trying to win at all costs."

Like the political polarization it reflects, such undemocratic behavior by former pro-democracy activists undermines democracy and is itself an authoritarian legacy. As pointed out by Jang-Jip Choi (2000; 2012), Korea is an incomplete democracy because political parties still compete primarily along the former pro-democracy ("progressive") versus former authoritarian ("conservative") axes. He also argues that the new progressive elites are living in the past and reprising their glory days as bold young activists; instead of promoting democratic values such as tolerance and compromise, they are running the government as if they were still fighting against authoritarianism (J.-J. Choi 2019). Research in social psychology have shown us that in-group identity and solidarity are a function of out-group (us versus them) contention.[9] It should come as no surprise, then, that Korean activists, who fought against dictatorships for decades, have developed "a collective self-concept that bears all the hallmarks of an oppositional social identity" (P. Y. Chang 2015b).

To be clear, though, it is not just the behavior of the Moon administration and the democratic-activists-turned-politicians of the 386 generation that raised concerns about the future of democracy in Korea. As pointed out by Aurel Croissant (2019), there were "near misses" (Ginsburg and Huq 2018) of backsliding episodes from 2009 to 2015 under the conservative governments of Lee Myung-bak and Park Geun-hye. These included illegal government surveillance of the opposition and journalists and state power abuse scandals of both administrations.

Moreover, these worrisome developments are nested in a broader problem in Korean politics: ineffectual representative politics. The democratization literature emphasizes the importance of effective parties and party system institutionalization for democracy and democratic consolidation (e.g., Clapham 1993; Dix 1992; Mainwaring 1999; Mainwaring and Scully 1995), but Korea's party system is characterized by unstable (or fluid) party organizations and high electoral volatility.

The first of these—party instability—is evidenced by the high rate of change: a total of 53 parties competed in the six legislative elections that occurred between 1987 and 2007, and only three parties among them continued to exist as of 2010 (K. Park 2010, 531). In contrast, an average of only 1.4 new parties emerged in any given election in 22 OCED democracies surveyed in the period from 1960 to 2002 (Tavits 2006, 106). Korean parties are also mired by frequent splits, mergers, and name changes—for example, since 1955, the main conservative party has changed its name approximately 10 times, and the main progressive (center-left) party has changed its identity 20 times (Gale 2016). These frequent changes to personalist (i.e., not programmatic) political parties, in both name and substance, drive the second issue: high electoral volatility. Because voter identification with parties is weak, their electoral support is inconsistent (Wong 2015, 262–63). Moreover, because parties are not viewed as the institutional vehicles for consistent policy platforms, people's dissatisfaction with them has increased while Korea's civic groups have "come to acquire moral, social and political hegemony" (Seong 2000, 92). Correspondingly, social mobilizations have increased since the late 1990s (e.g., 1997 Workers' General Strike, 2000 Blacklisting Campaign, 2004 Anti-Impeachment Rallies, 2008 Anti-US Beef Candlelight Protests, and 2016–17 Candlelight Revolution). Because it has acquired these characteristics in the democratic era, Korean democracy has been described as a "contentious democracy" (S. Kim 2012) and a "democracy without parties" (Y. Lee 2009).

Again, these features of Korean democracy—a weakly institutionalized party system and strong civic activism—are the products of the country's authoritarian past and the democratic transition process. According to Yoonkyung Lee, because the authoritarian regime in Korea was personalist rather than party-based, neither the ruling party nor the opposition parties developed into stable organizations with clear programmatic positions. The weakness of political parties was reinforced in the post-transition period when parties relied on regional appeals (as opposed to clearly articulated policy agendas) as a swifter method of mobilizing votes (Y. Lee 2014, 434–35). As Joseph Wong (2015) adds, the fact that the democratic transition occurred during relatively "good economic times" for the incumbent authoritarian regime (Slater and Wong 2013) not only allowed the ruling party to stay in power but also permitted ideological fluidity and flexibility in the political system, which undermined the development of salient political cleavages in Korea's political party system. In these ways, authoritarian legacies help explain why parties have failed to expand their social bases and channel various interests in representative politics.

Party behavior is not the only driver of Korea's "contentious democracy," however. Scholars of political culture have argued that the political attitudes of a country's masses affect its democratization and democratic consolidation (e.g., Almond and Verba 1963; Booth and Seligson 2009; Cleary and Stokes 2006; Eckstein 1966; Eckstein et al. 1998; Gilley 2009; Inglehart 2003). These scholars claim that the political stability of a democracy depends on the congruence between the performance of democratic political institutions and the mass expectations for those institutions. In explaining why Korean citizens set aside representative government and take part in social movements, Cho, Kim, and Kim (2019) focus on the Korean general public and their orientations toward democracy. Based on a nationwide survey conducted in 2015, the authors find that despite the institutional advancement of representative democracy in the country, "most Koreans disagree with the current form of representative democracy but aspire to participatory democracy, demanding more mass participation in politics" (Cho, Kim, and Kim 2019, 287). The authors explain that this incongruence between public attitudes toward democracy and the existing form of democracy is what's driving Koreans to engage in social movements in lieu of utilizing the political system's representative institutions by voting or contacting their representatives.

Moreover, the same study also reveals that "populist non-democrats" (those who do not fully endorse democracy and view authoritarian alternatives as favorable) in Korea are older, conservative, and Saenuri (now People's Power) Party supporters (Cho, Kim, and Kim 2019, 291). It should then come as no surprise that in 2017 the elderly radical conservatives who organized the aforementioned *taegukgi* protests (in support of Park Geun-hye) not only demanded that the Candlelight protestors (who were calling for Park's impeachment) be arrested but also that the army rise up, the National Assembly be dissolved, and martial law be imposed to restore order in Korean society (Sommerfeldt 2017). As discussed earlier in this chapter, political and economic legacies, including authoritarian nostalgia, persist and contribute to political polarization that was evident in Park Geun-hye's election and impeachment. And, as demonstrated in chapter 6, it is people's formative experiences of economic growth and authoritarianism (or lack thereof) that generated distinct political attitudes and behaviors, including civic participation patterns, across different generations. Thus, the authoritarian legacy—originating from people's varying experiences of authoritarianism—also influences mass political culture and ultimately the workings of (and challenges to) democracy in the country.

As a result of these challenges, Korean democracy is considered to be incomplete (e.g., J.-J. Choi 2012; D. C. Shin 2018), in stagnation (J. Kim 2018), limited (Yeo 2020), or backsliding (e.g., Haggard and You 2015; Kang and Kang 2014; G.-W. Shin 2020). Although assessing the current state of democracy in South Korea is beyond the scope of this book, we may nevertheless want to reconsider the idea that it is simply a degenerative form of democracy; we may want to consider it instead to be a democracy with its own unique characteristics. After all, theories of democratization—including modernization theory—have been developed based on Euro-American philosophical and historical experiences. As Mary Alice Haddad (2012) illustrates with Japan's democracy, the types of democracies that formed in non-Western countries represent an amalgamation of liberal democratic *and* indigenous political traditions, including cultural values and practices that are sometimes considered "illiberal" or "undemocratic" when compared to idealized versions of Western European and American values and institutions. Likewise, Korea's democracy is not only shaped by the political and social legacies of Confucianism (e.g., Sungmoon Kim 2014, 2018; D. C. Shin 2012, 2018) but also authoritarian legacies (Y. Lee 2009, 2014; Hong, Park, and Yang 2022). When democracy is built on indigenous political traditions and preexisting conditions (such as the authoritarian past), it is bound to take different forms and become "differently democratic." Hence, when evaluating the current state of democracy in countries like South Korea, it is important that we not only clearly identify its undemocratic aspects but also investigate and identify the ways in which democracy still works, even if it does so in ways that reflect the country's unique experiences that have been shaped in part by its authoritarian past.

As demonstrated in this book, authoritarian legacies have lasting effects on people's political attitudes and behavior in the democratic period. Just as autocrat-led economic development initially acted as a double-edged sword (by stabilizing dictatorship first but bringing it down later), it con-

190   Seeds of Mobilization

tinues to do so even post-democratization by leaving behind authoritarian baggage that creates challenges to the newly emerging democracy. The vestiges of dictators' economic development efforts thus remain in the democratic period, even after the dictators and dictatorships are supposedly gone. These observations have important implications for democracies worldwide, especially those that have followed (or are following) trajectories similar to South Korea's. Just as in Korea, where understanding the generational differences caused by the authoritarian past can help illuminate ways of reconciling the country's political divide, understanding each country's legacy is key to supporting well-functioning democracies worldwide.

Appendix

Datasets and Data Sources

Archival Sources from the Korea Democracy Foundation

The Korea Democracy Foundation (KDF; Minjuhwa Undong Kinyŏm Saophoe) serves as a centralized location for scholarly and cultural activities on South Korea's democracy and the democratization movement. Its publications and archival materials have greatly informed my research and understanding of the South Korean democracy movement, especially regarding the events that occurred outside of Seoul. The KDF was established in 2002 by the South Korean government in accordance with the Korea Democracy Foundation Act (legislated on June 28, 2001), "with the mission of inheritance of the democratization movement legacy and further development of the Korean democracy through various memorialization projects" (http://en.kdemo.or.kr/about/about-kdf). The KDF Open Archives was created based on article 6, paragraph 2 of the Korean Democracy Foundation Act: the KDF will manage the collection, preservation, computerization, management, exhibition, publicity, investigation, and research of historical records of the South Korean democracy movement (http://archives.kdemo.or.kr/intro/archive). As part of this effort to collect, preserve, and publicize information on South Korea's democracy movement, the KDF created three sourcebooks: the *KDF Dictionary of Events Related to the Democracy Movement* (KDF Events Dictionary; *Minjuhwa undong kwallyŏn sakŏn sajŏn*), the *KDF Dictionary of Organizations Related to the Democracy Movement* (KDF Organization Dictionary; *Minjuhwa*

191

192   *Appendix*

undong kwallyŏn tanch'e sajŏn), the *KDF Reports on the History of South Korea's Regional Democracy Movement* (KDF Regional History Report; *Chibang minjuhwa undongsa*).

The *KDF Events Dictionary* provides narrative accounts of events related to the democracy movement from 1954 to 1992. It includes detailed information on democracy-related protest events, including individuals and organizations involved in the event and the state's response to the event. The *KDF Organization Dictionary* is a directory of social movement organizations involved in the democracy movement from 1954 to 1992. It includes various information, including the date founded, formation process, relationships with other organizations, main activities, organizational structure, principal individuals involved, and major statements produced. The *KDF Regional History Report* provides narrative accounts of events related to the democracy movement from the same period as the *KDF Events Dictionary* but focuses on the events in the provincial areas (*chibang*; areas outside the capital city, Seoul). It covers all regions of South Korea, including Ch'ungbuk, Taejŏn and Ch'ungnam, Wŏnju and Ch'unch'ŏn (in Kangwon Province), T'aebaek and Ch'ŏngsŏn (in Kangwon Province), Inch'ŏn, Kyŏnggi, Cheju, Chŏnbuk, Kwangju and Chŏnnam, Taegu and Kyŏngbuk, and Pusan and Kyŏngnam.

In creating these sourcebooks, the KDF drew from many sources, including newspapers (local, national, and school), organizations' documents, pamphlets, publications, government records and documents, personal memoirs, and other primary and secondary sources. However, as pointed out by the Stanford Korea Democracy Project researchers (Chang 2015a; Shin et al. 2011), the KDF sourcebooks have possible limitations. First, there is a potential problem of omission. Events that were not found in any source were not included because there was no way for the foundation to collect information on them and report them in their sourcebooks. The second is the problem of data reliability. Since the KDF used any or all sources of information available, the quality and amount of information on each protest event vary by sourcebook. Nevertheless, the KDF sourcebooks represent the most exhaustive effort to provide a comprehensive qualitative account of the democracy movement.

In 2006, based on the *KDF Events Dictionary* and the *KDF Organization Dictionary*, the KDF published the *Timeline of the Korean Democracy Movement* (*Han'guk minjuhwa undong yŏnp'yo*). From 2011 to 2019, based on the *KDF Regional History Report*, the KDF has also published six volumes on the regional history of the Korean democracy movement in Ch'ungbuk (in 2011), Chŏnbuk (2012), Cheju (2013), Taejŏn and Ch'ungnam (2016), Kyŏnggi (2017), and Inch'ŏn (2019).

Appendix 193

The 1987 Great Workers' Struggle

Data for the dataset on the "Great Workers' Struggle" (July to August 1987; introduced in chapter 2) come from the *KDF Events Dictionary*, the *KDF Regional History Report*, and the *Timeline of the Korean Democracy Movement* (Minjuhwa Undong Kinyŏm Saophoe 2006). I also consulted the following primary and archival sources (in Korean) to either identify protest events that are not reported in the KDF sourcebooks or to obtain more detailed information on the event:

- Han'guk Kidokkyo Sahoe Munje Yŏn'guwŏn [Christian Institute for the Study of Justice and Development]. 1987. *7–8-wŏl nodongja taejung t'ujaeng* [The July–August Mass Struggle of the Workers]. Seoul: Minjungsa.
- Chŏn'guk Nodong Chohap Hyŏbŭihoe Paeksŏ Palgan Wiwŏnhoe [National Trade Union Council White Paper Publication Committee] and Nodong Undong Yŏksa Charyosil [Labor Movement History Archives]. 2003. *Chŏn'guk nodong chohap hyŏbŭihoe paeksŏ* [National Trade Union Council White Paper] (vol. 1). Seoul: Ch'aek Tongmu Nonjang.
- KDF Open Archives No. 00368511: Chŏn'guk Nodong Undong Tanch'e Hyŏbhŭihoe nodongja t'ujaeng ilchi (87-yŏn 7-wŏl 1-il~9-wŏl 7-il) [National Trade Union Council Workers Struggle Journal (July 1–September 7, 1987)].
- KDF Open Archives No. 00055565: Minju Hŏnpŏp Chaengch'wi Kungmin Undong Pusan Ponbu Nodong Munje T'ŭkpyŏl Taech'aek Wiwŏnhoe. Chanŏb ŏpnŭn sesang e salgosipta—Pusan chiyŏk 7,8-wŏl nodongja t'ujaeng charyojip [National Movement for Democratic Constitution Pusan Headquarters Special Countermeasures Committee on Labor Issues—I want to live in a world without overtime—Pusan area, July and August Workers Struggle data collection].
- KDF Open Archives No. 00063998: Nodong tae t'ujaeng ch'wijae ilchi Masan, Ch'angwŏn Kŏje chiyŏk [Journal of the Great Labor Struggle in Masan, Ch'angwŏn Kŏje area]
- 87 t'ujaeng chiyŏkpyŏl [87 Struggle by Region], Han'guk Nodong Net'ŭwŏk'ŭ Hyŏbŭihoe [Korea Labor Network Council].[1]

Using a coding scheme based on the template of the Stanford Korea Democracy Project Events Dataset coding manual (Chang 2015a; Shin et al. 2011), I identified and coded 1,285 events.[2] For each event, the follow-

194 *Appendix*

ing information was collected (if available): date, location, group(s) participating in the event, number of participants, issue(s) raised by the protesting group(s), tactic(s) used by the protesting group(s), individual(s) or group(s) repressing the event, type of repression used by repressive force(s), and links between events already coded.

According to the Christian Institute for the Study of Justice and Development publication on the Great Workers' Struggle, there were 1,796 events in the manufacturing sector, 1,247 among transportation workers (buses and taxis), and 127 in mining (Han'guk Kidokkyo Sahoe Munje Yŏn'guwŏn 1987b, 44). I do not include events in the transportation industry as my outcome of interest is mobilization among factory workers. I also code protest events that occurred over an extended time as a single event and record that event's duration. Therefore, my dataset's exact number of events may differ from the recorded number in the Christian Institute for the Study of Justice and Development publication. I also used *Hoesa yŏn'gam* (Company Yearbook) published by the Maeil Kyŏngje Sinmunsa (Maeil Business Newspaper) in 1987 to obtain additional information on the exact location of each factory when such information was unavailable in the above-listed sources.

The 1987 June Democratic Uprising

The data for the dataset on the "June Democratic Uprising" (April to June 1987; introduced in chapter 5) come from the *KDF Regional History Report* and the *6-wŏl minjuhwa tae tujaeng* (The Great June Uprising for Democratization) published by the Christian Institute for the Study of Justice and Development (Han'guk Kidokkyo Sahoe Munje Yŏn'guwon). Using the same coding scheme used to create the Great Workers' Struggle dataset, I identified and coded 1,194 protest events. The exact number of protests during the June Democratic Uprising is unknown. According to the South Korean government's official statistics, there were 3,362 demonstrations of all sorts (not limited to the protests that were part of the June Uprising) in June 1987 (C. Chung 2011, 171–72).

Student Protests in the 1980s

The data on Korean student protests in the 1980s (introduced in chapter 4) comes from the *KDF Dictionary of Events Related to the Democracy*

Movement and the *Timeline of the Korean Democracy Movement* (Minjuhwa Undong Kinyŏm Saophoe 2006) and news articles from *Chosun Ilbo, Dong-A Ilbo, Kyunghyang Sinmun,* and *Maeil Kyŏngje* (archived in the Naver News Library, https://newslibrary.naver.com). I used two keywords to locate news articles on student protests: student protest (*haksaeng siwi*) and student demonstration (*haksaeng demo*). For each event, the following information was collected (if available): date, name of the college or university students belonged to, number of participants, location of protest (if it was off-campus or at another school), issues being raised, and tactics being used. Using these sources, I identified 3,032 student protest events between 1980 and 1987 and obtained detailed information on 1,834 events.

Notes

CHAPTER 1

1. To be sure, as pointed out by Gerardo L. Munck (2018, 40), the majority of quantitative studies exploring the income–democracy link, especially since the publication of Adam Przeworski and Fernando Limongi's 1997 article in *World Politics*, found no (causal) or negative relationship between economic development and democracy.

2. According to Samuel Huntington (1991), democratic consolidation occurs when (1) the winners of the founding election are defeated and peacefully hand over power to the former opposition in a subsequent election, and (2) the new winners later peacefully turn over power to the winners of a later election. In the case of South Korea, the founding election was held on December 16, 1987. The first peaceful transfer of power to the former opposition occurred in 1997, when the opposition (progressive) candidate Kim Dae Jung won the presidency. The second was in 2007, when the conservative presidential candidate Lee Myung-bak won the election. Although the first power transfer after democratization occurred from Roh Tae Woo to Kim Young Sam in 1993 (following the December 1992 election), it is debatable as to whether there was a peaceful transfer of power to the former opposition given that Kim won the election by merging his Reunification Democratic Party with the ruling Democratic Justice Party (led by Roh Tae Woo) and forming the Democratic Liberal Party.

3. A large body of literature in comparative politics, including modernization theory, claims that the middle class is a critical force for democratic transition and consolidation (Almond and Powell 1966; Almond and Verba 1963; Lipset 1959; Moore 1966; Pye 1990). In the South Korean case, it is commonly understood that the middle class played an important role in democratization because of the large number of white-collar workers joining street demonstrations during the June Democratic Uprising. Although they did participate, members of the Korean

198 *Notes to Pages 9–21*

middle class were not active in the democracy movement before or after the June Democratic Uprising. Students and workers played a far more important and integral role—they were in fact the most dominant groups in the democracy movement throughout the authoritarian period (Shin et al. 2011, 24).

4. They also establish this dependency among some segments of the middle class, who are traditionally understood to be the driving force for democracy (Rosenfeld 2020).

5. Mass media is another aspect of modernization, but it is not the focus of this book.

6. There is extensive evidence in sociology that social ties are important for recruiting movement participants (e.g., Gould 1991; Hedström 1994; McAdam and Paulsen 1993; Opp and Gern 1993; Snow, Zurcher, and Ekland-Olson 1980).

7. In *Polyarchy*, Robert Dahl (1971) specifically lists having selected officials, free elections, inclusive suffrage, the right to run for office, freedom of expression, alternative information, and associational autonomy as the institutional guarantees of a polyarchy. He eventually pared down the list to include the following six criteria: elected officials; free, fair, and frequent elections; freedom of expression; alternative sources of information; associational autonomy; and inclusive citizenship (Dahl 2005, 188).

8. Various labels have been created by political scientists to describe these hybrid regimes, including "semi-democracy," "electoral democracy," "illiberal democracy," "electoral authoritarianism," and "competitive authoritarianism."

9. It rose from 6.4% in 1986 to 17.2% in 1987, 13.5% in 1988, and 17.5% in 1989 (Chai 1996, 273).

10. Detailed information on the Korea Democracy Foundation and its archive is found in the appendix.

11. Due to the foundation's efforts to collect information and document events on democracy movements in areas outside of the capital, this particular set of sourcebooks does not include a separate volume on Seoul. The *KDF Dictionary of Events Related to the Democracy Movement* provides data on events that happened in Seoul.

12. The Naver News Library provides a digital archive service for articles published between 1920 and 1999 from major Korean newspapers, including *Dong-A Ilbo, Hankyoreh Sinmun, Kyŏnghyang Sinmun, Maeil Kyŏngje Sinmun, and Chosŏn Ilbo*.

13. The literature focuses heavily on the events that were happening in Seoul in 1987, such as the announcement made by the Catholic Priests' Association for Justice regarding the torture death of a Seoul National University student named Pak Chongch'ol; the death of a Yonsei University student Yi Hanyŏl, who was injured by a tear gas grenade; and the student-led hunger strike at the Myŏngdong Cathedral. These were significant events, but they were not the only ones.

14. In the *danwei* system, necessities are distributed through one's work unit in a state-owned enterprise. In the *hukou* system of household registration, access to public services is contingent upon fixed and state-mandated residence in a particular district (Albertus, Fenner, and Slater 2018, 63).

Notes to Pages 26–35 199

CHAPTER 2

1. See W. Kang (2016a, 2016b) and S. Moon (2009) on Park Chung Hee nostalgia or syndrome in contemporary South Korea.

2. The import-substitution industrialization strategy was unsuccessful because the country had few natural resources, a small domestic market, low capital endowment, and unsophisticated technology (H. B. Im 1986, 242–43).

3. Another reason for Park's focus on the heavy chemical industry was his determination that the country would manufacture its own weapons, especially given the partial withdrawal of U.S. troops following President Richard Nixon's announcement of the 1969 Guam Doctrine.

4. Scholars have debated the impacts of Japanese colonialism on South Korea's economic growth, including the development and role of the bureaucracy; for example, see Kohli (1994; 1997) and Haggard, Kang, and Moon (1997). Additionally, while earlier developmental state literature (e.g., B.-K. Kim 1987; Evans 1995; T. Cheng, Haggard, and Kang 1998) have accredited Park for having created a meritocracy in Korea's bureaucracy, Jong-Sung You (2015) finds that the meritocratic bureaucracy was gradually developed over time since the latter part of the Rhee regime (1953 to 1960).

5. Until 1962, when the First FYED Plan began, there were no planned industrial sites or regulations on land use. Industrial sites were developed without government input and by individual corporations—mainly those in light industries located in large metropolises such as Seoul, Pusan, Taegu, and the surrounding areas.

6. The Free Export Zone 2 in Piin-Kunsan zone and the Nakdong River estuary steel industry base were not developed as originally planned. While Onsan was also chosen as a site for a free export zone, it was not developed due to a change in business category.

7. The figure excludes agricultural industrial complexes.

8. *Chaebŏls* are family-controlled conglomerates such as Samsung, Hyundai, LG, and SK Group. In Korean, *chae* (財) means wealth and *bŏl* (閥) means clan or faction. E. Kim and G.-S. Park (2011) provide three characteristics of the *chaebŏl*: (1) All firms in the group are controlled by a central company, which is typically operated by an owner-manager family; (2) most of the member firms are of a significant size and coordinated under centralized management at the top; and (3) they are usually involved in multiple sectors, with managers transferred from one sector to another to ensure unity of strategy and cross-fertilization of experience.

9. According to Carter Eckert (1991), the origins of Korean capitalism and the modern *chaebŏl* can be traced back to the Japanese colonial period, when the Japanese colonial government, for both political and economic reasons, promoted the rise of a Korean capitalist class.

10. According to the United Sates Department of Labor Bureau of Labor Statistics, in 1975, the income of Korean workers in manufacturing was only 5% of what it was for American manufacturing workers. Even when compared to other East Asian countries that were pursuing export-led industrialization, until the late 1980s the hourly rate of pay in South Korean manufacturing was low—it was 75%

of the rate in Taiwan and 80% of the rate in Hong Kong (Minns 2006, 151). Similarly, labor statistics compiled by the International Labour Office (https://www.bls.gov/fls/ichcc_pwmfg.htm) reveal that South Korea had the longest workweek in the world throughout the 1980s. In 1980, for example, the average workweek for Korean manufacturing workers was 53.1 hours, compared with 39.7 hours for those in the U.S., 38.8 hours for those in Japan, and 51 hours for those in Taiwan (H. Kim 1988, 316, cited in Koo 2001, 49).

11. See Greene (2007) and Magaloni (2006) on Mexico and Blaydes (2011) and Lust-Okar (2006) on the Middle East and North Africa.

12. From 1963 to 1985, the voter turnout rate in legislative (National Assembly) elections fluctuated between 71.4% and 84.6%. These elections were competitive in the sense that the ruling parties never won an outright majority. These elections were politically relevant and significant, as they reflected popular support for the ruling and opposition parties (J. B. Lee 2001, 146). The elections in 1971, 1978, and 1985, in particular, became a "window of opportunity for the opposition to challenge the authoritarian regime" (Croissant 2002, 241).

13. In a separate study, my coauthors and I examine the political impact of another national project: subway construction. We use a difference-in-difference analysis of neighborhood-level panel data on a subway system from 1971 to 1987 in South Korea and find that incumbent vote share increased in neighborhoods surrounding newly constructed subway stations. We show that subway construction was effective at boosting regime support in neighborhoods where people were more likely to read the government propaganda regarding that construction in newspapers. Similar to the findings of Hong and Park (2016) on the industrial complexes, we also find that the ruling party vote share is positive for both authoritarian tenures under Park Chung Hee and Chun Doo Hwan, but the size of the effect is larger for Park's ruling party. See Cho, Lee, and Song (2019).

14. According to Atul Kohli (1994), the repression and exclusion of the lower classes (i.e., peasants and workers) was integral to the colonial political economy led by a state-dominated, state-private sector alliance. The colonial state collaborated with Japanese and Korean capitalists to control labor and workers were prohibited from forming any organizations of their own, including labor unions.

15. An exception to this general portrayal of weak labor movement in the 1960s is the unionization efforts by the Korea Shipbuilding and Engineering Corporation workers in Pusan under the Park Chung Hee regime. See H. B. Nam (2009).

16. Nevertheless, the 1970s brought two iconic labor-related events that would become significant in the development of Korea's democracy movement. First was an incident that generated student interest in labor issues: Chŏn T'aeil's self-immolation protest on November 30, 1979. A 22-year-old male garment worker at Py'ŏnghwa (Peace) Market, Chŏn burned himself to death during a workers' demonstration in which he shouted slogans such as "We are not machines" and "Guarantee the three basic labor rights." The second significant event was the 1979 Y.H. Worker Protest (or Y.H. Incident), which externalized and politicized the labor struggle and contributed to the "fusion of labor struggles and pro-democracy political struggles" (Koo 2001, 91).

17. These firms include Dongil Textiles, Wonpoong Textiles, Bando Trading Company, Pangrim Textiles, Y.H. Trading Company, Control Data, Crown Electronics, Signetics, and Tongkwang Textiles.

Notes to Pages 40–50

18. This transformation began in the 1970s with Dongil Textile and Y.H. Company labor protests.

19. The Korea Trade Union Congress was dissolved in 1995 when the Korean Confederation of Trade Unions was established.

20. There are three administrative divisions in South Korea: provincial-level (*do, tŭkpyŏl chach'i-do, kwangyŏk-si, tŭkpyŏl-si*), municipal-level (*si, gun, gu*), and submunicipal-level (*eup, myeon, dong*) divisions. This study uses municipal-level divisions (i.e., counties) as the unit of analysis.

21. The authors use four different measurements to capture the influence of an industrial complex: *IC_Dummy* (whether a county has an industrial complex within 50 km), *IC_Appointment* (the space of the nearest appointed industrial cluster divided by the distance between the cluster and a county at the time of the public announcement), *IC_Beginning* (the influence of an industrial complex for which construction has begun), and *IC_Completion* (the influence of completed complexes).

22. Regional dummies (*Honam Region* and *Yŏngnam Region*) are included to control for regionalism that affected the electoral results in the 1987 presidential election (Honam being more supportive of the opposition, especially Kim Dae Jung). *Honam Region* includes Chŏnbuk and Chŏnnam Provinces and the *Yŏngnam Region* includes Kyŏngbuk and Kyŏngnam Provinces. *Urbanization* and *(Log) College Student Population* are included as controls, as urban areas were known to be more supportive of the opposition during the authoritarian period and college students were the vanguard of South Korea's democracy movement. Data for the New Korea Democratic Party vote share comes from the Korea National Election Commission (https://www.nec.go.kr/), and data for urbanization and college student population comes from the *1985 Population and Housing Census Report* (Kyŏngje Kihoegwŏn 1987a).

23. Although the Ministry of Commerce's *Kongŏp tanji hyŏnhwang* (*An Overview of Industrial Complexes*) contains comprehensive information on all of the industrial complexes in Korea, the data and information it includes on factories *inside* each industrial complex are inconsistent. The data for the number of manufacturing firms in 1987 is available for all counties and is found in the *1987 Mining and Manufacturing Census Report* (Kyŏngje Kihoegwŏn 1987b).

24. The data for the 1985 post-treatment covariates come from the *1985 Population and Housing Census Report* (Kyŏngje Kihoegwŏn 1987a).

25. Distance to nearest port was calculated using GIS ArcMap using the near tool. Data on the location of ports comes from *Han'guk ŭi hangman* (*Ports in Korea*) (Kŏnsŏlbu 1969). Data on population in manufacturing and population in 1960 come from the *1960 Population and Housing Census of Korea* (Kyŏngje Kihoegwŏn 1963).

26. The exact procedure for implementing the sequential g-estimation is as follows: first, I estimate the effect of the mediator on labor protests in 1987 controlling for all of my pretreatment and post-treatment covariates. I then transform the dependent variable by subtracting this effect. Lastly, I estimate the effect of industrial complexes on the transformed variable, which is the controlled direct effect of industrial complexes.

27. For the *Presence of IC*, using the estimates from columns (1) and (2) in table 2.4, (ATE - ACDE)/ATE = (11.924 - 7.636)/11.924 = 0.360.

202 *Notes to Pages 51–69*

28. The log population variable is set to the mean value, whereas the June Democratic Uprising variable is set to zero as it is a dummy variable. The results remain the same when setting the log population to the mean versus zero.

29. See online appendix tables A2.3 and A2.4 for full results.

30. Using the estimates from columns (1) and (2) in table A2.3, (ATE - ACDE)/ATE = (11.924 - 9.600)/11.924 = 0.195. And using the estimates from columns (1) and (2) in table A2.4, (ATE - ACDE)/ATE = (11.924 – 11.122)/11.924 = 0.067.

CHAPTER 3

1. See Zhang and Zhao (2018) for an overview of the literature on the social and spatial ecological contexts of social movements.

2. This number excludes the number of agricultural complexes.

3. Although some of those in the inland areas, like the Korean Export Industrial Complex (1,977 thousand m^2 in size), had 263 firms and 73,200 workers, the ones that were designated for shipbuilding in the southeastern coastal region of the country were occupied by one or two *chaebŏl* companies.

4. https://justice.gov

5. The formula for the Herfindahl-Hirschman Index is $HHI = s_1^2 + s_2^2 + s_3^2 + \ldots s_n^2$ where s_n = the market share percentage of firm n expressed as a whole number, not a decimal. The average value I obtain by excluding the miscellaneous category that might lump various industries into one category is 4,988. The average HHI value that includes the miscellaneous category is 4,570. Industrial complex data comes from *An Overview of Industrial Complexes* published by the Chungso Kiŏp Hyŏptong Chohap Chunganghoe (Korea Federation of Small and Medium Business) in 1989.

6. It is worth noting that, to some degree, the company provided these new facilities in response to the demands made by the independent union at Dongil Textiles.

7. Seung-kyung Kim (1997, 27) also points out that women workers preferred to live in the dormitory to protect their reputations for their prospective husbands and in-laws.

8. The Mining and Manufacturing Census Report produced annually by the Economic Planning Board in 1987 categorizes firm sizes by 5–19 workers, 20–99 workers, 100–499 workers, and 500 or more workers. Firms with 100 or more employees are considered large-scale firms.

9. A *p'yŏng* is a unit of the size of rooms or buildings in Korea. One *p'yŏng* equals approximately 3 square meters or 35 square feet.

10. This event started when roughly two hundred female workers of the Y.H. Trading Company held a sit in strike at the Seoul headquarters of the opposition party, the New Democratic Party, to protest the mismanagement and closing of their factory. Until that point, the NDP had been more or less aloof from the labor movement (Koo 2001, 91), but because they allowed the protest to occur at their headquarters, NDP leader Kim Young Sam was charged with inciting violence and social instability and was ousted from the National Assembly. Kim's ouster triggered protests in his congressional district of Pusan, which then spread to the nearby industrial city of Masan. These protests became known as the Pu-Ma

Notes to Pages 69–71

Uprising, which contributed to escalating disunity among key state actors. Specifically, the head of the Korean Central Intelligence Agency (Kim Chaegyu) and the head of the Presidential Security Service (Cha Chich'ŏl) disagreed about how the protests in Pusan and Masan should be managed, and their rivalry led to Kim Chaegyu's assassination of Park Chung Hee. The Y.H. Worker Protest thus played a role in the demise of Park's nearly two decades of authoritarian rule.

11. This claim that the UIM was an antiproductive organization that would lead companies to bankruptcy came in part from the fact that the Korean acronym for the UIM (*tosan*; 都産) has the same pronunciation as the Korean word (도산) for bankruptcy (*tosan*; 倒産) (Hong 2001).

12. Reverend Chŏng Chindong of the Ch'ŏngju UIM was sentenced to one year in jail with a stay of execution for two years for his involvement with the labor disputes at Sinhŭng Jebun (Sinhŭng Mill Company) in 1978. Reverend In Myŏngjin of the YDP-UIM was jailed four times in total for his involvement in the labor movement, including the Y.H. Incident. Reverend Cho Wha-Soon of the Inchŏn UIM was also jailed in 1972 on charges that she was a hidden communist. In 1974–75, three foreign clergymen—Reverend George Ogle (American), Father James Sinnott (American), and Reverend Stephen V. Lavender (Australian)—were deported for actively participating in "international political affairs" and "causing disorder" (Y.-S. Chang 1998, 459). These missionaries spoke out against the imprisonment and execution of eight pro-democracy student activists who were accused of having communist ties—known as the Inhyŏktang (People's Revolutionary Party) Incident—and publicized labor disputes in foreign news media.

13. Although workers at Dongil Textiles, Bando Trading Company, and Wonpoong Textiles were able to form independent unions with the help from the UIM and the JOC, workers at Y.H. Company and Ch'ŏnggye Garments were able to unionize with almost no support from the Christian organizations (W. Kim 2004, 129; 2006, 490).

14. According to the May 18 Memorial Foundation (https://518.org), 154 were killed, 74 were missing, and 4,141 were wounded (including those who died from their wounds) and placed under arrest by the martial law force.

15. Translated as the masses or the common people, *minjung* refers to those who have been "oppressed" but are "capable of rising up" against oppression (N. Lee 2007, 5). The *minjung* sentiment, especially among college students in the 1980s, became the driving force of the Korean democracy movement and was manifest not only in political rhetoric but also in music, art, literature, philosophy, and theology (P. Y. Chang 2015b).

16. Until the early 1980s, most Koreans viewed the United States positively, given U.S. support for South Korea during the Korean War. This positive image changed with the alleged involvement of the U.S. in the 1980 Kwangju Massacre. Koreans expected that the U.S. would and should actively intervene to stop the armed confrontation between Chun Doo Hwan's military government and Kwangju citizens. In the aftermath of the massacre, many Koreans, especially university students, came to believe that the U.S. was just using their country for its own strategic purposes and that all the talk about democracy and human rights was empty rhetoric.

17. See Namhee Lee, "Representing the Worker: The Worker-Intellectual

204 *Notes to Pages 72–79*

Alliance of the 1980s in South Korea" and *The Making of Minjung: Democracy and the Politics of Representation in South Korea* for the historical context of the worker-student alliance and the practice of disguised employment.

18. Although both the JOC and UIM played a significant role in facilitating the democratic union movement in the 1970s, there were some differences between the two Christian organizations. The UIM was a loose network of church-based labor organizers from five Protestant denominations. The denominations only played a supporting role to the city branches of the UIM, and staff members of each branch managed the organization. The UIM's primary activity was running small groups, each of which had a staff member (selected from among the workers) to run the group. In contrast, the JOC had a more centralized organizational structure with a clear hierarchy. There were different levels within each "section" (cell unit), and each section had an advising priest. Perhaps stemming from the differences in their organizational structures, the UIM perceived the JOC as being less active and slow in aiding the workers, whereas the JOC was critical of the UIM for being too aggressive and hindering the workers' autonomy in the movement. See Hong (2005) and W. Kim (2006, 490–95).

19. The history of night schools (*yahak*) in Korea dates to the end of the Chŏson period (1392–1897), when night schools were set up to complement the existing village schools (*sŏdang*). The first *yahak* movement started in 1907 as a part of the nationalist movement and became increasingly active during the colonial period (1910–45). During the authoritarian period, the Park Chung Hee government also set up "reconstruction schools" (*chaegŏn hakkyo*) for the urban poor and farmers. For more information on night schools, see Namhee Lee, "The Alliance between Labor and Intellectuals," in *The Making of Minjung*.

20. The Korean Student Christian Federation was a nationwide organization of young Christians (composed of youth, university students, and university graduates) that became active in the democracy movement in the 1970s and 1980s.

21. Kim Chisŏn was a labor activist who was arrested several times for her involvement in the Easter Service Incident in 1978 and the 1983 Inch'ŏn Blacklist Incident. Kim Yŏngmi was the president of the Hyosŏng Products union, which co-organized the Kuro Solidarity Strike in 1985.

22. The initial impetus for this political relaxation was external. The Reagan administration pressured the Chun government to liberalize the economy in exchange for regime support, which "opened up a path towards gradual political liberalization" (S.-C. Kim 2016, 24).

23. The government timed the arrests so that they were less likely to attract attention from the public and the media. On the day they chose, the National Assembly had been on recess for two days, and it was final examination period for college students. The student movement had also been repressed since May, when 73 college students occupied the U.S. Cultural Center in Seoul and demanded that the U.S. government apologize for its complicity in the repression of the Kwangju Uprising.

24. The Y.H. Worker Protest in 1979, held at the New Democratic Party headquarters, was the first instance during which the labor struggle was externalized and politicized.

25. In total, 279 workers from Daewoo Apparel, Hyosŏng, and Sŏnil companies

Notes to Pages 79–91 205

received leadership training together three times in 1984 (September 22–23, 1984, September 29-October 1, 1984, and October 6–7, 1984). Forty union leaders from Sŏnil and Puhŭngsa received training on June 17, 1984 (K. Yu 2001, 44).

26. "Fighting" is a commonly used word of encouragement as well as a cheer in South Korea.

27. There was also a sit-in demonstration by 36 Daewoo Apparel workers at the Sinmin (New Democratic) Party district office from June 26 to July 1.

28. For example, the Daewoo Apparel union was first formed on June 9, 1984 by 105 workers, many of whom were members of the hiking club. Karibong Electronics union members were also active in their reading, drama, and hiking clubs (K. Yu 2001, 37, 42).

29. The Council of Hyundai Group was formed during the Great Workers' Struggle on August 8, 1987, not before. During the 1987 Hyundai Workers Struggle, the council orchestrated a mass gathering of Hyundai-affiliated workers and their families on the streets of Ulsan and in the Ulsan public stadium on August 17–18; this action resulted in a successful wage negotiation between Kwŏn Yŏngmok and the deputy minister of labor. However, the Hyundai management ignored what was promised to the Hyundai workers by the deputy minister of labor.

30. Ojwabul later also served as the headquarters for the second episode of the Hyundai Workers Struggle, which occurred at Hyundai Heavy Industries for 128 days toward the end of 1988—the longest strike recorded in contemporary Korean history.

31. The information regarding the location of the firms inside the Ch'angwŏn Industrial Complex comes from the *Korean Industrial Complex Report* (*Han'guk kongdan hyŏnhwang*) (Han'guk Kongdan Yŏn'guso 1987).

CHAPTER 4

1. It also seems to echo related studies that link rising educational levels and greater occupational specialization with democratic values (Lipset 1960) and the resources to participate in democratic politics (Almond and Verba 1963; Inkeles 1969).

2. Alice Amsden (1992) refers to Korea's industrial process as late industrialization, one in which a "backward" country had to struggle to compete with the world of international business. "Learning" is referred to as the means by which the country managed to catch up and compete with the industrialized economies. In *Asia's Next Giant*, Amsden argues that late-industrializing countries, including Korea, achieved economic growth through a process of learning rather than a process of generating inventions or innovation.

3. The Daewoo Auto Strike of 1985 and T'ongil Corporation workers' strike in 1985 are the exceptions.

4. According to Michael Robinson (2007, 124), "A hierarchy of universities came into being, with Seoul National, Yonsei, Korea, Sogang and Ewha universities forming the top tier. A number of newer, private schools were considered second tier, and finally, the poorly funded national universities in the provinces brought up the rear." Moreover, as Namhee Lee (2007, 172) states, "Given that elite universities tended to have longstanding traditions of well-established circles

(extracurricular clubs) and that protest organizers were mostly circle members, it is not surprising that elite universities dominated the student movement in the early 1970s."

5. See appendix for more information on the dataset.

6. North Korea, which was seen as a competitor and as posing an ongoing threat, offered an alternative vision of national development based on communist ideals. South Korean autocrats focused on anticommunism to counter the possibilities that their vision offered.

7. In Korea, placing high value on education is attributable not only to the Confucian tradition, which emphasizes the importance of education, but also on the population's belief that providing children with quality education could facilitate upward mobility, which was dubbed "education fever" (Seth 2002) or "educational aspirations" (Nakamura 2003, 2005).

8. The mechanical technical high schools focused on training precision workers needed for the defense goods manufacturing and heavy machinery sectors. The experimental technical high schools focused on training certified technicians in machine assembly, metal plating, welding, electric works, and laying pipelines. Many of the experimental technical high school students were sent to the Middle East during the Middle East construction boom in the 1970s. Specialized technical high schools focused on training skilled technicians in electronics, chemicals, construction, iron, and railroads. Lastly, the general technical high schools focused on training a wide range of craftspeople to meet the general demand from shop floors.

9. Although the high school equalization policy was designed to equalize (and, theoretically, improve) the quality of schools, it didn't achieve that goal. As prestigious high schools were abolished and the quality of high school education suffered, wealthy families became more reliant on private tutoring or cram schools (*hakwon*) to prepare their children for college entrance examinations. This cycle drove the problem of overheated private tutoring.

10. Although public goods are defined as nonexcludable and nonrival goods, even public goods could be reversible as in the regime can extend public goods but later (threaten to) retract them (Stokes et al. 2013).

11. In the 1960s, there were a series of North Korean provocations that threatened Park's regime (e.g., the Blue House raid and the capture of the USS *Pueblo* in 1968). U.S. involvement in the Vietnam War created fears that there would be a decrease in U.S. troops and military aid to South Korea, which would compromise the country's national security. This anxiety was further heightened by the announcement of the Nixon Doctrine (June 25, 1969), which stated that U.S. allies should prepare to be responsible for their own military defense.

12. According to Sheena Greitens (2016), elite threats were greater starting around the establishment of the Yusin constitution in 1972. As a result, Park reconfigured the coercive apparatus by making it more exclusive and increased fragmentation within it by balancing power among the Korean Central Intelligence Agency, the Presidential Security Service, and the Army Security Command. As for Chun Doo Hwan, popular threat was greater than threats from the elites.

13. Although the origins of Korean capitalists are found in the Japanese colonial period (Eckert 1991), many of the big industrial bourgeoisie were formed in the postliberation period through acquisition of former Japanese properties at bargain

Notes to Pages 103–109

prices and privileged access to foreign aid, bank loans, and public contracts (H. B. Im 1986). The big industrial bourgeoisie made political contributions in exchange for economic favors (H. B. Im 1986).

14. Such expansion of vocational education was remarkable given that the public at the time tended to avoid vocational education and preferred advancing to universities (J.-H. Lee and Hong 2014, 91).

15. Although the increase in demand for unskilled women workers was augmented by the expanding light manufacturing sector in the 1960s, the HCI Drive in the 1970s increased the demand for skilled male workers.

16. For instance, from 1971 to 1978, Park made five visits to the Pusan National Mechanical High School alone and delivered funding to build faculty and staff housing (67 houses and one apartment-style building) and a student dormitory (Joongang Ilbo 2008). During his visit in July 1978, Park shook hands with students preparing for the International Vocational Training Competition and encouraged them by stroking their shoulders (DongA Ilbo 1978).

17. The machinery technical high school received the most financial and technical support, including a total of ₩12.6 billion between 1973 and 1978 and another ₩6.5 billion and ₩1 billion in 1979 and 1980, respectively (H.-A. Kim 2020, 32). The specialized technical high schools also received ₩4.8 billion, whereas the experimental technical high schools were allocated ₩3.6 billion in 1979. In fostering the growth of specialized technical high schools, the government also provided 50% of the experimental facilities in schools, all of the dormitory costs, and the experimental facilities outside of schools (J.-H. Lee and Hong 2014, 76).

18. Conscription has existed since 1957 and requires male citizens between the ages of 18 and 28 to perform compulsory military service. Park introduced a new Military Service Special Cases Law that mobilized graduates of specialized technical high schools as "special soldiers" (*t'ŭngnyebyŏng*) for the construction of core industries, especially the defense industry and the heavy chemical industry. This particular law "removed the distinction between soldiers and skilled workers, engineers, and researchers, among other technologically relevant groups" (H.-A. Kim 2020, 22).

19. Note, however, that the privilege was reserved for the elite *yangban* class during the Chosŏn dynasty (1392–1897).

20. The National Defense Student Corps was initially set up in 1949, during Syngman Rhee's rule, to lead progovernment and anticommunist student rallies. It was dissolved when the Rhee regime ended, following the April Student Revolution in 1960.

21. It is worth noting that despite the official withdrawal of state agents from college campuses, security agents in plainclothes were still present and aimed to install progovernment students in student council leadership; they also coerced student activists to become spies to report on their activist colleagues.

22. The ideological orientations and goals of the student movement (regarding the role of student activism in social change in particular) affected the direction of the movement. In the early 1980s, an ideological debate arose between the "Murim" group and the "Haklim" group (which was later continued as the "Flag versus Anti-Flag" debate in 1985). The Murim group believed that, rather than focusing on targeting the Chun regime, the student movement should focus on

208   *Notes to Pages 110–113*

issues of student welfare and then move gradually to political issues. The Haklim group, on the other hand, emphasized the importance of raising political issues, such as demanding democratization. After experiencing severe repression following the 1980 Kwangju Massacre, student activists focused on expanding the popular base of the student movement through daily activities on campus (Minjuhwa Undong Kinyŏm Saophoe 2010, 203). The movement upheld the Murim group's position—that students should focus on issues of student welfare and the organization of student power on campus first and then move gradually to political issues (H. Choi 1991). In doing so, student activists thought it was best to make full use of officially recognized student organizations, even including the state-controlled National Defense Student Corps, to reach and mobilize as many students as possible. This context helps explain why students focused their energy on rebuilding student councils once Chun announced the campus autonomy measures in December 1983. See H. Choi (1991), N. Lee (2007), and M. Park (2008) for more details on the ideological debates of the student movement in the 1980s.

23. The three *min* are national reunification (*minjok t'ongil*), liberation of people (*minjung haebang*), and achieving democracy (*minju chaengch'wi*).

24. On May 23, 1985, 73 students belonging to the Struggle Committee for the Kwangju Incident of the National Federation of Student Associations (Chŏnguk Haksaeng Ch'ongyŏnhap Kwangju Sa'tae T'ujaeng Wiwŏnhoe) occupied the U.S. Information Service building in Seoul to protest the U.S. government's tacit support of the 1980 Kwangju Massacre.

25. The Chungbu branch was formed on April 19, 1985, and was made up of Hanshin, Suwon, Aju, Kyonggi, Kyunghee (Suwon campus), Sungkyunkwan (Suwon campus), Seoul National Agricultural, and Seoul National Medical (Yongin campus) Universities. The Honam branch was formed on April 23, 1985, and included Chonnam National, Chonbuk National, Woosuk, Mokpo, and Kwangju Education Universities. As of July 19, 1985, the Yŏngnam branch, led by the student council president of Pusan University, had not had an official formation ceremony (Chosun Ilbo 1985).

26. The southern branch (formed on April 29, 1985, at Chungang University) included Seoul National, Chungang, Dankuk, Sookmyung Women's, Soongchon (now Soongsil), and Dongguk Universities as well as the Seoul National University of Education. The northern branch (formed on May 9, 1985, at Duksung Women's University) included Sungkyunkwan, Sungshin Women's, Kukmin, Hangsung, and Duksung Women's Universities. The western branch (formed on May 13, 1985, at Sokang University) included Yonsei, Ewha Women's, Sogang, Hongik, Methodist Theological, Sangmyung Women's, Kyonggi, and Myungji Universities. The eastern branch (formed on May 8, 1985, at Seoul National Medical University) included Korea, Seoul National Medical, Kyunghee, Kunkuk, Hanyang, Sejong, Kwangwoon, Dongduk Women's, and Seoul Women's Universities, as well as the University of Seoul (Chosun Ilbo 1985).

27. Figure A4.1 in the online appendix displays the number of protests *per* school to account for the correlation between the number of schools in Seoul versus non-Seoul areas and the number of protests shown in figure 4.3. The general patterns of student protests are similar in figures 4.3 and A4.1.

Notes to Pages 128–130

CHAPTER 5

1. Most college students were eligible to vote because the voting age was 19 (based on the international age-counting system).

2. The Youth Coalition for Democracy Movement was established in September 1983 and was composed of former student activists who were engaged in labor and social movements. It not only connected the older and younger generations of student activists but also connected student activists to professors, journalists, and other sympathetic intellectuals and professionals (Ch'oe 1990, 250–56, cited in Kim 2000, 83).

3. Reporting rallies (*pogo daehoe*) in Korea are large-scale, public briefing sessions held by private and public entities.

4. In 1974 Park Chung Hee declared Emergency Decree (ED) 4 that "contained twelve articles intended permanently to break the power of the student movement" (P. Y. Chang 2015b, 71). The government subsequently arrested individuals related to the National League for Democratic Youth and Students. Of the 1,024 students taken into custody, 253 of them were sent to the Emergency Martial Court to be prosecuted, and 180 of them were convicted and sentenced (C. Yi 2011, 274). The ED 4 was replaced with ED 7 on April 8, 1975, and ED 9 on May 13, 1975. The infamous ED 9 effectively silenced the student movement. With ED 9, the Park regime reestablished the National Defense Student Corps, dissolved autonomous student organizations, revised student regulations (to make it difficult to reinstate dismissed students), legalized the presence of security agents and the military on college campuses, extended students' military training, and curtailed various extracurricular activities.

5. The PMCDR was formed in March 1985 through a merger between the Council of Movement for People and Democracy (Minminhyŏp) and the National Congress for Democracy and Reunification (NCDR; Kungmin Hoeŭi). Both organizations were established in 1984. The NCDR was a successor to the National Coalition for Democracy and Reunification of 1979, which led the anti-Yusin struggle. While the NCDR consisted of intellectuals and religious leaders who were politically moderate and supportive of liberal democracy, the Council of Movement for People and Democracy was considered more radical, stressing the "mass line" and class-based struggle.

6. In early 1987, the nominal leader of the NKDP (Yi Min U) indicated to the ruling party DJP that he would abandon his insistence on direct presidential elections and instead consider the DJP's formula of parliamentarism in exchange for the guarantee of basic democratic reforms. In response, Kim Young Sam and Kim Dae Jung, the de facto leaders of the NKDP, along with the hardliners (69 out of 90 NKDP legislators), left the NKDP and formed the Reunification Democratic Party. The NMHDC consisted of 2,191 inaugural members from the PMCDR and 25 other social movement groups, covering all geographical areas of South Korea and all major sectoral groups (including Protestant pastors, Buddhist monks, opposition politicians, women's movement leaders, peasant activists, labor activists, urban poor activists, publishers and journalists, authors and writers, artists, educators, youth movement leaders, and lawyers).

210 *Notes to Pages 133–140*

7. http://aparc.fsi.stanford.edu/research/stanford_korea_democracy_project

8. As a measure of protest intensity, I also consider the number of days during the June Uprising on which protests occurred in a given county. The results, reported in table A5.5, column 2 in the online appendix, remain similar using this alternative measure of protest intensity.

9. http://info.nec.go.kr

10. The results are reported in table A5.4 in the online appendix.

11. Found in the 1984 *Korean University Yearbook*, this data is the latest available prior to the 1987 June Democratic Uprising. The quantity and quality of information in the yearbook vary depending on the college in question, and there is no way to determine the exhaustiveness of the data. One outlier—Korea Correspondence University (in Seoul)—was removed from the bivariate correlation. However, even with the inclusion of the outlier, a strong positive correlation between the two variables remains ($r = 0.87$).

12. Because more than one candidate from a party was able to contest in a given electoral district during the 1981 National Assembly election, I use total number of candidates instead of the widely used measure of total number of effective parties.

13. Column 1 gives the original results as a baseline comparison. Column 2 shows the results with number of days as the dependent variable. Column 3 provides the results using number of events from a subset of observations on days when the NMHDC was involved.

14. There are 76 nonzero districts among the 211 counties (36%) that were contested by the NKDP candidates. The negative binomial model is more appropriate than the Poisson model because the mean and variance of my dependent variable are not equal to each other ($\sigma = 12.83 > \mu = 5.08$). I also perform the Vuong test and find the zero-inflated negative binomial model to be an improvement over a standard negative binomial model (test statistic = 3.086 and p-value = 0.001).

15. The results displaying the coefficients for the control variables are found in tables A5.2 (for the protest events equation) and A5.3 (for the inflate equation) in the online appendix. The inflate equation in table A5.3, column 2, shows that districts with more electoral competitiveness, population density, and population employed in the industrial sector had a higher probability of seeing at least one protest event.

16. I follow Hilbe (2011) to calculate the IRR and the standard errors of the IRR and create a marginal effects plot visualizing the conditional effect of *NKDP Vote Share* on *Protest Intensity* at different levels of *Proportion of College Students*. $IRR_{NKDP\ Vote\ Share\ x\ Proportion\ of\ College\ Students} = \exp[-1.033 + 0.543^*\text{Proportion of College Students}]$ where $IRR_{NKDP\ Vote\ Share\ x\ Proportion\ of\ College\ Students}$ is the interaction of binary *NKDP Vote Share* and continuous *Proportion of College Students* predictors. The coefficients of the *NKDP Vote Share* and the interaction term come from table 5.4, column 2. The IRR standard errors for the interactions at each level of *Proportion of College Students* are determined by first calculating the variance using the variance-covariance matrix: $V_{NKDP\ Vote\ Share\ x\ Proportion\ of\ College\ Students} = 0.289 + \text{Proportion of College Students}^2{}^*0.037 + 2 * \text{Proportion of College Students} * -0.075$. Subsequently, I take the square root of the variance to obtain the standard error.

CHAPTER 6

1. For the rest of the chapter, the terms "cohort effect" and "generational effect" are used interchangeably. The same applies to "age effect" and "life cycle effect."

2. As time has passed, the 386 generation has been called the 486 generation in the 2000s and the 586 generation since the 2010s. This generation is also referred to as the 86 generation.

3. The protest began after the Lee Myung-bak administration reversed a ban on U.S. beef imports in 2008. The ban had been in place since December 2003, when mad cow disease was detected in U.S. beef cattle. At its height, the protest involved tens of thousands of people.

4. This view is reflected in the state-sanctioned narrative of the Korean War that dubs the war as "*yugio*" (literally "6/25" or June 25 [1950]). According to Jae-Jung Suh, by officially sanctioning the date of the war's beginning as June 25 (the date on which North Korea fired the proverbial first shot), the *yugio* narrative in South Korea erases the colonial origins of the war and positions South Korea as the victim and North Korea as the aggressor (J.-J. Suh 2010).

5. There is an ongoing discussion regarding the true meanings of progressivism and conservatism in Korea (S. Kim 2020; Lankov 2017). For the purpose of this chapter, progressiveness is defined as demonstrating support for the progressive (center-left) political parties. The progressive parties have been more willing to advocate for engagement with North Korea.

6. As mentioned in chapter 4, in the 1980s, U.S. government facilities in Korea (in Kwangju, Pusan, and Seoul) frequently became targets of high-profile attacks and occupation attempts by student movement groups. The main demands made by protestors included a thorough investigation of the Kwangju Uprising, punishment of those involved, and clarification of the U.S. role in the suppression of that uprising. Students also protested President Ronald Reagan's state visit to South Korea in 1983.

7. The other main faction in the late 1980s was the People's Democracy group that advocated an orthodox Marxist-Leninist revolution, emphasizing class struggle and labor issues.

8. Chuch'e, translated as "self-reliance," is Kim Il Sung's creative application of Marxist-Leninist principles to the modern political realities of North Korea (Socialist Constitution of the Democratic People's Republic of Korea 1972, 2).

9. Their language reflects these experiences. Some common phrases used by this generation include those indicating that Korea is hell ("Hell Joseon"), that one's family background predetermines one's life course ("golden spoon, dirt spoons"), that the powerful pick on the weak ("gapjil"), and that their generation was forced to give up (*pogi*) on three (*sam*) things—courtship, marriage, and children ("sampo generation") (G.-W. Shin and Moon 2017, 11–12).

10. South Korea's left-of-center political parties are commonly referred to as "progressive" rather than "liberal."

11. The Blue House is the executive office and official residence of the president (much like the White House in the United States).

212   *Notes to Pages 155–183*

12. The KGSS is the South Korean version of the General Social Survey of the National Opinion Research Center at the University of Chicago.

13. The cumulative data from 2003 to 2016 (excluding 2015) was not available when I was conducting the analysis.

14. Regionalism, particularly the antagonism between the Chŏlla and Kyŏngsang region dating back to the authoritarian period, has been addressed in other parts of this book. The dummy variables for Chŏlla and Kyŏngsang are included to capture the effects of regionalism, as people born in Chŏlla tend to vote for candidates from Chŏlla, and those born in Kyŏngsang tend to vote for candidates from Kyŏngsang.

15. The table of results is found in table A6.2 in the online appendix.

16. The Korean term *chinbo* (진보) is translated as progressive or liberal in English.

17. The table of results is found in table A6.3 in the online appendix.

18. The table of results is found in table A6.4 in the online appendix.

CHAPTER 7

1. In 1989, direct elections were introduced for the first time for local councils, the Legislative Yuan (the legislative branch), and executive posts at various levels, including county magistrates and city mayors. Direct elections for Taiwan provincial governors and the mayors of two municipalities, Taipei and Kaohsiung, were introduced in 1994, and for the president in 1996. In 2000, Taiwan experienced its first peaceful transfer of power when the Democratic Progressive Party candidate Chen Shui-bian won the presidential election. The second peaceful transfer of power occurred in 2008, when the KMT regained the presidency.

2. For example, the Wild Lily student movement occurred in 1990.

3. The "party organization provided the basis for selective incorporation and for the penetration of the educational system, the unions, and the country life—of civil society generally" (Haggard and Kaufman 1995, 280).

4. According to the 1971 Commission of Industrial and Commercial Census of Taiwan, large industrial establishments (with over 100 employees) accounted for only one-third of rural manufacturing employment while establishments with fewer than 10 employees accounted for 41% of such employment (Stites 1982, 249).

5. These areas included Seoul-Inch'ŏn, Pusan, and other cities (Taegu and Ulsan) along the expressway connecting Seoul and Pusan.

6. Until 1994, when the University Law was revised, the Ministry of Education dominated almost every aspect of higher education, including controls over the establishment of new higher education institutions, their size and scale, the tuition charged, the courses offered, the students recruited, and the appointment of each college's president.

7. Various terms such as deconsolidation, democratic backsliding, and democratic erosion have been used by political scientists to describe the political global trend. For example, see Bermeo (2016), Foa and Mounk (2017), Haggard and Kaufman (2021), Levitsky and Ziblatt (2018), and Democracy Reports by the Varieties of Democracy (https://v-dem.net/publications/democracy-reports).

8. A recent empirical study by Hong, Park, and Yang (2022) shows that the New Village Movement—through Park Chung Hee's positive legacy associated with the rural development plan and the overall economic success of his regime—helped his daughter's electoral victory in 2012.

9. Social identity theory, originally formulated by social psychologists Henri Tajfel and John C. Turner (e.g., Tajfel 1978, 1982; Tajfel and Turner 1979), addresses the ways that social identities (i.e., people's self-concepts that are based on their membership in social groups) affect people's attitudes and behaviors regarding their in-group and the out-group.

APPENDIX

1. Han'guk Nodong Net'ŭwŏk'ŭ Hyŏbŭihoe (http://nodong.net) is a South Korean nongovernmental organization that started as the Labor Information Project Group in 1996.

2. When the source reports several protests occurring simultaneously in a given locality, these events were coded as separate events if the participants (belonging to different groups) are not physically protesting with one another. Protest events that were planned but did not occur (due to repression or other reasons specified in the source) are not counted as events. Gatherings (*unjip*) without any additional information are also not coded as events.

Bibliography

Acemoglu, Daron, and James A. Robinson. 2001. "A Theory of Political Transitions." *American Economic Review* 91: 938–63.

Acemoglu, Daron, and James A. Robinson. 2006. *Economic Origins of Dictatorship and Democracy*. Cambridge: Cambridge University Press.

Acharya, Avidit, Matthew Blackwell, and Maya Sen. 2016. "Explaining Causal Findings without Bias: Detecting and Assessing Direct Effects." *American Political Science Review* 110 (3): 512–29.

Albertus, Michael, Sofia Fenner, and Dan Slater. 2018. *Coercive Distribution*. Elements in the Politics of Development. Cambridge: Cambridge University Press.

Almond, Gabriel A., and G. Bingham Powell. 1966. *Comparative Politics: A Developmental Approach*. Boston: Little, Brown.

Almond, Gabriel A., and Sidney Verba. 1963. *The Civic Culture: Political Attitudes and Democracy in Five Nations*. Center for International Studies, Princeton University. Princeton: Princeton University Press.

Amsden, Alice. 1992. *Asia's Next Giant: South Korea and Late Industrialisation*. Rev. ed. New York: Oxford University Press.

Andrews, Kenneth T. 1997. "The Impacts of Social Movements on the Political Process: The Civil Rights Movement and Black Electoral Politics in Mississippi." *American Sociological Review* 62 (5): 800–819.

Andrews, Kenneth T. 2004. *Freedom Is a Constant Struggle: The Mississippi Civil Rights Movement and Its Legacy*. Chicago: University of Chicago Press.

Barro, Robert J. 1990. "Government Spending in a Simple Model of Endogenous Growth." *Journal of Political Economy* 98 (S5): 103–25.

Beaulieu, Emily. 2014. *Electoral Protest and Democracy in the Developing World*. New York: Cambridge University Press.

Beaulieu, Emily, and Susan D. Hyde. 2009. "In the Shadow of Democracy Promotion: Strategic Manipulation, International Observers, and Election Boycotts." *Comparative Political Studies* 42 (3): 392–415.

Beissinger, Mark. 2002. *Nationalist Mobilization and the Collapse of the Soviet State.* Cambridge: Cambridge University Press.

Benford, Robert D. 2013. "Master Frame." In *The Wiley-Blackwell Encyclopedia of Social and Political Movements*, edited by David A. Snow, Donatella della Porta, Bert Klandermans, and Doug McAdam. Malden, MA: Wiley.

Benford, Robert D., and David A. Snow. 2000. "Framing Processes and Social Movements: An Overview and Assessment." *Annual Review of Sociology* 26: 611–39.

Bermeo, Nancy. 2016. "On Democratic Backsliding." *Journal of Democracy* 27 (1): 5–19.

Bernhard, Michael, Amanda B. Edgell, and Staffan I. Lindberg. 2020. "Institutionalising Electoral Uncertainty and Authoritarian Regime Survival." *European Journal of Political Research* 59: 465–87.

Bernhard, Michael, Christopher Reenock, and Timothy Nordstrom. 2004. "The Legacy of Western Overseas Colonialism on Democratic Survival." *International Studies Quarterly* 48 (1): 225–50.

Birch, Sarah. 2010. "Perceptions of Electoral Fairness and Voter Turnout." *Comparative Political Studies* 43 (12): 1601–22.

Blaydes, Lisa. 2011. *Elections and Distributive Politics in Mubarak's Egypt.* New York: Cambridge University Press.

Blee, Kathleen M., and Ashley Currier. 2006. "How Local Social Movement Groups Handle a Presidential Election." *Qualitative Sociology* 29 (3): 261–80.

Boix, Carles. 2003. *Democracy and Redistribution.* Cambridge: Cambridge University Press.

Boix, Carles. 2018. "Richer, More Equal, and More Democratic." *Annals of Comparative Democratization* 16 (3): 12–16.

Boix, Carles, and Susan C. Stokes. 2003. "Endogenous Democratization." *World Politics* 55 (4): 517–49.

Boix, Carles, and Milan Svolik. 2013. "The Foundation of Limited Authoritarian Government: Institutions, Commitment, and Power-Sharing in Dictatorships." *Journal of Politics* 75 (2): 300–316.

Bollen, Kenneth. 1979. "Political Democracy and the Timing of Development." *American Sociological Review* 44 (4): 572–85.

Booth, John A., and Mitchell A. Seligson. 2009. *The Legitimacy Puzzle in Latin America: Political Support and Democracy in Eight Nations.* Cambridge: Cambridge University Press.

Brazinsky, Gregg. 2009. *Nation Building in South Korea: Koreans, Americans, and the Making of a Democracy.* Chapel Hill: University of North Carolina Press.

Brownlee, Jason. 2007. *Authoritarianism in an Age of Democratization.* Cambridge: Cambridge University Press.

Brownlee, Jason. 2012. "Executive Elections in the Arab World: When and How Do They Matter?" *Comparative Political Studies* 44 (7): 807–28.

Buehler, Matt. 2013. "Safety-Valve Elections and the Arab Spring: The Weakening (and Resurgence) of Morocco's Islamist Opposition Party." *Terrorism and Political Violence* 25 (1): 137–56.

Bueno de Mesquita, Bruce, Alastair Smith, Randolph M. Siverson, and James D. Marrow. 2004. *The Logic of Political Survival.* Cambridge: MIT Press.

Bunce, Valerie J., and Shannon L. Wolchik. 2006. "International Diffusion and Postcommunist Electoral Revolution." *Communist and Post-Communist Studies* 39 (3): 283–304.

Bunce, Valerie J., and Shannon L. Wolchik. 2011. *Defeating Authoritarian Leaders in Post-Communist Countries*. Cambridge: Cambridge University Press.

Burkhart, Ross E., and Michael S. Lewis-Beck. 1994. "Comparative Democracy: The Economic Development Thesis." *American Political Science Review* 88 (4): 903–10.

Caryl, Christian. 2017. "South Korea Shows the World How Democracy Is Done." *Washington Post*, March 10.

Case, F. Duncan. 1981. "Dormitory Architecture Influences." *Environment and Behavior* 13 (1): 23–41.

Chae, Jae-eun. 2013. "The Education Development Plan for Algeria: With a Focus on Vocational Education and Training and Higher Education." In *Establishment of Algeria's National Vision 2030*, edited by Hong Tack Chun and MoonJoong Tcha. Seoul: Ministry of Strategy and Finance and Korea Development Institute.

Chae, Jae-Eun, and Hee Kyung Hong. 2009. "The Expansion of Higher Education Led by Private Universities in Korea." *Asia Pacific Journal of Education* 29 (3): 341–55.

Chai, Goo Mook. 1996. "Intellectuals in the South Korean Labor Movement in the 1980s." *International Journal of Politics, Culture, and Society* 10 (2): 273–90.

Chang, Paul Y. 2015a. *Protest Dialectics: State Repression and South Korea's Democracy Movement, 1970–1979*. Stanford: Stanford University Press.

Chang, Paul Y. 2015b. "The Polarization of South Korea: The Legacy of Authoritarianism and People's Movements." *Stanford University Press blog*, https://stanfordpress.typepad.com/blog/2015/03/the-polarization-of-south-korea.html

Chang, Paul Y., and Kangsan Lee. 2021. "The Structure of Protest Cycles: Inspiration and Bridging in South Korea's Democracy Movement." *Social Forces* 100 (2): 879–904.

Chang, Yun-Shik. 1998. "The Progressive Christian Church and Democracy in South Korea." *Journal of Church and State* 40 (2): 437–68.

Chen, Jie. 2013. *A Middle Class without Democracy: Economic Growth and the Prospects for Democratization in China*. New York: Oxford University Press.

Cheng, Tun-Jen. 1989. "Democratizing the Quasi-Leninist Regime in Taiwan." *World Politics* 41 (4): 471–99.

Cheng, Tun-jen, Stephan Haggard, and David Kang. 1998. "Institutions and Growth in Korea and Taiwan: The Bureaucracy." *Journal of Development Studies* 34 (6): 87–111.

Cheng, Tun-jen, and Eun Mee Kim. 1994. "Making Democracy: Generalizing the South Korean Case." In *The Politics of Democratization: Generalizing East Asian Experience*, edited by Edward Friedman. Boulder: Westview Press.

Cheon, Jung-Hwan. 2018. "Laboring Intellectuals, Writing Workers: A New Critical Perspective on 1980s-1990s South Korean Cultural History." *Ex-Position* 40: 37–56.

Cho, Joan E., and Paul Y. Chang. 2017. "The Socioeconomic Foundations of South Korea's Democracy Movement." In *Routledge Handbook of Korean Culture and Society*, edited by Youna Kim. London: Routledge.

Cho, Joan E., Jae Seung Lee, and B. K. Song. 2017. "Media Exposure and Regime Support under Competitive Authoritarianism: Evidence from South Korea." *Journal of East Asian Studies* 17 (2): 145–66.

Cho, Joan E., Jae Seung Lee, and B. K. Song. 2019. "Mind the Electoral Gap: The Effect of Investment in Public Infrastructure on Authoritarian Support in South Korea." *Studies in Comparative International Development* 54 (4): 473–500.

Cho, Sŭnghyŏk. 1981. *Tosi sanŏp sŏn'gyo ŭi inshik* [Understanding the Urban Industrial Mission]. Seoul: Minjungsa.

Cho, Youngho, Mi-son Kim, and Yong Cheol Kim. 2019. "Cultural Foundations of Contentious Democracy in South Korea." *Asian Survey* 59 (2): 272–94.

Choe, Hyun, and Jiyoung Kim. 2012. "South Korea's Democratization Movements, 1980–1987: Political Structure, Political Opportunity, and Framing." *Inter-Asia Cultural Studies* 13 (1): 55–86.

Ch'oe, Yŏn Ku. 1990. "80-yŏndae ch'ŏngnyŏn undong ŭi sŏnggyŏk kwa kŭ chŏn'gae" [The Nature and Evolution of the Youth Movement in the 1980s]. In *Han'guk sahoe undongsa* [History of Social Movements in Korea], edited by Hŭi-yŏn Cho. Seoul: Hanul.

Choi, Hee Jun, and Ji-Hye Park. 2013. "Historical Analysis of the Policy on the College Entrance System in South Korea." *International Education Studies* 6 (11): 106–21.

Choi, Hyaeweol. 1991. "The Societal Impact of Student Politics in Contemporary South Korea." *Higher Education* 22 (2): 175–88.

Choi, Jang-Jip. 1989. *Labor and the Authoritarian State: Labor Unions in South Korean Manufacturing Industries, 1961–1980*. Seoul: Korea University Press.

Choi, Jang-Jip. 1993. "Political Cleavages in South Korea." In *State and Society in Contemporary Korea*, edited by Hagen Koo. Ithaca: Cornell University Press.

Choi, Jang-Jip. 1997. *Han'guk ŭi nodong undong kwa kukka* [The Labor Movement and the State in Korea]. Seoul: Nanam.

Choi, Jang-Jip. 2002. *Minjuhwa ihu minjujuŭi* [Democracy after Democratization]. Seoul: Humanitas.

Choi, Jang-Jip. 2012. *Democracy after Democratization: The Korean Experience*. Stanford: Walter H. Shorenstein Asia-Pacific Research Center, Stanford University.

Choi, Jang-Jip. 2019. "Kim Dae Jung and Democracy: Thought and Practice." Presented as a keynote speech on the nineteenth anniversary of Kim Dae Jung receiving the Nobel Peace Prize, Seoul, December 9.

Chŏn'guk Nodong Chohap Hyŏbŭihoe Paeksŏ Palgan Wiwŏnhoe [National Trade Union Council White Paper Publication Committee] and Nodong Undong Yŏksa Charyosil [Labor Movement History Archives]. 2003. *Chŏn'guk nodong chohap hyŏbŭihoe paeksŏ* [National Trade Union Council White Paper]. Vol. 1. Seoul: Ch'aek Tongmu Nonjang.

Chŏn'guk Taehak Yŏn'gam P'yŏnch'an Wiwŏnhoe [Korean University Yearbook Compilation Committee]. 1984. *Han'guk taehak yŏn'gam* [Korean University Yearbook]. Seoul: Aedŭ Yŏng.

Chosun Ilbo. 1985. "Chŏn'guk haksaeng ch'ongyŏnhap kigup'yo" [National Federation of Student Associations Organizational Chart]. July 19.

Chung, Chulhee. 2011. "Mesomobilization and the June Uprising: Strategic Cultural Integration in Pro-democracy Movements in South Korea." In *East Asian*

Social Movements: Power, Protest, and Change in a Dynamic Region, edited by Jeffrey Broadbent and Vicky Brockman. New York: Springer.

Chung, Hae-Gu, Hye-Jin Kim, and Sang-Ho Chung. 2004. *6-wŏl hangjaeng kwa Han'guk ŭi minjujuŭi* [June Democratic Struggle and Korea's Democracy]. Seoul: Minjuhwa Undong Kinyŏm Saŏphoe.

Chung, Jin Min. 2012. "Han'guk yugwŏnjadŭl ŭi t'up'yo hyŏngt'ae wa sadae: 2010-yŏn chibang sŏn'gŏ rŭl chungsim ŭro" [Korean Voting Behavior and Generation in the 2010 Local Elections]. *Han'guk chŏngch'i yŏn'gu* [Journal of Korean Politics] 21 (2): 1–21.

Chungso Kiŏp Hyŏptong Chohap Chunganghoe [Korea Federation of Small and Medium Business]. 1989. *Kongŏp tanji hyŏnhwang* [An Overview of Industrial Complexes]. Seoul: Sanggongbu: Chungso Kiŏp Hyŏptong Chohap Chunganghoe.

Clapham, Christopher. 1993. "Democratisation in Africa: Obstacles and Prospects." *Third World Quarterly* 14 (3): 423–38.

Clark, David H., and Patrick M. Regan. 2003. "Opportunities to Fight: A Statistical Technique for Modeling Unobservable Phenomena." *Journal of Conflict Resolution* 47 (1): 94–115.

Cleary, Matthew R., and Susan C. Stokes. 2006. *Democracy and the Culture of Skepticism: The Politics of Trust in Argentina and Mexico*. New York: Russell Sage Foundation.

Clemens, Elisabeth S. 1996. "Organization Form as Frame: Collective Identity and Political Strategy in the American Labor Movement, 1880–1920." In *Comparative Perspectives on Social Movements: Political Opportunities, Mobilizing Structures, and Cultural Framings*, edited by Doug McAdam, John D. McCarthy, and Mayer N. Zald. Cambridge: Cambridge University Press.

Croissant, Aurel. 2002. "Electoral Politics in South Korea." In *Electoral Politics in Southeast & East Asia*, edited by Gabriele Bruns, Aurel Croissant, and Marei John. Singapore: Friedrich Ebert Stiftung.

Croissant, Aurel. 2019. "Beating Backsliding? Episodes and Outcomes of Democratic Backsliding in Asia-Pacific in the Period 1950 to 2018." Working Paper.

Cumings, Bruce. 1997. *Korea's Place in the Sun: A Modern History*. New York: W.W. Norton.

Dahl, Robert A. 1971. *Polyarchy: Participation and Opposition*. New Haven: Yale University Press.

Dahl, Robert A. 2005. "What Political Institutions Does Large-Scale Democracy Require?" *Political Science Quarterly* 120 (2): 187–97.

Davies, James C. 1962. "Toward a Theory of Revolution." *American Sociological Review* 27 (1): 5–19.

della Porta, Donatella. 1996. "Social Movements and the State: Thoughts on the Policing of Protest." In *Comparative Perspectives on Social Movements: Political Opportunity Structures, Mobilizing Structures, and Cultural Framings*, edited by Doug McAdam, John D. McCarthy, and Mayer N. Zald. Cambridge: Cambridge University Press.

Deyo, Frederic. 1989. *Beneath the Miracle: Labor Subordination in the New Asian Industrialism*. Berkeley: University of California Press.

Dix, Robert. 1992. "Democratization and the Institutionalization of Latin American Political Parties." *Comparative Political Studies* 24 (4): 488–511.

Doner, Richard F., and Ben Ross Schneider. 2016. "The Middle-Income Trap: More Politics Than Economics." *World Politics* 68 (4): 608–44.

Dong, Wonmo. 1987. "University Students in South Korean Politics: Patterns of Radicalization in the 1980s." *Journal of International Affairs* 40 (2): 233–55.

DongA Ilbo. 1978. "Pusan kigye konggo sach'al" [Inspection of Pusan Mechanical High School]. July 21. Naver News Library.

DongA Ilbo. 1980. "Tosi kongwŏn chibang yŏngnyu" [City Factory Workers Returning to the Countryside]. January 15. Naver News Library.

DongA Ilbo. 1985. "Taehaksaeng 3-baek yŏmyŏng chongnosŏ hanttae siwi" [About 300 College Students Protest in Chongno]. February 9. Naver News Library.

Donno, Daniela. 2013. "Elections and Democratization in Authoritarian Regimes." *American Journal of Political Science* 57 (3): 703–16.

Dunning, Thad. 2008. *Crude Democracy: Natural Resource Wealth and Political Regimes.* Cambridge: Cambridge University Press.

Eckert, Carter J. 1991. *Offspring of Empire: The Koch'ang Kims and the Colonial Origins of Korean Capitalism, 1876–1945.* Seattle: University of Washington Press.

Eckstein, Harry. 1966. *Division and Cohesion in Democracy.* Princeton: Princeton University Press.

Eckstein, Harry, Frederic J. Fleron, Erik P. Hoffmann, and William M. Reisinger. 1998. *Can Democracy Take Root in Post-Soviet Russia?* Lanham, MD: Rowman and Littlefield.

Edgell, Amanda B., Valeriya Mechkova, David Altman, Michael Bernhard, and Staffan I. Lindberg. 2018. "When and Where Do Elections Matter? A Global Test of the Democratization by Elections Hypothesis, 1900–2010." *Democratization* 25 (3): 422–44.

Eisenstadt, Todd. 2007. *Courting Democracy in Mexico: Party Strategy and Electoral Institutions.* Cambridge: Cambridge University Press.

Epstein, David L., Robert Bates, Jack Goldstone, Ida Kristensen, and Sharyn O'Halloran. 2006. "Democratic Transitions." *American Journal of Political Science* 50 (3): 551–69.

Evans, Peter. 1995. *Embedded Autonomy: States and Industrial Transformation.* Princeton: Princeton University Press.

Festinger, Leon, Stanley Schachter, and Kurt Back. 1950. *Social Pressures in Informal Groups.* Stanford: Stanford University Press.

Foa, Roberto Stefan, and Yascha Mounk. 2017. "The Signs of Deconsolidation." *Journal of Democracy* 28 (1): 5–16.

Fu, Diana, and Greg Distelhorst. 2018. "Grassroots Participation and Repression under Hu Jintao and Xi Jinping." *China Journal* 79: 100–122.

Fukuyama, Francis. 2014. *Political Order and Political Decay.* London: Profile Books.

Gale, Alastair. 2016. "A Korean Political Party by Any Other Name Is Probably Still the Same." *Wall Street Journal*, April 11. https://www.wsj.com/articles/a-korean-political-party-by-any-other-name-is-probably-still-the-same-1460410892

Gamson, William A., and David S. Meyer. 1996. "Framing Political Opportunity." In *Comparative Perspectives on Social Movements: Political Opportunities, Mobilizing*

Structures, and Cultural Framings, edited by Doug McAdam, John D. McCarthy, and Mayer N. Zald. Cambridge: Cambridge University Press.

Gandhi, Jennifer. 2008. *Political Institutions under Dictatorship*. Cambridge: Cambridge University Press.

Gandhi, Jennifer, and Adam Przeworski. 2007. "Authoritarian Institutions and the Survival of Autocrats." *Comparative Political Studies* 40 (11): 1279–1301.

Gans, Herbert J. 1967. *The Levittowners: Ways of Life and Politics in a New Suburban Community*. New York: Pantheon Books.

Gates, Hill. 1979. "Dependency and the Part-Time Proletariat in Taiwan." *Modern China* 5 (3): 381–407.

Geddes, Barbara. 2005. "Why Parties and Elections in Authoritarian Regimes?" Paper presented to the Annual Meeting of the American Political Science Association.

Gerring, John. 2007. "Is There a (Viable) Crucial-Case Method?" *Comparative Political Studies* 40 (3): 231–53.

Gilley, Bruce. 2009. *The Right to Rule: How States Win and Lose Legitimacy*. New York: Columbia University Press.

Ginsburg, Tom, and Aziz Huq. 2018. "Democracy's 'Near Misses.'" *Journal of Democracy* 29 (4): 16–30.

Giraudy, Agustina, Eduardo Moncada, and Richard Snyder. 2019. "Subnational Research in Comparative Politics." In *Inside Countries: Subnational Research in Comparative Politics*, edited by Agustina Giraudy, Eduardo Moncada, and Richard Snyder. Cambridge: Cambridge University Press.

Goldstone, Jack A., and Adriana Kocronik-Mina. 2013. "Democracy and Development: New Insights from Graphic Analysis." Working paper of the Center for the Study of Social Change, Institutions, and Policy, George Mason University.

Gould, Roger V. 1991. "Multiple Networks and Mobilization in the Paris Commune, 1871." *American Sociological Review* 56 (6): 716–29.

Gould, Roger V. 1995. *Insurgent Identities: Class, Community, and Protest in Paris from 1848 to the Commune*. Chicago: University of Chicago Press.

Graham, Edward M. 2003. *Reforming Korea's Industrial Conglomerates*. Washington, DC: Peterson Institute for International Economics.

Greene, Kenneth. 2007. *Why Dominant Parties Lose: Mexico's Democratization in Comparative Perspective*. Cambridge: Cambridge University Press.

Greitens, Sheena Chestnut. 2016. *Dictators and Their Secret Police*. Cambridge: Cambridge University Press.

Gurr, Ted. 1970. *Why Men Rebel*. Princeton: Princeton University Press.

Haddad, Mary Alice. 2012. *Building Democracy in Japan*. Cambridge: Cambridge University Press.

Hadenius, Axel, and Jan Teorell. 2007. "Pathways from Authoritarianism." *Journal of Democracy* 18 (1): 143–57.

Hafner-Burton, Emilie M., Susan D. Hyde, and Ryan S. Jablonski. 2014. "When Do Governments Resort to Election Violence?" *British Journal of Political Science* 44 (1): 149–79.

Haggard, Stephan. 2018. *Developmental States*. Elements in the Politics of Development. Cambridge: Cambridge University Press.

Haggard, Stephan, David Kang, and Chung-In Moon. 1997. "Japanese Colonialism and Korean Development: A Critique." *World Development* 25 (6): 867–81.

Haggard, Stephan, and Robert R. Kaufman. 1995. *The Political Economy of Democratic Transitions*. Princeton: Princeton University Press.

Haggard, Stephan, and Robert R. Kaufman. 1997. "The Political Economy of Democratic Transitions." *Comparative Politics* 29 (3): 263–83.

Haggard, Stephan, and Robert R. Kaufman. 2016. *Dictators and Democrats: Masses, Elites, and Regime Change*. Princeton: Princeton University Press.

Haggard, Stephan, and Robert R. Kaufman. 2021. *Backsliding: Democratic Regress in the Contemporary World*. Elements in the Political Economy. Cambridge: Cambridge University Press.

Haggard, Stephan, and Jong-Sung You. 2015. "Freedom of Expression in South Korea." *Journal of Contemporary Asia* 45 (1): 167–79.

Han, Seung-Mi. 2004. "The New Community Movement: Park Chung Hee and the Making of State Populism in Korea." *Pacific Affairs* 77 (1): 69–93.

Han'guk Kidok Haksaenghoe Ch'ongyŏnmaeng [Korean Student Christian Federation]. 1981. "Yahak hwaldong annaesŏ" [Guidelines for Night School Activism]. 00871651. Korea Democracy Foundation Open Archives.

Han'guk Kidok Haksaenghoe Ch'ongyŏnmaeng [Korean Student Christian Federation]. 1984. "Kongjang hwaldong annaesŏ" [Guidelines for Factory Activism]. 00063840. Korea Democracy Foundation Open Archives.

Han'guk Kidokkyo Kyohoe Hyŏbŭihoe [National Council of Churches of Korea]. 1984. *Nodong hyŏnjang kwa chŭngŏn* [The Scene and Testimony of Labor]. Seoul: P'ulpit.

Han'guk Kidokkyo Sahoe Munje Yŏn'guwŏn [Christian Institute for the Study of Justice and Development]. 1987a. *6-wŏl minjuhwa tae tujaeng* [The Great June Democratic Uprising]. Seoul: Han'guk Kidokkyo Sahoe Munje Yŏn'guwŏn.

Han'guk Kidokkyo Sahoe Munje Yŏn'guwŏn [Christian Institute for the Study of Justice and Development].1987b. *7–8-wŏl nodongja taejung t'ujaeng* [The July–August Mass Struggle of the Workers]. Seoul: Minjungsa.

Han'guk Kongdan Yŏn'guso [Korea Industrial Complex Research Institute]. 1987. *Han'guk kongdan hyŏnhwang* [Korea Industrial Complex Report]. Seoul: Han'guk Kongdan Yŏn'guso.

Han'guk Minjujuŭi Yŏn'guso [Institute for Korean Democracy]. 2016. *1980-yŏndae kaehŏn undong kwa 6.10 minju hangjaeng* [1980s Constitutional Reform Movement and the 6.10 Democratic Uprising]. Seoul: Minjuhwa Undong Kinyŏm Saŏphoe.

Han'guk Nodongja Pokchi Hyŏbŭihoe [Korean Workers' Welfare Council]. 1984. *YH nodong chohap sa* [History of YH Labor Union]. Seoul: Hyŏngsŏngsa.

Han'guk Ŭnhaeng [Bank of Korea]. 1970. "Kongŏp tanji kyŏngjejŏk ŭiŭi wa uri nara ŭi kongŏp tanji chosŏng" [Economic Significance of the Industrial Complex and South Korea's Composition of Industrial Complexes]. *Chugan naeoe kyŏngje* [Weekly Domestic and Foreign Economy] 439.

Han'guk Ŭnhaeng Chosabu [Bank of Korea Research Department]. 1985. *Kyŏngje t'onggye yŏnbo* [Economics Statistics Yearbook]. Seoul: Han'guk Ŭnhaeng.

Hedström, Peter. 1994. "Contagious Collectivities: On the Spatial Diffusion of Swedish Trade Unions, 1890–1940." *American Journal of Sociology* 99 (5): 1157–79.

Bibliography 223

Hellmann, Olli. 2018. "High Capacity, Low Resilience: The 'Developmental' State and Military–Bureaucratic Authoritarianism in South Korea." *International Political Science Review* 39 (1): 67–82.

Heston, Alan, Robert Summers, and Bettina Aten. 2002. "Penn World Table Version 6.1." Philadelphia: Center for International Comparisons at the University of Pennsylvania.

Hilbe, Joseph M. 2011. *Negative Binomial Regression*. 2nd ed. Cambridge: Cambridge University Press.

Hirschman, Albert O. 1979. *Shifting Involvements: Private Interest and Public Action*. Princeton: Princeton University Press.

Ho, Samuel P. S. 1982. "Economic Development and Rural Industry in South Korea and Taiwan." *World Development* 10 (11): 973–90.

Hong, Hyŏnyŏng. 2005. "'Tosi sanŏp sŏn'gyohoe wa 1970-yŏndae nodong undong" [The Urban Industrial Mission and the 1970s Labor Movement]. In *1970-yŏndae minjung undong yŏn'gu* [Research on the 1970s Minjung Movement], edited by Sŏngwan Ch'a, Kyŏngsun Yu, Muyong Kim, Hyŏnyŏng Hong, T'aeil Kim, and Imha Yi. Seoul: Minjuhwa Undong Kinyŏm Saŏphoe.

Hong, Ji Yeon, and Sunkyoung Park. 2016. "Factories for Vote? How Dictators Gain Popular Support Using Targeted Industrial Policy." *British Journal of Political Science* 46 (3): 501–27.

Hong, Ji Yeon, Sunkyoung Park, and Hyunjoo Yang. 2022. "In Strongman We Trust: The Political Legacy of the New Village Movement in South Korea." *American Journal of Political Science* (August). https://doi.org/10.1111/ajps.12716

Hong, Sang-Wun. 2001. "Manyŏ sanyang, tosi sanŏp sŏn'gyohoe" [Witch Hunt, Urban Industrial Mission]. *Ijenŭn marhal su itta* [We Can Speak Now]. Seoul: Munhwa Broadcasting Corporation.

Huang, Chang-Ling. 1999. "Labor Militancy and the Neo-Mercantilist Development Experience: South Korea and Taiwan in Comparison." PhD diss., University of Chicago.

Huh, Sang-Soo. 1989. "Choekŭn sahoe pyŏnhyŏk undong kwa nodong undong" [The Recent Social Movements and the Labor Movement]. In *Han'guk sahoe pyŏnhyŏk undong kwa nodong undong* [Social Movements and the Labor Movement in Korea], edited by Han'guk Kidokkyo Sahoe Kaebalwon. Seoul: Chungam Munhwasa.

Huntington, Samuel. 1968. *Political Order in Changing Societies*. New Haven: Yale University Press.

Huntington, Samuel. 1991. *The Third Wave: Democratization in the Late 20th Century*. Norman: University of Oklahoma Press.

Hwang, Ah-Ran. 2009. "Chŏngch'i sedae wa inyŏm sŏnghyang: Minjuhwa sŏngch'wi sedae rŭl chungsim ŭro" [Ideological Dispositions of the Political Generation: Its Continuity and Change in Korea]. *Kukkajŏlyak* [National Strategy] 15 (2): 123–52.

Hwang, Kyung Moon. 2017. "Great Labor Uprising of Summer 1987." *Korea Times*, August 2. https://www.koreatimes.co.kr/www/opinion/2019/04/633_234082.html

Im, Hyug Baeg. 1986. "The Rise of Bureaucratic Authoritarianism in South Korea." *World Politics* 39 (2): 231–57.

Bibliography

Im, Hyug Baeg. 2011. "The Origins of the Yushin Regime: Machiavelli Unveiled." In *The Park Chung Hee Era: The Transformation of South Korea*, edited by Byung-Kook Kim and Ezra F. Vogel. Cambridge, MA: Harvard University Press.

Im, Hyug-Baeg. 1994. *Sijang, kukka, minjujuŭi: Han'guk minjuhwa wa chŏngch'i kyŏngje iron* [The Market, the State, and Democracy: Democratic Transition in Korea and Theories of Political Economy]. Seoul: Nanam.

Im, Seong-ho. 2010. "Kukhoe ŭi yŏksajŏk pyŏnch'ŏn" [Historical Transformation of the National Assembly]. In *Han'guk kukhoe wa chŏngch'i kwajŏng* [Korean National Assembly and Its Political Process], edited by National Assembly Research Institute. Seoul: Orum.

Inch'ŏn Urban Industrial Mission. 1976. "Inch'ŏn Kidokkyo Sanŏp Sŏn'gyohoe: Sogae wa hwaltong" [Inch'ŏn Urban Industrial Mission: Introduction and Activities]. 00441922. Korea Democracy Foundation Open Archives.

Inglehart, Ronald. 1990. *Culture Shift in Advanced Industrial Society*. Princeton: Princeton University Press.

Inglehart, Ronald. 1997. *Modernization and Postmodernization*. Princeton: Princeton University Press.

Inglehart, Ronald. 2003. "How Solid Is Mass Support for Democracy—and How Can We Measure It?" *PS: Political Science & Politics* 36 (1): 51–57.

Inglehart, Ronald, and Christian Welzel. 2005. *Modernization, Cultural Change, and Democracy: The Human Sequence*. Cambridge: Cambridge University Press.

Inglehart, Ronald, and Christian Welzel. 2009. "How Does Development Lead to Democracy? What We Know about Modernization." *Foreign Affairs* 88 (2): 33–48.

Inkeles, Alex. 1969. "Participant Citizenship in Six Developing Countries." *American Political Science Review* 63 (4): 1120–41.

Jackman, Robert W. 1973. "On the Relations of Economic Development to Democratic Performance." *American Journal of Political Science* 17 (3): 611–21.

Jennings, M. Kent. 1987. "Residue of a Movement: The Aging of the American Protest Generation." *American Political Science Review* 81 (2): 367–82.

Jeong, Taek-su. 2008. "Chigŏp nŭngnyŏk kaebal chedo ŭi pyŏnch'ŏn kwa kwaje" [Changes and Challenges of the Vocational Competency Development System]. Seoul: Korea Research Institute for Vocational Education and Training.

Joffe, Marshall M., and Tom Greene. 2009. "Related Causal Frameworks for Surrogate Outcomes." *Biometrics* 65 (2): 530–38.

Johnson, Chalmers. 1982. *MITI and the Japanese Miracle*. Stanford: Stanford University Press.

Jones, Leroy, and Il Sakong. 1990. *Government, Business, and Entrepreneurship in Economic Development: The Korean Case*. Cambridge, MA: Harvard University Press.

JoongAng Ilbo. 2008. "Pak Chŏng-hŭi ga sŏllip'an Pusan kigongŭn ŏttŏn hakkyo?" [What Kind of School Is Pusan Mechanical High School, a School Founded by Park Chung Hee?], August 12. https://news.joins.com/article/3257317

JoongAng Ilbo. 2019. "Korea Is 386ers' Nation." *Joongang Ilbo*, September 23. https://www.joongang.co.kr/article/23583819

Jung, Heon Joo. 2010. "The Rise and Fall of Anti-American Sentiment in South Korea: Deconstructing Hegemonic Ideas and Threat Perception." *Asian Survey* 50 (5): 946–64.

Kang, Hyun-kyung. 2015. "Sweatshop Workers Laid Foundation for 'Miracle on Han River.'" *Korea Times*, September 11. http://www.koreatimes.co.kr/www/nation/2019/08/113_186627.html

Kang, Sin-ch'ŏl. 1988. *80-yŏndae haksaeng undongsa: Sasang iron kwa chojik nosŏn ŭl chungsim ŭro* [The History of the Student Movement in the 1980s: Ideological Theories and Organizational Guidelines]. Seoul: Hyŏngsŏngsa.

Kang, Won-Taek. 2009. "386 sedaenŭn ŏdiro kanna? 2007-yŏn taesŏn kwa 2008-yŏn ch'ongsŏn esŏŭi inyŏm kwa sedae" [Where Are the '386 Generation'? The Ideologies and the Generations in the 17th Presidential Election and the 18th General Election]. In *Pyŏnhwahanŭn Han'guk yugwŏnja 3* [Changing Korean Voters 3], edited by Nae-Young Lee and Min-Jun Kim. Seoul: EAI.

Kang, Woojin. 2016a. "Democratic Performance and Park Chung-hee Nostalgia in Korean Democracy." *Asian Perspective* 40 (1): 51–78.

Kang, Woojin. 2016b. "The Past Is Long-Lasting: Park Chung Hee Nostalgia and Voter Choice in the 2012 Korean Presidential Election." *Journal of Asian and African Studies* 53 (2): 233–49.

Kang, Woojin, and Mun Gu Kang. 2014. "Yi Myŏngbak chŏngbu wa Han'guk minjujuŭi ŭi chil: Bubun ch'eje chŏpkŭn bŏbŭl chungsim ŭro" [The Lee Myung-bak Government and the Quality of Democracy in Korea: Focusing on the Partial Regimes Approach]. *Kyŏngjewa Sahoe* [Economy and Society] 104: 265–98.

Kennedy, Ryan. 2010. "The Contradiction of Modernization: A Conditional Model of Endogenous Democratization." *Journal of Politics* 72 (3): 785–98.

Kim, Byung-Kook. 1987. "Bringing and Managing Socioeconomic Change: The State in Korea and Mexico." PhD diss., Harvard University.

Kim, Charles. 2017. *Youth for Nation: Culture and Protest in Cold War South Korea.* Honolulu: University of Hawaii Press.

Kim, Chŏng-ho. 2015. *Kkŭnnaji anŭn chŏhang, 1985–2015: T'ongil-S&T chunggongŏp nojo undong 30-yŏnsa* [The Unending Struggle, 1985–2015: The 30-Year History of T'ongil-S&T Heavy Industries]. Seoul: Hannae.

Kim, Eun Mee, and Gil-Sung Park. 2011. "The Chaebol." In *The Park Chung Hee Era: The Transformation of South Korea*, edited by Byung-Kook Kim and Ezra F. Vogel. Cambridge, MA: Harvard University Press.

Kim, Hagyŏng, and Mach'ang Noryŏnsa Palgan Wiwŏnhoe [The Publishing Committee on the History of the Council of Masan and Ch'angwŏn Unions]. 1999. *Nae sarang mach'ang noryŏn* [My Love, Trade Union Confederation in Masan-Ch'angwŏn]. Seoul: Kalmuri.

Kim, Hyung-A. 2013. "Industrial Warriors: South Korea's First Generation of Industrial Workers in Post-Development Korea." *Asian Studies Review* 37 (4): 577–95.

Kim, Hyung-A. 2015. "South Korea's Skilled Workers of the 1970s: Pioneers of Korea's Industrialization." *Journal of Contemporary Korean Studies* 2 (1): 57–79.

Kim, Hyung-A. 2020. *Korean Skilled Workers: Toward a Labor Aristocracy.* Seattle: University of Washington Press.

Kim, Hyung-ki. 1988. *Han'guk ŭi tokchŏm chabon kwa imkŭm nodong* [Monopoly Capital and Wage Labor in South Korea]. Seoul: Kkachi.

Kim, Jisŏn. 2009. "Kim Chisŏn Interview Transcript (Interviewer Yi Kyŏngŭn)." Korea Democracy Foundation Open Archives.

226　　Bibliography

Kim, Jiyoon, Karl Friedhoff, Chungku Kang, and Euicheol Lee. 2015. "South Korean Attitudes toward North Korea and Reunification." Seoul: Asan Institute for Policy Studies.

Kim, Jiyun, and Hee Sun Kim. 2013. "Globalization and Access to Higher Education in Korea." In *Fairness in Access to Higher Education in a Global Perspective: Reconciling Excellence, Efficiency, and Justice*, edited by Maia Chankesellani, Heinz-Dieter Meyer, Edward P. St. John, and Lina Uribe. Rotterdam: Sense Publishers.

Kim, Jun. 1993. "Asia kwŏnwijuŭi kukka ŭi nodong chŏngch'i wa nodong undong" [Labor Politics and Labor Movements in Asian Authoritarian States]. PhD diss., Seoul National University.

Kim, Jung. 2018. "South Korean Democratization: A Comparative Empirical Appraisal." In *Routledge Handbook of Democratization in East Asia*, edited by Tunjen Cheng and Yun-han Chu. Abingdon, Oxon: Routledge.

Kim, Seong-kon. 2020. "True Meanings of Progressivism and Conservatism." *Korea Herald*, January 14. https://www.koreaherald.com/view.php?ud=202001 13000821

Kim, Seung-kyung. 1997. *Class Struggle or Family Struggle? The Lives of Women Factory Workers in South Korea*. Cambridge: Cambridge University Press.

Kim, Sookyung, Paul Y. Chang, and Gi-Wook Shin. 2013. "Past Activism, Party Pressure, and Ideology: Explaining the Vote to Deploy Korean Troops to Iraq." *Mobilization: An International Quarterly* 18 (3): 243–66.

Kim, Sun-Chul. 2016. *Democratization and Social Movements in South Korea: Defiant Institutionalization*. Abingdon, Oxon: Routledge.

Kim, Sungmoon. 2014. *Confucian Democracy in East Asia: Theory and Practice*. New York: Cambridge University Press.

Kim, Sungmoon. 2018. "Candlelight for Our Country's Right Name: A Confucian Interpretation of South Korea's Candlelight Revolution." *Religions* 9 (11): 330.

Kim, Sunhyuk. 2000. *The Politics of Democratization in Korea: The Role of Civil Society*. Pittsburgh: University of Pittsburgh Press.

Kim, Sunhyuk. 2009. "Civic Engagement and Democracy in South Korea." *Korean Observer* 40 (1): 1–26.

Kim, Sunhyuk. 2012. "'Contentious Democracy' in South Korea." *Taiwan Journal of Democracy* 8 (2): 51–61.

Kim, Won. 2004. "1970-yŏndae 'yŏgong' ŭi munhwa: Minju nojo saŏpchang ŭi kisuksa wa somoim munhwa rŭl chungsim ŭro" [The Culture of 'Factory Girls' in the 1970s: On Factory Dormitories and Small Group Culture]. *Feminism yŏn'gu* [Feminism Studies] 4 (1): 101–48.

Kim, Won. 2005. "1970-yŏndae kat'ollik nodong ch'ŏngnyŏnhoe wa nodong undong" [The Young Catholic Workers and the Labor Movement in the 1970s]. In *1970-yŏndae minjung undong yŏn'gu* [Research on the 1970s Minjung Movement], edited by Sŏngwan Ch'a, Kyŏngsun Yu, Muyong Kim, Hyŏnyŏng Hong, T'aeil Kim, and Imha Yi. Seoul: Minjuhwa Undong Kinyŏm Saŏphoe.

Kim, Won. 2006. *Yŏgong 1970, kŭnyŏdŭl ŭi pan yŏksa* [1970 Factory Girls: A Counterhistory]. Seoul: Imaejin.

Kim, Won. 2015. *Karibong ogŏri* [Karibong Five-Way Intersection]. Seoul: Sŏul Yŏksa Pangmulgwan [Seoul Museum of History].

Kim, Won. 2016. "Between Autonomy and Productivity: The Everyday Lives of Korean Women Workers during the Park Chung-hee Era." In *Everyday Life in Mass Dictatorship*, edited by Alf Lüdtke. London: Palgrave Macmillan.

Kim, Wonik, and Jennifer Gandhi. 2010. "Coopting Workers under Dictatorship." *Journal of Politics* 72 (3): 646–58.

Kim, Yŏngmi. 2005. "Kim Yŏngmi Interview Transcript (Interviewer Yu Kyŏngsun)." Korea Democracy Foundation Open Archives.

Kim, Young Jak. 2011. "Park Chung Hee's Governing Ideas: Impact on National Consciousness and Identity." In *Reassessing the Park Chung Hee Era, 1961–1979: Development, Political Thought, Democracy, and Cultural Influence*, edited by Hyung-A Kim and Clark W. Sorenson. Seattle: University of Washington Press.

Kim, Yun-t'ae. 2002. "Han'guk injŏk chawŏn kaebal chŏngch'aek ŭi punsŏk mit p'yŏngga 1962–2002" [An Analysis and Assessment of Korea's Human Resource Development Policy, 1962–2002]. Seoul: Han'guk Chigŏp Nŭngnyŏk Kaebarwŏn [Korea Research Institute for Vocational Education and Training].

Kitschelt, Herbert P. 1986. "Political Opportunity Structures and Political Protest: Anti-Nuclear Movements in Four Democracies." *British Journal of Political Science* 16 (1): 57–85.

Klandermans, Bert. 1997. *The Social Psychology of Protest*. Cambridge: Blackwell.

Knutsen, Carl Henrik, John Gerring, Svend-Erik Skaaning, Jan Teorell, Matthew Maguire, Michael Coppedge, and Staffan I. Lindberg. 2019. "Economic Development and Democracy: An Electoral Connection." *European Journal of Political Research* 58 (1): 292–314.

Knutsen, Carl Henrik, Håvard Mokleiv Nygård, and Tore Wig. 2017. "Autocratic Elections: Stabilizing Tool or Force for Change?" *World Politics* 69 (1): 98–143.

Ko, Insi. 2002. "Ko Insi Interview Transcript (Interviewer Yun Taeklim), Han'guk sanŏp nodongja ŭi hyŏngsŏng kwa saenghwal segye yŏn'gu" [Research on the Formation and Life-World of Industrial Workers]. Seoul: Songkonghoe University Center for Culture and Information Studies.

Kohli, Atul. 1994. "Where Do High Growth Political Economies Come From? The Japanese Lineage of Korea's 'Developmental State.'" *World Development* 22 (9): 1269–93.

Kohli, Atul. 1997. "Japanese Colonialism and Korean Development: A Reply." *World Development* 25 (6): 883–88.

Kohli, Atul. 2004. *State-Directed Development: Political Power and Industrialization in the Global Periphery*. Cambridge: Cambridge University Press.

Kong, Kye-chin. 2005. "Kong Kyejin Interview Transcript (Interviewer Yu Kyŏngsun)." Korea Democracy Foundation Open Archives.

Kŏnsŏlbu [Ministry of Construction]. 1969. *Han'guk ŭi hangman* [Ports in Korea]. Seoul: Kŏnsŏlbu.

Koo, Hagen. 1991. "Middle Classes, Democratization, and Class Formation: The Case of South Korea." *Theory and Society* 20 (4): 485–509.

Koo, Hagen. 2001. *Korean Workers: The Culture and Politics of Class Formation*. Ithaca: Cornell University Press.

Koo, Hagen. 2011. "Labor Policy and Labor Relations during the Park Chung Hee Era." In *Reassessing the Park Chung Hee Era, 1961–1979: Development, Political*

228   *Bibliography*

Thought, Democracy, and Cultural Influence, edited by Hyung-A Kim and Clark W. Sorenson. Seattle: University of Washington Press.

Korea Exposé. 2017. "What 'Progressive' Means in South Korea." *Korea Exposé*. https://www.koreaexpose.com/progressive-meaning-south-korea/

Kornhauser, William. 1959. *The Politics of Mass Society*. Glencoe, IL: Free Press.

Kurzman, Charles. 1996. "Structural Opportunity and Perceived Opportunity in Social Movement Theory." *American Sociological Review* 61 (1): 153–70.

Kwŏn, Yŏngmok. 1988. "Hyŏndae Kŭrup nodong undongsa" [The History of the Labor Movement at Hyundai Group]. *Saepyŏk* [Dawn] 3: 285-303.

Kyŏnghyang Sinmun. 1985. "Taehaksaeng 3-baek yŏmyŏng siwi ŏje Chongnosŏ, 28-myŏng yŏnhaeng" [300 College Students Protest in Chongno Yesterday, 28 Taken to the Police Station]. February 9. Naver News Library.

Kyŏngje Kihoegwŏn [Economic Planning Board]. 1963. *1960 in'gu chut'aek kukse chosa pogo* [1960 Population and Housing Census of Korea]. Seoul: Kyŏngje Kihoegwŏn.

Kyŏngje Kihoegwŏn [Economic Planning Board]. 1987a. *1985 in'gu mit chut'aek sensŏsŭ pogo* [1985 Population and Housing Census Report]. Seoul: Kyŏngje Kihoegwŏn Chosa T'onggyeguk.

Kyŏngje Kihoegwŏn [Economic Planning Board]. 1987b. *Kwanggongŏp t'onggye chosa pogosŏ* [Mining and Manufacturing Census Report]. Seoul: Kyŏngje Kihoegwŏn.

Lankov, Andrei. 2008. "Fiascos of 386 Generation." *Korea Times*, February 5. http://www.koreatimes.co.kr/www/news/special/2008/12/180_18529.html

Lankov, Andrei. 2017. "Conservatives vs. Progressives." *Korea Times*, May 28. https://www.koreatimes.co.kr/www/nation/2019/04/304_230176.html

Lee, HyunChool. 2018. "Silver Generation's Counter-Movement in the Information Age: Korea's Pro-Park Rallies." *Korea Observer* 49 (3): 465–91.

Lee, Ju-Ho, and Soong Chang Hong. 2014. "2013 Modularization of Korea's Development Experience: The Development of Vocational High Schools in Korea during the Industrialization Period." Seoul: Ministry of Education and KDI School of Public Policy and Management.

Lee, Jung Bock. 2001. "The Political Process in Korea." In *Understanding Korean Politics: An Introduction*. SUNY Series in Korean Studies. Albany: SUNY Press.

Lee, Junhan. 2004. "Who Votes and Why in Korea?" *International Journal of Public Opinion Research* 16 (2): 183–98.

Lee, Junhan, and Wonjae Hwang. 2012. "Partisan Effect of Voter Turnout in Korean Elections, 1992–2010." *Asian Survey* 52 (6): 1161–82.

Lee, Kye-Woo. 2005. *Training by Small and Medium Scale Enterprises in the Knowledge Economy: A Case Study of Korea*. Seoul: Ewha Womans University Press.

Lee, Manwoo. 1990. *The Odyssey of Korean Democracy: Korean Politics, 1987–1990*. New York: Praeger.

Lee, Nae-Young. 2010. "6.2 chibang sŏn'gŏ wa sedae kyunyŏl ŭi puhwal" [6.2 Local Elections and the Revival of the Generational Rift]. In *Pyŏnhwahanŭn Han'guk yugwŏnja 4* [Changing Korean Voters Vol. 4], edited by Nae-Young Lee and Seong-Hak Lim. Seoul: EAI.

Lee, Nae-Young. 2014. "Politics of Polarization and Democracy in South Korea." Asian Barometer Working Paper Series No. 103. A Comparative Survey of

Democracy, Governance and Development. Taipei: National Taiwan University, Asian Barometer.

Lee, Nam Young. 2008. "Chiyŏkchuŭi wa sedae galtŭng: Che 17-tae taet'ongnyŏng sŏn'gŏ rŭl chungsim ŭro" [Regionalism and Generational Conflict: The 17th Presidential Election]. *P'yŏnghwahak yŏn'gu* [The Journal of Peace Studies] 9 (3): 283–305.

Lee, Namhee. 2005. "Representing the Worker: The Worker-Intellectual Alliance of the 1980s in South Korea." *Journal of Asian Studies* 64 (4): 911–37.

Lee, Namhee. 2007. *The Making of Minjung: Democracy and the Politics of Representation in South Korea*. Ithaca: Cornell University Press.

Lee, Namhee. 2009. "The Theory of Mass Dictatorship: A Reexamination of the Park Chung Hee Period." *Review of Korean Studies* 12 (3): 41–69.

Lee, Sook-Jong. 2005. "Democratization and Polarization in Korean Society." *Asian Perspective* 29 (3): 99–125.

Lee, Soo-Won. 1994. *Hyŏndae Kŭrup nodong undong: Kŭ kyŏkdong ŭi yŏksa* [The Labor Movement at Hyundai Group: The History of the Great Upheaval]. Seoul: Daeryuk.

Lee, Yoonkyung. 2009. "Democracy with Parties? Political Parties and Social Movements for Democratic Representation in Korea." *Korea Observer* 40 (1): 27–52.

Lee, Yoonkyung. 2011. *Militants or Partisans: Labor Unions and Democratic Politics in Korea and Taiwan*. Stanford: Stanford University Press.

Lee, Yoonkyung. 2014. "Diverging Patterns of Democratic Representation in Korea and Taiwan: Political Parties and Social Movements." *Asian Survey* 54 (3): 419–44.

Lehoucq, Fabrice, and Ivan Molina. 2002. *Stuffing the Ballot Box: Fraud, Electoral Reform, and Democratization in Costa Rica*. New York: Cambridge University Press.

Lemke, Douglas, and William Reed. 2001. "The Relevance of Politically Relevant Dyads." *Journal of Conflict Resolution* 45 (1): 125–44.

Lerner, Daniel. 1958. *The Passing of Traditional Society: Modernizing the Middle East*. Glencoe, IL: Free Press.

Levitsky, Steven, and Lucan Way. 2005. "International Linkage and Democratization." *Journal of Democracy* 16 (3): 20–34.

Levitsky, Steven, and Lucan Way. 2010. *Competitive Authoritarianism: Hybrid Regimes after the Cold War*. Cambridge: Cambridge University Press.

Levitsky, Steven, and Daniel Ziblatt. 2018. *How Democracies Die*. New York: Crown.

Lijphart, Arend. 1997. "Unequal Participation: Democracy's Unresolved Dilemma." *American Political Science Review* 91 (1): 1–14.

Lindberg, Staffan I. 2006a. *Democracy and Elections in Africa*. Baltimore: Johns Hopkins University Press.

Lindberg, Staffan I. 2006b. "The Surprising Significance of Elections in Africa." *Journal of Democracy* 17 (1): 139–51.

Linz, Juan J., and Alfred C. Stepan. 1996. "Toward Consolidated Democracies." *Journal of Democracy* 7 (2): 14–33.

Lipset, Seymour Martin. 1959. "Some Social Prerequisites of Democracy: Economic Development and Political Legitimacy." *American Political Science Review* 53 (1): 69–105.

Lipset, Seymour Martin. 1963. *Political Man: The Social Bases of Politics*. Garden City, NY: Doubleday.

Liu, Hwa-Jen. 2015. *Leverage of the Weak: Labor and Environmental Movements in Taiwan and South Korea*. Minneapolis: University of Minnesota Press.

Lo, William Yat Wai. 2014. *University Rankings: Implications for Higher Education in Taiwan*. Singapore: Springer.

Londregan, John B., and Keith T. Poole. 1990. "Poverty, the Coup Trap, and the Seizure of Executive Power." *World Politics* 42 (2): 151–83.

Loxton, James. 2015. "Authoritarian Successor Parties." *Journal of Democracy* 26 (3): 157–70.

Lust-Okar, Ellen. 2006. "Elections under Authoritarianism: Preliminary Lessons from Jordan." *Democratization* 13 (3): 456–71.

Lust-Okar, Ellen. 2009. "Competitive Clientelism in the Middle East." *Journal of Democracy* 20 (3): 122–35.

Lust-Okar, Ellen, and Amaney Jamal. 2002. "Rulers and Rules: Re-Assessing the Influence of Regime Type on Electoral Law Formations." *Comparative Political Studies* 35 (3): 337–66.

Ma, Kyoung Hee, and Hye-Kyung Kim. 2015. "Collective Memory and Formation of the 'Unconscious' Political Generation: Focusing on the Former Period Baby Boomers in Korea." *Development and Society* 44 (1): 77–116.

Maeil Kyŏngje Sinmun [Maeil Business Newspaper]. 1987. *Hoesa yŏn'gam* [Company Yearbook]. Seoul: Maeil Kyŏngje Shinmunsa.

Magaloni, Beatriz. 2006. *Voting for Autocracy: Hegemonic Party Survival and Its Demise in Mexico*. Cambridge: Cambridge University Press.

Magaloni, Beatriz. 2010. "The Game of Electoral Fraud and the Ousting of Authoritarian Rule." *American Journal of Political Science* 54 (3): 751–65.

Magaloni, Beatriz, and Ruth Kricheli. 2010. "Political Order and One-Party Rule." *Annual Review of Political Science* 13: 123–43.

Mainwaring, Scott. 1999. *Rethinking Party Systems in the Third Wave of Democratization*. Stanford: Stanford University Press.

Mainwaring, Scott, and Timothy Scully. 1995. *Building Democratic Institutions: Party Systems in Latin America*. Stanford: Stanford University Press.

Mannheim, Karl. 1952. "The Problem of Generations." In *Essays on the Sociology of Knowledge*, edited by Paul Kecskemeti. London: Routledge and Kegan Paul.

Marshall, Monty, Keith Jaggers, and Ted Robert Gurr. 2003. "POLITY IV Project." http://www.systemicpeace.org/polity/polity4.htm

Mason, Edward S., Mahn J. E. Kim, Dwight H. Perkins, Kwang Suk Kim, David C. Cole, Leroy Jones, Il Sakong, Donald R. Snodgrass, and Noel F. McGinn. 1980. *The Economic and Social Modernization of the Republic of Korea*. 1st ed. Cambridge, MA: Harvard University Asia Center.

McAdam, Doug. 1982. *Political Process and the Development of Black Insurgency, 1930–1970*. Chicago: University of Chicago Press.

McAdam, Doug. 1988. *Freedom Summer*. Chicago: University of Chicago Press.

McAdam, Doug. 2017. "Social Movement Theory and the Prospect for Climate Change Activism in the United States." *Annual Review of Political Science* 20: 189–208.

McAdam, Doug, John D. McCarthy, and Mayer N. Zald, eds. 1996. *Comparative*

Bibliography 231

Perspectives on Social Movements: Political Opportunities, Mobilizing Structures, and Cultural Framings. Cambridge Studies in Comparative Politics. Cambridge: Cambridge University Press.

McAdam, Doug, and Ronnelle Paulsen. 1993. "Specifying the Relationship between Social Ties and Activism." *American Journal of Sociology* 99 (3): 640–67.

McAdam, Doug, and Sidney Tarrow. 2010. "Ballots and Barricades: On the Reciprocal Relationship between Elections and Social Movements." *Perspectives on Politics* 8 (2): 529–42.

McAdam, Doug, Sydney Tarrow, and Charles Tilly. 2012. *Dynamics of Contention.* Cambridge: Cambridge University Press.

Merriam-Webster. 2021. "There Is Strength in Numbers." https://www.merriam -webster.com/dictionary/there%20is%20strength%20in%20numbers

Meyer, David S. 2004. "Protest and Political Opportunities." *Annual Review of Sociology* 30: 125–45.

Michelson, William H. 1976. *Man and His Urban Environment: A Sociological Approach.* Reading: Addison-Wesley.

Miller, Michael K. 2012. "Economic Development, Violent Leader Removal, and Democratization." *American Journal of Political Science* 56 (4): 1002–20.

Miller, Warren E. 1992. "The Puzzle Transformed: Explaining Declining Turnout." *Political Behavior* 14 (1): 1–40.

Miller, Warren E., and J. Merrill Shanks. 1996. *The New American Voter.* Cambridge, MA: Harvard University Press.

Minjuhwa Undong Kinyŏm Saophoe [Korea Democracy Foundation]. 2006. *Han'guk minjuhwa undongsa yŏnp'yo* [Timeline of the Korean Democracy Movement]. Seoul: Minjuhwa Undong Kinyŏm Saŏphoe.

Minjuhwa Undong Kinyŏm Saophoe [Korea Democracy Foundation]. 2010. *Han'guk minjuhwa undongsa: Sŏul ŭi pom put'ŏ munmin chŏngbu surip kkaji* [History of the Korean Democratization Movement: From the Spring of Seoul to the Establishment of the Civil Government]. Vol. 3. Paju: Dolbegae.

Minns, John. 2006. *The Politics of Developmentalism: The Midas States of Mexico, South Korea and Taiwan.* International Political Economy Series. Basingstoke: Palgrave Macmillan.

Mobrand, Erik. 2019. *Top-Down Democracy in South Korea.* Seattle: University of Washington Press.

Moon, Jae-in. 2019. "Opening Remarks by President Moon Jae-in at New Year Press Conference." January 10. https://www.korea.net/Government/Briefing -Room/Presidential-Speeches/view?articleId=167057

Moon, Seungsook. 2009. "The Cultural Politics of Remembering Park Chung Hee." *Asia-Pacific Journal: Japan Focus* 7, no. 19 (5). https://apjjf.org/-Seungso ok-Moon/3140/article.html

Moore, Barrington. 1966. *Social Origins of Dictatorship and Democracy: Lord and Peasant in the Making of the Modern World.* Boston: Beacon Press.

Morgenbesser, Lee, and Thomas Pepinsky. 2019. "Elections as Causes of Democratization: Southeast Asia in Comparative Perspective." *Comparative Political Studies* 52 (1): 3–35.

Muller, Edward N. 1985. "Income Inequality, Regime Repression, and Political Violence." *American Sociological Review* 50 (1): 47–61.

Munck, Gerardo L. 2018. "Modernization Theory as a Case of Failed Knowledge Production." *Annals of Comparative Democratization* 16 (3): 37–41.

Mun'gyobu [Ministry of Education]. 1965. *Kyoyuk t'onggye yŏnbo* [Statistical Yearbook of Education]. Seoul: Mun'gyobu.

Mun'gyobu [Ministry of Education]. 1987. *Kyoyuk t'onggye yŏnbo* [Statistical Yearbook of Education]. Seoul: Mun'gyobu.

Nakamura, Takayasu. 2003. "Educational Aspirations and the Warming-Up/Cooling Down Process: A Comparative Study between Japan and South Korea." *Social Science Japan Journal* 6 (2): 199–220.

Nakamura, Takayasu. 2005. "Educational System and Parental Education Fever in Contemporary Japan: Comparison with the Case of South Korea." *KEDI Journal of Educational Policy* 2 (1): 25–49.

Nam, Hwasook Bergquist. 2009. *Building Ships, Building a Nation: Korea's Democratic Unionism under Park Chung Hee*. Seattle: University of Washington Press.

Nam, Jeong-Lim. 2000. "Gender Politics in Transition to Democracy." *Korean Studies* 24: 94–112.

Nathan, Andrew J. 2016. "The Puzzle of the Chinese Middle Class." *Journal of Democracy* 27 (2): 5–19.

National Museum of Korean Contemporary History. 2018. *The 1987 Korean Democratization Movement in Retrospective: A Critical Oral History*. Seoul: National Museum of Korean Contemporary History.

Neundorf, Anja, and Kaat Smets. 2017. "Political Socialization and the Making of Citizens." In *Oxford Handbook Online in Political Science*. Oxford: Oxford University Press.

Newcomb, Theodore M. 1961. *Acquaintance Process*. New York: Holt, Rinehart & Winston.

Nodongch'ŏng [Office of Labor Affairs]. 1973. *Yŏsŏng chejoŏp shilt'ae josa pogosŏ: Chejoŏpch'e, unsuŏpch'e chungshim ŭro* [Report on Women in Manufacturing: Focusing on Manufacturing and Transportation Companies]. Seoul: Nodongch'ŏng.

Noh, Hwanhee, Jungmin Song, and Won-Taek Kang. 2013a. "Generation Effects Remain Salient? An Analysis of the South Korean Presidential Elections between 1997 and 2012." *Korean Party Studies Review* 12 (1): 113–40.

Noh, Hwanhee, Jungmin Song, and Won-Taek Kang. 2013b. "Sedae kyunyŏl e taehan koch'al: Sedae hyogwa in'ga yŏllyŏng hyogwa in'ga" [Considerations on the Generational Cleavage: Is It the Generation Effect or the Age Effect]. In *2012-yŏn taet'ongnyŏng sŏn'gŏ punsŏk* [Analysis of the 2012 Presidential Election], edited by Chan Wook Park and Won-Taek Kang. Seoul: Nanam.

Oberschall, Anthony. 1996. "Opportunities and Framing in the Eastern European Revolts of 1989." In *Comparative Perspectives on Social Movements: Political Opportunity Structures, Mobilizing Structures, and Cultural Framings*, edited by Doug McAdam, John D. McCarthy, and Mayer N. Zald. Cambridge: Cambridge University Press.

O'Donnell, Guillermo, Philippe C. Schmitter, and Laurence Whitehead, eds. 1986. *Transitions from Authoritarian Rule: Comparative Perspectives*. Baltimore: Johns Hopkins University Press.

Ogle, George E. 1990. *South Korea: Dissent within the Economic Miracle*. London: Zed Books.

Oh, John Kie-chiang. 1999. *Korean Politics: The Quest for Democratization and Economic Development*. Ithaca: Cornell University Press.

Oh, Saejae. 2015. "386-sedae sedae hyogwa ŭi t'ŭkching yŏn'gu: Sedae hyogwa ŭi chogŏnjŏk p'yoch'urŭl chungsim ŭro" [Analysis of the Characteristics of the 386-Generation: Focusing on the Conditional Effect of the Generation]. *21-segi chŏngch'i hakhoebo* [21st Century Political Science Review] 25 (1): 133–64.

Oh, Saejae, and Hyeon-Woo Lee. 2014. "386-sedae ŭi chogŏnjŏk sedae hyogwa: inyŏm sŏnghyang kwa taesŏn t'up'yo rŭl chungsim ŭro" [Conditional Effects of the 386 Generation: Focusing on Political Ideology and Voting Decisions in Presidential Elections]. *Ŭijŏng yŏn'gu* [Korean Journal of Legislative Studies] 20 (1): 199–230.

Opp, Karl-Dieter, and Christiane Gern. 1993. "Dissident Groups, Personal Networks, and Spontaneous Cooperation—the East-German Revolution of 1989." *American Sociological Review* 58 (5): 659–80.

Orru, Marco, Nicole Woosely Biggart, and Gary G. Hamilton. 1997. *The Economic Organization of East Asian Capitalism*. Thousand Oaks, CA: Sage.

Pak, Chŏng-hŭi. 1972. "Sinnyŏn Mesiji" [New Year's Message]. In *Pak Chŏng-hŭi taet'ongnyŏng yŏnsŏl munjip* [Collection of President Park Chung Hee's Speeches], 9:24–25. Seoul: Taet'ongnyŏng Pisŏsil.

Pak, Hyŏn-jung. 2003. "T'onggye ro pon chungdŭng kyoyuk" [Secondary Education Viewed through Statistics]. Seoul: Korean Educational Development Institute.

Pan, Jennifer. 2020. *Welfare for Autocrats: How Social Assistance in China Cares for Its Rulers*. New York: Oxford University Press.

Pang, Yŏngsŏk. 2010. "Pang Yongsŏk Interview Transcript (Interviewer Im Songja)." Korea Democracy Foundation Open Archives.

Park, Chan Wook. 2008. "Sahoe kyunyŏl kwa t'up'yo sŏnt'aek: Chiyŏk, sedae, inyŏm ŭi yŏnghyang" [Social Rift and Voting Choice: Influence of Region, Generation, and Ideology]. In *Pyŏnhwa hanŭn Han'guk yugwŏnja 3* [Changing Korean Voters 3], edited by Meen-Geon Kim and Nae-Young Lee. Seoul: EAI.

Park, Chung Hee. 1966. "The 8th Labor Day." Speech, March 10. http://pa.go.kr/research/contents/speech/index.jsp

Park, Chung Hee. 1979. *Saemaul: Korea's New Community Movement*. Seoul: Korea Textbook Co.

Park, Jaehoo. 2011. "The Conservatization of the 386 Generation: Cohort Effects in Voting Behavior of a Political Generation in South Korea." Sanford School of Public Policy, Duke University.

Park, Kyungmee. 2010. "Party Mergers and Splits in New Democracies: The Case of South Korea (1987–2007)." *Government and Opposition* 45 (4): 531–52.

Park, Mi. 2005. "Organizing Dissent against Authoritarianism: The South Korean Student Movement in the 1980s." *Korean Journal* 45 (3): 262–89.

Park, Mi. 2008. *Democracy and Social Change: A History of South Korean Student Movements, 1980–2000*. Bern: Peter Lang.

Park, Mi. 2012. "South Korea: Passion, Patriotism, and Student Radicalism." In *Student Activism in Asia: Between Protest and Powerlessness*, edited by Meredith L. Weiss and Edward Aspinall. Minneapolis: University of Minnesota Press.

Park, Myung-Ho. 2009. "2008 Ch'ongsŏnesŏ nat'anan sedae hyogwa wa yŏllyŏng hyogwae kwanhan punsŏk: 386 sedaerŭl chungsimŭro" [A Study on the Gen-

234 *Bibliography*

eration and Age Effects in the 2008 General Election: Focusing on the 386 Generation]. *Han'guk chŏngdang hakhoebo* [Korean Party Studies Review] 8 (1): 65–86.

Park, Sun-Young. 2007. "Shinsedae: Conservative Attitude of a 'New Generation' in South Korea and the Impact on the Korean Presidential Election." *East-West Center Insights* 2 (1): 1–4.

Park, Won-Ho. 2012. "Sedaegyunyŏrŭi chinhwa: '386sedae'ŭi somyŏlgwa 30tae yugwŏnja ŭi pusang" [The Evolution of the Generational Rift: The Disappearance of the '386 Generation' and the Rise of Voters in Their 30s]. In *Han'guk yukwŏnja ŭi sŏnt'aek. 1, 2012 ch'ongsŏn* [Korean Voter Choice. 1, 2012 General Election], edited by Chan Wook Park, Jiyoon Kim, and Jung-Yeop Woo. Seoul: Asan Institute for Policy Studies.

Park, Won-Ho. 2013. "Sedaeron ŭi chŏnhwan: Che 18-tae taet'ongnyŏng sŏn'gŏ wa sedae" [Transformation of Generation Theory: The 18th Presidential Election and Generation]. In *Han'guk yugwŏnja ŭi sŏnt'aek 2 (18-tae taesŏn)* [Korean Voters' Choice 2 (18th Presidential Election)], edited by Chan Wook Park, Jiyoon Kim, and Jung-Yeop Woo. Seoul: Asan Institute for Policy Studies.

Perry, Elizabeth J. 1980. *Rebels and Revolutionaries in North China, 1845–1945*. Stanford: Stanford University Press.

Perry, Elizabeth J. 1997. "From Native Place to Workplace: Labor Origins and Outcomes of China's Danwei System." In *Danwei: The Changing Chinese Workplace in Historical and Comparative Perspective*, edited by Xiaobu Lu and Elizabeth J. Perry. New York: M. E. Sharpe.

Philipp, Kuntz, and Mark Thompson. 2009. "More Than Just the Final Straw: Stolen Elections as Revolutionary Triggers." *Comparative Politics* 41 (3): 253–72.

Pierson, Paul. 2004. *Politics in Time: History, Institutions, and Social Analysis*. Princeton: Princeton University Press.

Piven, Frances Fox, and Richard A. Cloward. 1979. *Poor People's Movements: Why They Succeed and Why They Fail*. New York: Vintage Books.

Przeworski, Adam, and Fernando Limongi. 1997. "Modernization: Theories and Facts." *World Politics* 49 (2): 155–83.

Putnam, Robert D. 1994. *Making Democracy Work: Civic Traditions in Modern Italy*. Princeton: Princeton University Press.

Putnam, Robert D. 1995. "Tuning In, Tuning Out: The Strange Disappearance of Social Capital in America." *PS: Political Science & Politics* 28 (4): 664–83.

Putnam, Robert D. 2000. *Bowling Alone*. New York: Simon and Schuster.

Pye, Lucian. 1990. "Political Science and the Crisis of Authoritarianism." *American Political Science Review* 84 (1): 3–19.

Pyle, Kenneth B. 2008. "Political Generations in East Asia: The Policy Significance." In *Emerging Leaders in East Asia: The Next Generation of Political Leadership in China, Japan, South Korea, and Taiwan*, edited by Li Cheng. Seattle: National Bureau of Asian Research.

Ra, Young-Sun, and Soon-Hee Kang. 2012. "Vocational Training System for a Skilled Workforce." Seoul: Ministry of Strategy and Finance, Republic of Korea.

Radelet, Steven. 2015. "The Rise of the World's Poorest Countries." *Journal of Democracy* 26 (4): 5–19.

Robinson, Michael E. 2007. *Korea's Twentieth-Century Odyssey: A Short History*. Honolulu: University of Hawaii Press.

Rød, Espen Geelmuyden, Carl Henrik Knutsen, and Håvard Hegre. 2020. "The Determinants of Democracy: A Sensitivity Analysis." *Public Choice* 185 (1): 87–111.

Roessler, Philip G., and Marc M. Howard. 2006. "Post–Cold War Political Regimes: When Do Elections Matter?" In *Democratization by Elections*, edited by Staffan I. Lindberg. Baltimore: Johns Hopkins University Press.

Rosenfeld, Bryn. 2020. *The Autocratic Middle Class: How State Dependency Reduces the Demand for Democracy*. Princeton: Princeton University Press.

Ross, Michael L. 2012. *The Oil Curse: How Petroleum Wealth Shapes the Development of Nations*. Princeton: Princeton University Press.

Rueschemeyer, Dietrich, Evelyne Huber Stephens, and John D. Stephens. 1992. *Capitalist Development and Democracy*. Chicago: University of Chicago Press.

Rupp, Leila J., and Verta A. Taylor. 1987. *Survival in the Doldrums: The American Women's Rights Movement, 1945 to the 1960s*. Columbus: Ohio State University Press.

Ryu, Yongwook. 2013. "Does Political Generation Matter for Foreign Policy?" *Korean Journal of International Studies* 11 (1): 113–41.

Savada, Andrea Matles, and William Shaw, eds. 1990. *South Korea: A Country Study*. Washington, DC: Government Printing Office for the Library of Congress.

Schady, Norbert R. 2000. "The Political Economy of Expenditures by the Peruvian Social Fund (FONCODES), 1991–95." *American Political Science Review* 94 (2): 289–304.

Schedler, Andreas. 2001. "Taking Uncertainty Seriously: The Blurred Boundaries of Democratic Transition and Consolidation." *Democratization* 8 (4): 1–22.

Schedler, Andreas, ed. 2006. *Electoral Authoritarianism: The Dynamics of Unfree Competition*. Boulder: Lynne Rienner.

Schumpeter, Joseph. 1942. *Capitalism, Socialism, and Democracy*. New York: Harper & Brothers.

Seong, Kyuong-Ryung. 2000. "Civil Society and Democratic Consolidation in South Korea: Great Achievement and Remaining Problems." In *Consolidating Democracy in South Korea*, edited by Larry Diamond and Byung-Kook Kim. Boulder: Lynne Rienner.

Seoul Yŏksa Pangmulgwan [Seoul Museum of History]. 2013. *Karibong-dong: Kuro gongdan paehuji aesŏ tamunhwa ŭi konggan ŭro* [Karibong-Dong: From the Hinterland of the Kuro Industrial Complex to a Multicultural Space]. Seoul: Seoul Yŏksa Pangmulgwan.

Seoul Museum of History. 2015. *Research on Seoul: Garibong-Dong* [in English]. Seoul: Seoul Museum of History.

Seoul Nambu [Southern] Police. 1981. "Wonpoong Mobang kisuksaseang chiptan haengdong chosa pogo" [Research Report on the Collective Activity of Wonpoong Textiles Dormitory Members]. 00854038. Korea Democracy Foundation Open Archives.

Seth, Michael. 2002. *Education Fever: Society, Politics, and the Pursuit of Schooling in South Korea*. Honolulu: University of Hawaii Press.

Seth, Michael. 2012. "Education Zeal, State Control and Citizenship in South Korea." *Citizenship Studies* 16 (1): 13–28.

Shim, Jae-Seung, and Moosung Lee. 2008. *The Korean Economic System: Government, Big Business, and Financial Institutions*. Aldershot: Ashgate.

Shin, Doh Chull. 2012. *Confucianism and Democratization in East Asia*. New York: Cambridge University Press.

Shin, Doh Chull. 2018. "The Deconsolidation of Liberal Democracy in Korea: Exploring Its Cultural Roots." *Korea Observer* 49 (1): 107–36.

Shin, Gi-Wook. 2020. "South Korea's Democratic Decay." *Journal of Democracy* 31 (3): 100–114.

Shin, Gi-Wook, Paul Y. Chang, Jung-eun Lee, and Sookyung Kim. 2007. "South Korea's Democracy Movement (1970–1993): Stanford Korea Democracy Project Report." Stanford: Walter H. Shorenstein Asia-Pacific Center, Stanford University.

Shin, Gi-Wook, Paul Y. Chang, Jung-eun Lee, and Sookyung Kim. 2011. "The Korean Democracy Movement: An Empirical Overview." In *South Korean Social Movements: From Democracy to Civil Society*. Abingdon, Oxon: Routledge.

Shin, Gi-Wook, and Kyung Moon Hwang, eds. 2003. *Contentious Kwangju: The May 18 Uprising in Korea's Past and Present*. Lanham, MD: Rowman and Littlefield.

Shin, Gi-Wook, and Rennie J. Moon. 2017. "South Korea after Impeachment." *Journal of Democracy* 28 (4): 117–31.

Shin, Gwang-Yeong. 1994. *Kegŭp kwa nodong undong ŭi sahoehak* [The Sociology of Class and the Labor Movement]. Seoul: Nanam.

Simpser, Alberto. 2013. *Why Governments and Parties Manipulate Elections*. Cambridge: Cambridge University Press.

Siu, Kaxton, and Jonathan Unger. 2020. "Work and Family Life among Migrant Factory Workers in China and Vietnam." *Journal of Contemporary Asia* 50 (3): 341–60.

Slater, Dan. 2010. *Ordering Power: Contentious Politics and Authoritarian Leviathans in Southeast Asia*. Cambridge: Cambridge University Press.

Slater, Dan. 2012. "Southeast Asia: Strong-State Democratization in Malaysia and Singapore." *Journal of Democracy* 23 (2): 19–33.

Slater, Dan, and Sofia Fenner. 2011. "State Power and Staying Power: Infrastructural Mechanisms and Authoritarian Durability." *Journal of International Affairs* 65 (1): 15–29.

Slater, Dan, and Joseph Wong. 2013. "The Strength to Concede: Ruling Parties and Democratization in Developmental Asia." *Perspectives on Politics* 11 (3): 717–33.

Slater, Dan, and Joseph Wong. 2022. *From Development to Democracy: The Transformation of Modern Asia*. Princeton: Princeton University Press.

Snow, David A., Louis A. Zurcher, and Sheldon Ekland-Olson. 1980. "Social Networks and Social Movements: A Microstructural Approach to Differential Recruitment." *American Sociological Review* 45 (5): 787–801.

Sŏ, Chung-sŏk. 2011. *6-wŏl hangjaeng: 1987-yŏn minjung undong ŭi changŏmhan p'anorama* [The June Democratic Struggle: 1987 Minjung Movement's Grand Panorama]. Paju: Tolbegae.

Bibliography

Sommerfeldt, Chris. 2017. "Deadly Protests Break Out after the Removal of South Korea's Impeached President." Nydailynews.com, March 10. https://www.ny dailynews.com/news/world/removal-south-korea-president-triggers-deadly-pr otests-article-1.2993805

Song, Jŏngsun. 2002. "Song Jŏngsun Interview Transcript (Interviewer Shin Byŏnghyŏn), Han'guk sanŏp nodongja ŭi hyŏngsŏng kwa saenghwal segye yŏn'gu" [Research on the Formation and Life-World of Industrial Workers]. Seoul: Songkonghoe University Center for Culture and Information Studies.

Sŏng, Yubo, Dohyŏn Kim, Yŏngjun Im, Insŏng Hwang, and Yŏngshik Im. 2017. 6-wŏl hangjaeng kwa kukpon [The June Democratic Uprising and the National Headquarters for Democratic Constitution]. Seoul: Minjuhwa Undong Kinyŏm Saŏphoe.

Socialist Constitution of the Democratic People's Republic of Korea. 1972. Pyongyang: Foreign Languages Publishing House.

Sŏul Taehakkyo 60-yŏnsa P'yŏnch'an Wiwŏnhoe [Seoul National University 60 Year History Compilation Committee]. 2006. Sŏul taehakkyo 60-yŏnsa [Seoul National University since 1946]. Seoul: Sŏul Taehakkyo.

Stillerman, Joel. 2003. "Space, Strategies, and Alliances in Mobilization: The 1960 Metalworkers' and Coal Miners' Strikes in Chile." Mobilization: An International Quarterly 8 (1): 65–85.

Stites, Richard. 1982. "Small-Scale Industry in Yingge, Taiwan." Modern China 8 (2): 247–79.

Stokes, Susan C., Thad Dunning, Marcelo Nazareno, and Valeria Brusco. 2013. Brokers, Voters, and Clientelism: The Puzzle of Distributive Politics. New York: Cambridge University Press.

Suh, Doowon. 2001. "How Do Political Opportunities Matter for Social Movements? Political Opportunity, Misframing, Pseudosuccess, and Pseudofailure." Sociological Quarterly 42 (3): 437–60.

Suh, Jae-Jung. 2010. "Truth and Reconciliation in South Korea." Critical Asian Studies 42 (4): 503–24.

Svolik, Milan. 2012. The Politics of Authoritarian Rule. Cambridge: Cambridge University Press.

Tajfel, Henri, ed. 1978. Differentiation between Social Groups: Studies in the Social Psychology of Intergroup Relations. London: Academic Press.

Tajfel, Henri. 1982. "Social Psychology of Intergroup Relations." Annual Review of Psychology 33: 1–39.

Tajfel, Henri, and John C. Turner. 1979. "An Integrative Theory of Inter-Group Conflict." In The Social Psychology of Intergroup Relations, edited by William G. Austin. Monterey: Brooks Cole Publishing.

Tarrow, Sidney. 1996. "States and Opportunities: The Political Structuring of Social Movements." In Comparative Perspectives on Social Movements: Political Opportunity Structures, Mobilizing Structures, and Cultural Framings, edited by Doug McAdam, John D. McCarthy, and Mayer N. Zald. Cambridge: Cambridge University Press.

Tarrow, Sidney. 1998. Power in Movement. New York: Cambridge University Press.

Tavits, Margit. 2006. "Party System Change: Testing a Model of New Party Entry." Party Politics 12 (1): 99–119.

238 *Bibliography*

Tharoor, Ishaan. 2017. "South Korea Just Showed the World How to Do Democracy." *Washington Post*, May 10. https://www.washingtonpost.com/news/world views/wp/2017/05/10/south-korea-just-showed-the-world-how-to-do-democ racy/

Therborn, Göran. 1977. "The Rule of Capital and the Rise of Democracy." *New Left Review* 103: 3–41.

Treisman, Daniel. 2015. "Income, Democracy, and Leader Turnover." *American Journal of Political Science* 59 (4): 927–42.

Treisman, Daniel. 2018. "Triggering Democracy." *Annals of Comparative Democratization* 16 (3): 32–36.

Treisman, Daniel. 2020a. "Democracy by Mistake: How the Errors of Autocrats Trigger Transitions to Freer Government." *American Political Science Review* 114 (3): 792–810.

Treisman, Daniel. 2020b. "Economic Development and Democracy: Predispositions and Triggers." *Annual Review of Political Science* 23: 241–57.

Trejo, Guillermo. 2014. "The Ballot and the Street: An Electoral Theory of Social Protest in Autocracies." *Perspectives on Politics* 12 (2): 322–52.

Tsai, Ching-Hwa. 1996. "The Deregulation of Higher Education in Taiwan." *International Higher Education* 4.

Tucker, Joshua A. 2007. "Enough! Electoral Fraud, Collective Action Problems, and Post-Communist Colored Revolutions." *Perspectives on Politics* 5 (3): 535–51.

van de Walle, Nicolas. 2002. "Elections without Democracy: Africa's Range of Regimes." *Journal of Democracy* 13 (2): 66–80.

Vansteelandt, Sijin. 2009. "Estimating Direct Effects in Cohort and Case-Control Studies." *Epidemiology* 20 (6): 851–60.

V-Dem Institute. 2021. "Autocratization Turns Viral: Democracy Report 2021." Gothenburg: V-Dem Institute, University of Gothenburg.

Voss, Kim. 1993. *The Making of American Exceptionalism: The Knights of Labor and Class Formation in the Nineteenth Century*. Ithaca: Cornell University Press.

Wang, Ru-jer. 2003. "From Elitism to Mass Higher Education in Taiwan: The Problems Faced." *Higher Education* 46 (3): 261–87.

Wang, Yuhua. 2014. "Coercive Capacity and the Durability of the Chinese Communist State." *Communist and Post-Communist Studies* 47 (1): 13–25.

Whittier, Nancy. 2004. "The Consequences of Social Movements for Each Other." In *The Blackwell Companion to Social Movements*, edited by David A. Snow, Sarah A. Soule, and Hanspeter Kriesi. Malden, MA: Blackwell.

Whyte, William H. 1956. *Organization Man*. New York: Doubleday.

Won, Young-Mi. 2006. "1987-nyŏn ijŏn Ulsan nodongja ŭi saenghwal segye: Hyŏndae Chunggongŏp nodongja rŭl chungshim ŭro" [The Life World of Ulsan Workers before 1987: A Case of Hyundai Heavy Industries Workers]. Ulsan: Ulsan Development Institute.

Wong, Joseph. 2015. "South Korea's Weakly Institutionalized Party System." In *Party System Institutionalization in Asia: Democracies, Autocracies, and the Shadows of the Past*, edited by Allen Hicken and Erik Martinez Kuhonta. New York: Cambridge University Press.

Wonpoong Sanŏp Mobang Kongjang Kisuksa Chach'ihoe [Wonpoong Textiles

Bibliography

Dormitory Council]. 1982. "Kisuksa chach'ihoe kyujŏng" [Dormitory Council Regulations]. 00853553. Korea Democracy Foundation Open Archives.

Woo-Cumings, Meredith. 1999. *The Developmental State*. Ithaca: Cornell University Press.

Wright, Joseph. 2011. "Electoral Spending Cycles in Dictatorship." Unpublished manuscript. Pennsylvania State University.

Wright, Joseph, and Abel Escribà-Folch. 2012. "Authoritarian Institutions and Regime Survival: Transitions to Democracy and Subsequent Autocracies." *British Journal of Political Science* 42 (2): 283–309.

Wright, Teresa. 1999. "Student Mobilization in Taiwan: Civil Society and Its Discontents." *Asian Survey* 39 (6): 986–1008.

Wright, Teresa. 2012. "Taiwan: Resisting Control of Campus and Polity." In *Student Activism in Asia: Between Protest and Powerlessness*, edited by Meredith L. Weiss and Edward Aspinall. Minneapolis: University of Minnesota Press.

Xiang, Jun. 2010. "Relevance as a Latent Variable in Dyadic Analysis of Conflict." *Journal of Politics* 72 (2): 484–98.

Yeo, Andrew. 2020. "Has South Korean Democracy Hit a Glass Ceiling? Institutional-Cultural Factors and Limits to Democratic Progress." *Asian Politics & Policy* 12 (4): 539–58.

Yi, Chaeo. 2011. *Han'guk haksaeng nodongsa: 1945–1970-yŏn* [History of Korean Student Movements: 1945–1979]. Seoul: P'ara Puksŭ.

Yi, Chaesŏn. 1976. "Ŏche ŭi sŭlp'ŭm i onŭl ŭi haengpok ŭl" [Tomorrow's Sadness, Today's Happiness]. *Sanŏp kwa nodong* [Industry and Labor] 91.

Yi, Gyŏng-jae. 1987. "Minjung ŭi sŭngni: 5.17 esŏ 6.29 kkaji" [People's Victory: From 5.17 to 6.29]. *Shin Tonga*, August.

Yi, T'ae-ho, ed. 1986. "Taeu Ŏp'aerŏl nojo t'anap e taehan Kuro jiyŏk yŏndae t'ujaeng" [Solidarity Struggle in the Kuro Area regarding the Labor Repression against Daewoo Apparel]. In *Ch'oegŭn nodong undong kirok* [Recent Records of the Labor Movement]. Seoul: Ch'ŏngsa.

Yŏngdŭngp'o Sanŏp Sŏn'gyohoe 40-yŏnsa Kihoek Wiwŏnhoe [Yŏngdŭngp'o Urban Industrial Mission 40 Years History Planning Committee]. 1998. *Yŏngdŭngp'o sanŏp sŏn'gyohoe 40-yŏnsa* [40-Year History of Yŏngdŭngp'o Urban Industrial Mission]. Seoul: Yŏngdŭngp'o Sanŏp Sŏn'gyohoe.

Yoon, Sang Chul. 2009. "Sedae chŏngch'i wa chŏngch'i kyunyŏl 1997-yŏn ihu ch'urhyŏn kwa somyŏl ŭi tonghak" [Generation Politics and Political Cleavage—Appearance and Fadeout since 1997]. *Kyŏngje wa sahoe* [Economy and Society] 81: 61–88.

You, Jong-sung. 2015. *Democracy, Inequality and Corruption: Korea, Taiwan and the Philippines Compared*. Cambridge: Cambridge University Press.

Yu, Je-Ch'ŏl. 2010. "1970-yŏndae yŏsŏng nodongja ŭi yŏga sigan ŭl tullŏsan t'ujaeng" [Women Workers' Struggle Surrounding Leisure Time in the 1970s]. *Sahoe wa yŏksa* [Society and History] 85: 53–82.

Yu, Kyŏngsun. 2001. "1984-yŏn Kuro jiyŏk minju nodong undong ŭi chŏn'gae wa t'ŭkching: Kuro tongmaeng p'aŏp ŭi chuch'e hyŏngsŏng kwajŏng e taehaesŏ" [The Development and Characteristics of the 1984 Kuro-Area Democratic Union Movement: On the Progress of Subject Formation of the Kuro Solidarity Strike]. *Yŏksa yŏn'gu* [Journal of History] 9: 7–61.

240 *Bibliography*

Yu, Kyŏngsun. 2002. "1985-yŏn Kuro tongmaeng p'aŏp ŭi palsaeng kwa nodong undong yŏksajŏk wich'i" [The Origins of the 1985 Kuro Solidarity Strike and Its Historical Position]. *Yŏksa yŏn'gu* [Journal of History] 11: 109–48.

Yu, Kyŏngsun. 2006. "Kongjang ŭro kan chisigin, Kuro tongmaeng p'aŏp kwa nodong undong" [Intellectuals Who Went to the Factories: Kuro Solidarity Strike and the Labor Movement]. *Naeil rŭl yŏnŭn yŏksa* [History That Opens Tomorrow] 25: 200–227.

Yun, Hyeryŏn. 2005. "Yun Hyeryŏn Interview Transcript (Interviewer Yu Kyŏngsun)." Korea Democracy Foundation Open Archives.

Zhang, Yang, and Dingxin Zhao. 2018. "The Ecological and Spatial Contexts of Social Movements." In *The Wiley Blackwell Companion to Social Movements*, edited by David A. Snow, Sarah A. Soule, Hanspeter Kriesi, and Holly J. McCammon. Newark: John Wiley & Sons.

Zhao, Dingxin. 1998. "Ecologies of Social Movements: Student Mobilization during the 1989 Beijing Student Movement in Beijing." *American Journal of Sociology* 103 (6): 1493–1529.

Ziblatt, Daniel. 2006. "How Did Europe Democratize?" *World Politics* 58 (2): 311–38.

Ziblatt, Daniel. 2017. *Conservative Parties and the Birth of Democracy*. New York: Cambridge University Press.

Index

Act on Promoting the Development of Income Sources for Agricultural and Fishing Villages, 33
aging effects, 153
agriculture, 27–28, 33
alumni associations, 85, 106
Amsden, Alice, 90
anticommunism: and educational policy, 92; and generational differences in political attitudes, 150, 174; and labor policy, 39; and repression of Christian activists, 203n12
April Revolution of 1960, 4, 16, 112, 120, 132
Army Security Command, 206n12
Asian Barometer Survey, 170–71
Asian Financial Crisis, 4, 150, 151
Asian Games, 109
Association of Student Representatives, 131
authoritarian regime: China as, 20–21, 22–23; democratic concessions as survival strategy for, 6–7; increase in, 4; industrialization by, 2, 27–36, 180; legacy of polarization, 183–90; Taiwan as, 178. *See also* Chun Doo Hwan; co-optation; Park Chung Hee; repression

baby boomers (South Korea). *See* Yusin generation
baby boomers (US), 148

Bando Trading Company, 66, 67, 200n17, 203n13
banks, nationalization of, 102
Basic Press Law, 77, 127, 131, 133
Basic Vocational Training Act, 96–97
beef imports, 150. *See also* Candlelight protests (2008)
"beehive houses," 62
built environment. *See* ecology of industrial complexes and labor movement; ecology of student movement; housing

Candlelight generation: defined, 149, 150; and generational differences in political attitudes, 150, 151–52, 155–56, 163, 171, 172, 173
Candlelight protests (2008), 150, 151–52
"Candlelight Revolution" (2016–17), 4, 174, 184, 186, 188
Catholic Priests' Association for Justice, 130, 198n13
Cha Chich'ŏl, 203n10
chaebŏls: defined, 199n8; and industrialization, 34–36; and state management of elites, 102
Ch'angwŏn Carburetor Company, 87
Ch'angwŏn Industrial Complex: development of, 32, 52; and Great Workers' Struggle, 75, 83, 84, 85, 87–88, 106; and Kuro Solidarity Strike, 78

241

Index

Charter for National Education, 92
chemical industry. *See* heavy chemical
  industry (HCI)
Chen Shui-bian, 212n1
"chicken coop houses," 62
Chile, spatiality of social movements
  in, 56
Chin Yŏngkyu, 84
China: as authoritarian regime, 20–21,
  22–23; spatiality of social movements
  in, 56
Cho Ch'ŏlgwŏn, 78
Cho Sŭnghyŏk, 69
Cho Wha-Soon, 69, 203n12
Choi Soon-sil, 174
Ch'ŏlsan Apartment, 60, 66
Chŏn T'aeil, 200n16
Chŏng Chindong, 203n12
Ch'ŏnggye Garments, 203n13
Chŏnnam Democratic Youth Associa-
  tion, 141–42
Chonnam National University, 91, 107,
  110, 111, 115
Chosun University, 115
Christian activists, 41, 68–69, 71–74,
  77, 85
Ch'u Chaesuk, 77
Chu Yŏn-ok, 66
Chuch'e Sasangpa, 151
Chun Doo Hwan: coup, 126; economic
  policy, 2, 95–96; educational policy,
  77, 91, 95–98, 108–9, 116–18, 181;
  and elites, 206n12; and June Demo-
  cratic Uprising, 130; and Kwangju
  Massacre, 2, 70, 95, 113, 126, 151;
  labor policy, 35, 77; liberalization
  under, 12, 70, 77, 109, 120–21, 127,
  181; and 1985 National Assembly
  election, 127
Chungang University, 115
Chungnam National University, 115
civic engagement: and generational differences in political attitudes, 156–57,
  158, 165–68, 173; in Taiwan, 178–79.
  See also voter participation
civil society: and generational replacement, 147, 173; and 1985 National
  Assembly election, 121, 128, 129, 130;
  repression of under Chun, 126–27;

role in modernization theory, 3; Taiwan comparison, 180, 181–82. *See also*
  student movement
class: conflicts during colonial period,
  199n9, 200n14; consciousness and
  ecology of industrial complexes, 13,
  59, 63–66, 68, 75, 79, 82–83, 85, 88;
  consciousness and social activists, 68–
  74, 79; and education, 89, 94, 206n7;
  and geospatial patterns of development, 182; and June Democratic
  Uprising, 182, 197n3. *See also* middle
  class
coercion by state: coercive distribution
  of services and benefits, 21, 101–6,
  119; and "purification" by Chun
  regime, 126–27; and security apparatus, 35–36, 67–68, 108–9, 209n4. *See
  also* repression
cohort effects. *See* generational effects
colonial period: and anti-Japanese
  sentiment, 152; exploitation of class
  conflicts during, 199n9, 200n14;
  industrialization during, 27–28,
  206n13; labor organization during, 39;
  and moral education, 92; and night
  schools, 204n19
Committee of the Three *Min* Struggle,
  110
communism. *See* anticommunism
complexes. *See* industrial complexes
compulsory military service, 104–5
Confucian values, 106, 189, 206n7
constitution and constitutional reforms:
  and June Democratic Uprising, 1–2,
  130–32; and June 29 Declaration, 15,
  131; as master frame, 129–30, 144–45;
  and 1985 National Assembly election,
  121, 129–30; and presidential powers,
  126; and student movement, 121,
  129–30
Control Data Company, 200n17
co-optation: and democratization inflection point, 20–21; and generational
  differences in political attitudes, 146,
  147, 152, 156, 157, 173; of unions, 69.
  See also distribution, coercive
coordination, horizontal, 11
corruption, 28, 184, 187

Council of Hyundai Group, 205n29
Council of Masan and Ch'angwŏn
   Unions, 88
Council of Movement for People and
   Democracy, 209n5
Crown Electronics, 77, 200n17
cultural heritage, role in modernization
   theory, 3
curfews, 59, 60

Dae Dong Electronics, 77
Daehyup, 77
Daelim Motor Company, 87
Daewoo Apparel: first union at, 205n28;
   housing, 60; inter-union leadership
   training, 204n25; Kuro Solidarity
   Strike, 40, 77–82
Daewoo Auto Strike, 205n3
Daewoo *chaebŏl*, union federation formation at, 88
Dahl, Robert A., 14
danwei work unit system, 21
datasets, 18–19, 191–95
deaths and injuries: labor movement,
   200n16; student movement, 130,
   198n13. *See also* Kwangju Massacre
democratic consolidation: and backsliding, 183–84, 186–87, 188–89; defined,
   14; and peaceful transfer of power,
   197n2
Democratic Justice Party, 6–7, 38, 126,
   128, 197n2. *See also* Chun Doo Hwan
Democratic Korea Party, 126
Democratic Liberal Party, 197n2
Democratic Party (Minjoo), 153, 186
Democratic Progressive Party (Taiwan),
   178, 179
Democratic Republican Party, 38. *See
   also* Park Chung Hee
democratic transition, 14–15
democratization of South Korea: backsliding in, 4, 183–84, 186–87, 188–89;
   chronology of, 15; and democratic
   transition, 14–15; democratization,
   defined, 14; as example of modernization theory, 3–8, 175, 182–83; and
   generational differences in political
   attitudes, 145–50, 168–72, 173, 189;
   and geospatial patterns of develop-

ment, 8, 9–10, 176–83; and June 29
   Declaration, 1; long view of, 15; as
   mixture of from below/above, 2, 6–8;
   and peaceful transfer of power, 4;
   scholarship on, 7; and scope conditions, 20–23; Taiwan comparison, 176,
   178–83; as third-wave democracy,
   3. *See also* June Democratic Uprising; modernization theory; student
   movement; worker activism and labor
   movement
Development of Export Industrial Complexes Act, 32
dissident *(minjung)* groups: and Kuro
   Solidarity Strike, 78; and Kwangju
   Massacre, 70; *minjung* churches, 72,
   85; *minjung* term, 203n15; and 1985
   National Assembly election, 128; and
   solidarity strikes, 40
distribution, coercive, 21, 101–6, 119
Distribution of Industry Act, 33
Dongguk University, 115
Donghwan Industries, 87
Dongil Textile Company, 37, 60, 61, 66,
   67, 69, 200n17
Dongwoo/Kia Machine Tool Company,
   87
dormitories. *See* housing

Easter Service Incident, 204n21
ecology of industrial complexes and
   labor movement: in China, 22–23;
   and class consciousness, 13, 59,
   63–66, 68, 75, 79, 82–83, 85, 88;
   and concentration of workers, 55,
   58–59, 79–81, 176, 177, 180–82;
   ecological conditions, defined, 56;
   and ecology-dependent strategies,
   57, 66–68, 71–74, 75, 78–83, 106,
   176; and housing, 57, 59–68, 86–87;
   and interfirm solidarity actions and
   strikes, 57, 74–88; and leisure activities, 57, 59, 61, 65–66, 85, 205n28;
   and mobilizing structures, 12–13,
   56; overview of, 55–58; physical structure of, 60–63; and small
   group networks, 13, 56, 65–66, 68,
   69, 71–72, 82–83, 85, 88; and social
   activists, 71–74, 75, 88

244   *Index*

ecology of student movement: in China, 56; and concentration of students, 91, 106–8, 110, 134–41, 176, 177, 180–82; ecological conditions, defined, 56; and ecology-dependent strategies, 71–74, 79, 176

economic development: and education policy, 8–9, 10, 89–100; FYED Plans, 29, 31, 32–33, 93–95, 96; and GDP, 5, 28, 29; generational differences from, 149–50, 151, 152; and generational differences in political attitudes, 150, 168–72, 173, 189; industrialization under authoritarian regime, 2, 27–36, 180; nonlinear impact of, 8–14; and political polarization, 174; role in modernization theory, 3, 8–9, 11; social forces and stability of, 11–12; as stabilizing to authoritarian regime, 2, 8–9, 26, 29–30, 95–96, 102, 175; of Taiwan, 178, 179

economic development as destabilizing to authoritarian regime: and concentration of social actors, 9–10; and geospatial patterns, 176, 177, 182–83; overview of, 2, 9–14. *See also* education and educational policy; industrial complexes; worker activism and labor movement

Economic Planning Board, 31

economic policy: and Chun, 2, 95–96; and FYED Plans, 29, 31, 32–33, 93–95, 96; and industrialization under authoritarian regime, 2, 27–36, 180; and Park, 2, 26, 29–30, 36–37, 102, 150; and Rhee, 28

education and educational policy: and Chun, 77, 91, 95–98, 108–9, 116–18, 181; and Confucian values, 106, 206n7; and economic growth, 8–9, 10, 89–100; education levels and civic engagement, 168; education levels and democratic values, 205n1; liberalization of, 77, 109, 181; and morality, 92, 106; and night schools, 72–73; overview of, 89–91; and Park, 91, 92, 93–95, 102–4, 108, 109, 110–11, 204n19; primary, 89, 92, 93; reconstruction schools, 204n19; and Rhee,

91–92, 207n20; role in modernization theory, 89, 100; spending on, 94, 96, 104; as stabilizing to authoritarian regime, 8–9, 10, 91, 100–106, 118–19, 176; Taiwan comparison, 180–81. *See also* higher education; secondary education; student movement; vocational education

education fever, 94

education policy as destabilizing to authoritarian regime: and development of activism, 2, 10–13, 90–91, 105–19, 181; and failure to maintain programs, 13, 91, 105–6, 119; overview of, 2, 10–13, 90–91. *See also* higher education; student movement; vocational education

elections: and electoral volatility, 187; impact on social movements, 123–26, 143–44; and June 29 Declaration reforms, 131; for 1981 National Assembly, 127, 136; for 1985 National Assembly, 121, 127–30, 132–45; for 1997 presidential election, 197n2; and popular support for industrial complexes, 38; *vs.* protests as mobilizing structures, 124–26, 140–43; role in democracy, 14–15, 122; role in de/stabilizing authoritarian regime, 122–24, 143–44; role in modernization theory, 5; for 2007 presidential election, 197n2. *See also* voter participation

elementary education, 89, 92, 93

elites: decline in from vocational education, 103, 104, 118; and Taiwan comparison, 178; as threat to authoritarian regime, 102

Emergency Decree No. 4, 209n4

Emergency Decree No. 9, 108

entrance exams, 94, 97

events: economic crises and generational differences in political attitudes, 150, 151; economic crises and modernization theory, 5, 11; and generational effects, 148; triggering, 11

Ewha Women's University, 112, 115

export-oriented industrialization strategy, 29, 30–36, 180. *See also* industrial complexes

Factory New Village Movement, 30
Federation of Korean Trade Unions, 35, 70
586 generation. *See* 386 generation
Five-Year Economic Development (FYED) Plans, 29, 31, 32–33, 93–95, 96
Five-Year Technical School Promotion Plan, 94
Flag *vs.* Anti-Flag debate, 207n22
486 generation. *See* 386 generation framing, 125, 129–30, 144–45
FYED (Five-Year Economic Development) Plans, 29, 31, 32–33, 93–95, 96

GDP (Gross Domestic Product): South Korea, 5, 28, 29; Taiwan, 178, 179
gender. *See* women workers
generational differences in political attitudes: and Candlelight Revolution, 174, 188; and election results, 152–54; empirical analysis, 155–68; generational effects, defined, 147–48; generations, described, 147–52; and ideology, 145, 146–60, 162, 170, 173, 184–89; and intergenerational value change, 168–69, 172, 173; and North Korea relations, 150–51, 152, 154–55, 156, 157, 158–65, 173; and polarization, 173–74, 184–89; and political behavior, 156–58, 159, 161; and regionalism, 156; scholarship on, 153–55; and US relations, 148, 150–52, 154–55, 156, 157, 158, 160–65, 173
generational effects: defined, 147–48; and policymaking, 151
geospatial patterns of development: and concentration of students, 91, 106–8, 110, 134–41, 176, 177, 180–82; and concentration of workers, 55, 58–59, 79–81, 176, 177, 180–82; and democratization, 176–83; in Taiwan comparison, 176, 179–82. *See also* ecology of industrial complexes and labor movement; ecology of student movement
Gerring, John, 6
gongsuni term, 36
Gould, Roger V., 56

Graduation Quota Program, 99–100, 108, 116–18, 119, 181
Grand National Party, 185
Great Labor Uprising. *See* Great Workers' Struggle
Great National March of Peace, 131
Great Workers' Struggle: data analysis, 43–51; dataset, 18–19, 193–94; and ecology of industrial complexes, 75, 83–88, 106; and ecology-dependent strategies, 57, 106; and industrial complexes, 27, 43–54, 55, 57; and June Democratic Uprising, 47, 51, 83, 84; and middle class, 145; numbers of new protests, 87; numbers of participants, 41, 83, 90; numbers of protests, 41, 42, 43–47, 75, 76, 87, 194; role in democratization, 16–17, 41, 55; and vocational education, 13, 106; and wages, 17, 41
Guam Doctrine, 199n3
Gyeonggi College of Science and Technology, 115

Han Myŏnghŭi, 36
Hankuk University of Foreign Studies, 115
Hanyang University, 115
head residents (*sagam*), 60, 67
heavy chemical industry (HCI): and *chaebŏls* development, 34; and compulsory service, 104–5; concentration of workers in, 53; and defense, 199n3; as economic policy focus, 29, 32; and gender of workers, 207n15; industrial complexes for, 32; lack of labor activism in, 13, 101, 119; rise of labor activism in, 91, 106, 119; and vocational education, 90, 91, 94–95, 101, 104–5, 106, 119
Herfindahl-Hirschman Index, 58
high school. *See* secondary education
High School Equalization Policy, 94, 103, 118
higher education: elite schools as forefront of activism, 91, 103, 107, 110, 111; expansion of, 13, 70, 89–90, 93, 96, 97–100, 108, 169, 176, 181; increase in enrollments, 70, 97–100,

higher education (*continued*)
108, 117–18, 181; increase in numbers
of, 117; increase in private schools, 100;
liberalization of under Chun, 77, 109,
181; quotas on, 95, 97, 99–100, 108,
116–18, 119, 181; Taiwan comparison,
180–81. *See also* student movement
Hŏ Inhoe, 110
Hong Joon-pyo, 153
housing: costs, 60–61; and ecology of
industrial complexes, 57, 59–68, 74,
85, 86–87
hukou household registration system,
21, 22
hunger strikes, 82, 198n13
hybrid regimes, 15
Hyosŏng Products, 77–81, 82, 204n21
Hyundai Heavy Industries: and Great
Workers' Struggle, 75, 86–87; and
housing, 62; and leisure groups, 65–66
Hyundai industries: Council of Hyundai
Group, 205n29; and Great Workers'
Struggle, 75, 83, 85, 86–87; and housing, 62, 64–65, 85; and leisure groups,
65–66
Hyundai Workers Struggle, 85, 86–87

identity: in-group, 186; and neighborhood solidarity, 56; social, 186;
worker, 46
ideology: debates in student movement,
207n22; and economic policy, 29–30,
37, 38, 150; and educational policy,
91–92, 103–4; generational differences
in, 145, 146–60, 162, 170, 173, 184–
89; and life cycle effect, 159–60; and
polarization, 184–89
IMF generation: defined, 149, 150;
generational differences in political
attitudes, 155, 156, 162, 163, 171, 172
import-substitution industrialization
strategy, 28, 29
In Myŏngjin, 203n12
Inch'ŏn Blacklist Incident, 204n21
Inch'ŏn Council of the Labor Movement, 40
Inch'ŏn May 3 Uprising, 137
Inch'ŏn Region Social Movement Association, 142–43

income: and civic engagement, 168; in
modernization theory, 3, 4
Industrial Complex Development Promotion Act, 32
industrial complexes: in China, 22–23;
concentration of, 45–46, 56, 57, 58–
59, 84, 180; concentration of workers
in, 45–46, 50–54, 55, 58–59, 79–81,
84, 176, 180–82; development of,
31–33, 176; duration of, 43, 47–52;
and export-oriented industrialization
strategy, 30–36; and Great Workers' Struggle, 27, 43–54, 57, 75; and
infrastructure, 10, 31, 38; and light
industry, 32; and local residents, 37–
38; numbers of, 33, 59; numbers of
employees, 59; popular support for,
37–38; private, 32; and rural-urban
migration, 51; as stabilizing authoritarian regime, 2, 10, 26–27, 36–38,
176; and worker identity, 46. *See also*
ecology of industrial complexes and
labor movement; heavy chemical
industry (HCI)
industrial complexes as destabilizing
authoritarian regime: and development of worker activism, 2, 10–13,
26–27, 39–42, 180; and Great Workers' Struggle, 27, 43–54, 57, 75
industrialization and industrial policy:
under authoritarian regime, 2, 27–36,
180; and *chaebŏls*, 34–36; during colonial period, 27–28, 206n13; export-
oriented industrialization strategy,
29, 30–36, 180; import-substitution
strategy, 28, 29; and intergenerational
value change, 169; as stabilizing in
short term, 2, 10, 26–27, 36–38, 175–
76; in Taiwan, 180. *See also* ecology of
industrial complexes and labor movement; industrial complexes; industrial
complexes as destabilizing authoritarian regime; vocational education
infrastructure: destruction of during
Korean War, 28, 31; and industrial
complexes, 10, 31, 38
Inglehart, Ronald, 168, 173
in-group identity, 186
institutional weakness, 5

intelligence organizations and repression of labor, 35–36
intergenerational value change, 168–69, 172, 173

Japan: generational differences in attitudes toward, 152. *See also* colonial period
Jasic Incident, 22
Jasic Workers Support Group, 22–23
Jeunesse Ouvrière Chrétienne (JOC), 68–69, 72, 77, 85
June Democratic Uprising: in chronology of democratic transition, 15; and class, 182, 197n3; and constitutional reform, 1–2, 130–32; data analysis, 132–43; dataset, 18–19, 194; distribution of protests, 133, 134, 135; diversity of protest participants, 16; and Great Workers' Struggle, 47, 51, 83, 84; and middle class, 197n3; as national protest, 182; national rallies, 131, 137, 141, 142; number of events, 194; number of participants, 1, 131, 133, 134, 135, 137; origins in 1985 National Assembly election, 121; role in democratization of South Korea, 16–17; size of, 1–2; and student movement, 1, 7, 91, 119, 121, 130–43, 144, 176, 181, 198n3
June 29 Declaration, 1, 15, 17, 131

Kang Myŏngja, 77
Karibong Electronics, 66, 77–81, 205n28
Kim Chaegyu, 203n10
Kim Chisŏn, 204n21
Kim Chunyŏng, 77, 78
Kim Dae Jung, 128, 130, 131, 133, 150, 197n2
Kim Minsŏk, 110
Kim Yŏngmi, 204n21
Kim Young Sam, 128, 130, 133, 202n10
Kong Kyejin, 82
Konkuk University, 115
Korea Democracy Foundation, 191–92
Korea Export Industrial Complex Zones. *See* Kuro Industrial Complex
Korea Marvell Co., 77
Korea People's Party for Reform, 185

Korea Shipbuilding and Engineering Corporation, 200n15
Korea Tongkyŏng Electronics, 66
Korea Trade Union Congress, 41
Korea University, 91, 107, 110, 111, 113, 115
Korean Central Intelligence Agency, 35–36, 203n10, 206n12
Korean Confederation of Trade Unions, 35, 201n19
Korean Export Industrial Complexes. *See* industrial complexes
Korean General Social Survey, 155
Korean Nationalist Party, 126
Korean Student Christian Federation, 73
Korean War, 28, 31, 211n4
Korean War generation: defined, 148, 149; and generational differences in political attitudes, 148, 149, 155, 163, 171, 172
Kukmin University, 115
Kŭmo Technical High School, 104
Kŭmsŏngsa, 87
Kuomintang, 178, 181
Kuro Industrial Complex: and Christian activists, 72; housing, 60, 62; map, 80; size of, 202n1; solidarity strike, 40, 57, 66, 74–83, 204n21; wages at, 61
Kuro Solidarity Strike, 40, 57, 66, 74–83, 204n21
Kwangju Massacre: in analysis of June Democratic Uprising, 137; and Chun, 2, 70, 95, 113, 126, 151; diversity of protest participants, 16; and May Struggle protests, 113; and regional differences in civic engagement, 168; and student movement, 70, 132, 151, 204n23; and US, 70, 151, 152, 204n23
Kwangju Uprising. *See* Kwangju Massacre
Kwŏn Yŏngmok, 85, 205n29
Kyunghee University, 115
Kyungpook National University, 110, 111, 115

Labor Disputes Adjustment Act, 77
labor movement. *See* worker activism and labor movement

248   *Index*

labor policy: and Chun, 35, 77; and
export-oriented industrialization
strategy, 34–36; and Park, 13, 35, 39;
and Rhee, 35
Lavender, Stephen V., 203n12
Law Concerning Special Measures for
Safeguarding National Security, 35
Law on Assembly and Demonstration,
77
Lee Myung-bak, 164, 187, 197n2, 211n3
Legislative Council for National Security, 127
leisure activities and ecology of industrial complexes, 57, 59, 61, 65–66, 85,
205n28
liberalization under Chun, 12, 70, 77,
109, 120–21, 127, 181
Liberty Korea Party, 153
life cycle effect, 159–60
Lipset, Seymour Martin, 3, 183
literacy, 92, 93

Malaysia, coercive and administrative
power in, 20
Masan Free Export Zone: demonstrations and activism in, 16, 75, 85, 88,
106; and industrial complexes, 52, 60,
61, 66, 72
master frames, 129–30, 144–45
May Struggle, 113
Methodist Theological University, 115
Methodist Urban Industrial Mission,
68–69, 71–72, 77
methodology and research design, 14–
23, 43–47, 57, 132–39, 155–56
middle class: and educational policy,
89, 94; and Great Workers' Struggle,
145; and June Democratic Uprising,
197n3; role in modernization theory,
4, 7; and state dependency in China,
21
Middle School Equalization Policy, 94
migration, rural-urban, 51
military: and balance of power of elites,
206n12; compulsory service, 104–5;
and repression of labor, 36
Millennium Democratic Party, 152, 185
Minjoo Party, 153, 186
minjung churches, 72, 85

minjung groups. *See* dissident *(minjung)*
groups
"Miracle on the Han River," 2, 26, 30,
152
mobilizing structures: defined, 56, 108,
125; importance of in democratization, 144; industrial complexes as,
12–13, 56; and June Democratic
Uprising, 119, 131–32, 136, 144, 176;
role in social movements, 125; student
organizations as, 12–13, 108–10, 113,
119, 121, 131–32, 136, 144, 176;
and trade-off between elections and
protests, 124–26, 140–43
modernization theory: conditional, 5,
11; revised theory of and intergenerational value change, 173; role
of economics in, 3, 8–9, 11; role of
education in, 89, 100; South Korea
as classic example of, 3–8, 175; South
Korea as complicated example of,
8–14, 177, 182–83; South Korea as
pathway case, 6, 177
Mokwon University, 115
Moon Jae-in, 153, 183, 186
morality and education, 92, 106
multilevel theory building, 17–20
Mun Sŏnghyŏn, 83–84
Murim *vs.* Haklim ideological debates,
207n22

Namsŏng Electronics, 78, 80, 82
National Alliance of Student Associations Election Planning Committee,
128
National Alliance of Youth and Students
for the Protection of Democracy, 110
National Assembly: dissolution of, 127;
generational makeup of, 154, 185;
and June 29 Declaration, 15; 1981
election, 127, 136; 1985 election, 121,
127–30, 132–43; Special Committee
on Constitutional Revision, 130
National Coalition for Democracy
Movement, 129, 130
National Congress for Democracy and
Reunification, 209n5
National Council for Reunification,
126

Index

National Council of Student Representatives, 115–16
National Defense Student Corps, 108, 109, 207n20, 208n22, 209n4
National Democratic Youth and Student Alliance, 110–11
National Federation of Student Associations, 110–13
National League for Democratic Youth and Students, 129
National Liberation, 151
National Movement Headquarters for Democratic Constitution, 84, 130, 131, 137
National Rally for Banishment of Tear Gas Grenades, 131
nationalism: and economic policy under Park, 29, 36–37; and educational policy, 92; generational differences in, 152; and night schools, 204n19
natural resources, role in modernization theory, 3
New Democratic Party, 38, 127, 202n10, 204n24
New Korea Democratic Party: constitutional reforms, 129–30; 1985 election, 16, 24, 121, 127, 128–29, 132–37, 139–41
New Village/Saemaŭl Factory Movement, 30, 36, 184
night schools, 72–73
Nixon, Richard, 199n3
Nixon Doctrine, 206n11
North Korea: and anticommunist policies, 206n6; and generational differences in political attitudes, 150–51, 152, 154–55, 156, 157, 158–65, 173; as threat to authoritarian regime, 102

Ogle, George, 203n12
Olympic Games, 109
opposition, political: and alliance with student movement, 120–21, 128–29, 131–44, 176; and constitutional reforms, 121, 129–30; and framing, 125, 129–30, 144–45; and June Democratic Uprising, 130–32, 176; and 1985 election, 121, 127–30, 132–43; sponsored by regime, 126;

and trade-off between elections and protests, 124–26, 140–43
Osŏngsa, 87
out-groups and in-group identity, 186

Pak Chongch'ŏl, 130, 198n13
Pak Chŏngsuk, 67
Pangrim Textiles, 200n17
Park Chung Hee: assassination of, 70, 203n10; and compulsory service, 207n18; coup by, 4; economic policy, 2, 26, 29–30, 36–37, 102, 150; educational policy, 91, 92, 93–95, 102–4, 108, 109, 110–11, 204n19; and elites as threat to regime, 102; generational differences in attitudes on, 170, 184–85; labor policy, 13, 35, 39; and North Korea, 102
Park Geun-hye, 4, 153, 174, 184–85, 186, 187, 188
party instability, 187
peaceful transfer of power, 4, 212n1
People's Democracy, 211n7
People's Movement Coalition for Democracy and Reunification, 78, 130
period effects, 148, 154
Perry, Elizabeth, 56
polarization, political: and generational differences in political attitudes, 173–74, 184–89; as legacy of authoritarian regime, 183–90
police and repression of labor, 35–36, 67–68
Political Climate Renovation Law, 127
political opportunities: and ecology of industrial complexes and labor movement, 57, 75, 83–85; elections as, 123–24; and Great Workers' Struggle, 83–85; role in democratization, 12
political process theory, 12
Political Renovation Committee, 127
Poongsung Electric Company, 87
post-386 generations: defined, 149, 150; and generational differences in political attitudes, 150, 151–52, 155–68, 171; relative importance of economic development and democracy, 169–72

250 *Index*

postwar industrialization generation: defined, 149; and generational differences in political attitudes, 155, 163, 171, 172

pre-386 generations: defined, 149–50; and generational differences in political attitudes, 149–50, 155–68; and North Korean relations, 150, 173; relative importance of economic development and democracy, 150, 169–72; and US relations, 150, 173

presidency: Chun and election rules, 126; imperial, 184; and June 29 Declaration reforms, 131; and 1985 National Assembly election, 121; and Park's powers, 4

Presidential Security Service, 203n10, 206n12

primary education, 89, 92, 93

Private School Law, 100

Promotion of Industrial Education Act, 93

propaganda: on economy, 36–37; and educational policy, 91–92

protests and demonstrations: Candlelight protests, 150, 151–52; as contentious nature of democracy, 188; deaths and injuries from, 198n13, 200n16; distribution of, 10; *vs.* elections as mobilizing structures, 124–26, 140–43; frequency of, 10; increase in with electoral volatility, 187; May Struggle, 113; national coordination of, 11, 111–13; national rallies, 131, 138, 141, 142; numbers of, 41, 42, 43–47, 194; numbers of participants, 41; in Taiwan, 178; types of, 43. *See also* Great Workers' Struggle; June Democratic Uprising; Kuro Solidarity Strike; Kwangju Massacre

Provisional Exceptional Law Concerning Labor Unions, 35

public goods, 101

Puhŭngsa, 78, 82

Pu-Ma Uprising, 202n10

Pusan National Mechanical High School, 207n16

Pusan National University, 110, 111, 115, 131

Pusan-Masan Uprising, 137

Pyle, Kenneth, 169

Reagan, Ronald, 211n6

reconstruction schools, 204n19

Regional Industrial Development Act, 33

Regional Industrial Development Enterprise Zones, 33

regionalism and differences in political attitudes, 156, 168

representation, ineffectual, 187–88

repression: and analysis of 1985 National Assembly election, 137; of Christian activists, 69; and democratization inflection point, 20–21; of labor, 13, 34–36, 67–68, 77; of student movement, 70–71, 108–9, 110–11, 113, 130. *See also* Kwangju Massacre

research design and methodology, 14–23, 43–47, 57, 132–39, 155–56

Reunification Democratic Party, 130, 197n2

Rhee, Syngman: economic policy, 28; educational policy, 91–92, 207n20; and Federation of Korean Trade Unions, 35; labor policy, 35; resignation of, 4, 110

Roh Moo-hyun: and Candlelight generation, 150; education policy, 92; election of, 152; generational differences in support for, 152–53; generational makeup of administration, 154; and political polarization, 185

Roh Tae Woo, 15, 131

Rom-Korea, 66, 78, 80, 82

rooming houses, 62–63, 64. *See also* housing

rural-urban migration, 51

Saemaŭl Factory Movement. *See* New Village/Saemaŭl Factory Movement

Saenuri Party, 184, 188

sagam (head residents), 60, 67

Samsung Pharmaceutical Company, 78, 82

scope conditions, 20–23

secondary education: entrance exams, 94; expansion of, 92, 93–94; specialization of, 94–95, 96, 103, 105, 106, 118; standardization of, 89, 94, 97, 118; and tutoring, 97; and vocational education, 94–95, 96, 103–4, 105, 106, 118

security apparatus: and balance of power of elites, 206n12; and repression of labor, 35–36, 67–68; and repression of student movement, 108–9, 209n4

Sejin Electronics, 78, 80, 82

Seoul Council of the Labor Movement, 40

Seoul National University: enrollment at, 103; as forefront of student movement, 91, 103, 107, 110, 111, 115; and June Democratic Uprising, 107, 112, 115, 119, 128, 130; and Kuro Solidarity Struggle, 81, 83–84

Settlement of Labor Disputes in Foreign-Invested Firms, 35

7.30 Educational Reform Measure, 97, 99–100, 181

Shen Mengyu, 22

Signetics, 200n17

Sim Sang-jung, 79, 83

Singapore, coercive and administrative power in, 20

Sinnott, James, 203n12

Six-Year Compulsory Education Completion Plan, 92

small group networks: and social activists, 68, 69, 71–72, 75, 79, 82–83, 88; and student movement, 13, 71, 79, 82–83; and worker activism, 13, 56, 65–66, 68, 69, 71–72, 75, 79, 82–83, 85, 88

social activists: Christian activists, 41, 68–69, 71–74, 77, 85; and ecology-dependent strategies, 71–74, 75, 88; and labor movement development, 68–74, 75; national organization by, 10–13; and small group networks, 68, 69, 71–72, 75, 79, 82–83, 88. *See also* student movement

social capital, 3

social identity theory, 186

social movements: framing, 125, 129–30, 144–45; impact of elections on, 123–26, 143–44; role of mobilizing

structures in, 125; and spatiality, 55–56. *See also* student movement; worker activism and labor movement

Sogang University, 110, 111, 112, 115

Sŏnil Textile, 77–81

Sŏnkyung *chaebŏl*, 88

spatiality and social movements, 55–56. *See also* ecology of industrial complexes and labor movement

Special Act for Expropriation of Land for Manufacturing Zone Development, 31

Special Committee on Constitutional Revision, 130

Specialization Initiatives at Technical High Schools, 94, 96, 103, 105, 118

Spring of Seoul, 70, 77, 95

Ssangyong *chaebŏl*, 88

state capacity, role in modernization theory, 3, 5

state dependency: in China, 21; erosion of, 13; and social benefits, 9, 101; and support for democratization, 20–21; and vocational education, 91, 101, 102–5

Stillerman, Joel, 56

Struggle Committee for the Kwangju Incident of the National Federation of Student Associations, 208n24

Student Alliance for Democratic Elections, 128

student councils, as mobilizing structures, 13, 108, 109–10, 132

student movement: alliance with political opposition, 120–21, 128–29, 131–44, 176; alliance with workers, 1, 7, 13, 40, 41, 70–71, 198n3; and April Revolution of 1960, 16, 112, 120, 132; in China, 22–23; and class consciousness development of workers, 70–71, 73, 79; concentration of students, 91, 106–8, 110, 134–41, 176, 177, 180–82; and constitutional reforms, 121, 129–30; datasets, 18–19, 194–95; deaths and injuries, 130, 198n13; development of, 2, 12–13, 90–91, 105–19, 176; and distribution of protests, 113–18; ecology-dependent strategies, 71–74, 79, 176; elite schools' role in activism,

252

Index

student movement (*continued*)
91, 103, 107, 110, 111; and generational differences in politics, 148–49, 151; and Great Workers' Struggle, 86; historical background, 16; ideological debates in, 207n22; and June Democratic Uprising, 1, 7, 91, 119, 121, 130–43, 176, 181, 198n3; and Kuro Solidarity Strike, 78, 79, 81, 82–83; and Kwangju Massacre, 70, 132, 151, 204n23; and May Struggle protests, 113; and *minjung* movement, 203n15; and mobilizing structures, 12–13, 108–10, 113, 119, 121, 131–32, 136, 144, 176; national organization and coordination of, 11, 12, 110–13; and night schools, 73; and 1985 National Assembly election, 121, 128–30, 134–43; number of events, 195; number of participants, 107; protest repertoire, 111–12; repression of, 70–71, 108–9, 110–11, 113, 130; and small group networks, 13, 71, 79, 82–83; structures and organization of, 111–12; students-turned-workers, 22, 70–71, 73–74, 79, 86; against United States, 110, 151, 204n23. *See also* ecology of student movement
subnational approach, 17–20
subway construction, 200n13
Sungkyunkwan University, 110, 111, 115

Taiwan comparison, 176, 178–83
tertiary education. *See* higher education
textbooks, 92
third-wave democracies, 3, 15
3-3-3 structure, 111
386 generation: and aging effects, 153; defined, 148; and generational differences in politics, 148–68, 185–86; and relative importance of economic development and democracy, 169–72, 173; and period effects, 154; and polarization, 185–86
T'ong'il Industry, 78, 83–84, 85, 205n3
Tongkwang Textiles, 77
Trade Union Act, 35
triggering events, 11
tutoring, 97

UIM (Urban Industrial Mission), 68–69, 71–72, 77
Ulsan Mipo Industrial Complex: and Great Workers' Struggle, 75, 83, 85, 86, 106; housing, 32, 52, 62, 64–65
UNESCO, 90
unions: control of by authoritarian regime, 35; development of, 39–42; numbers of, 42; regional trade union councils, 41. *See also* worker activism and labor movement
United States: aid from, 28; and defense, 199n3, 206n11; generational differences in political attitudes toward, 148, 150–52, 154–55, 156, 157, 158, 160–65, 173; and Kwangju Massacre, 70, 151, 152, 204n23; pressure for democratic reforms from, 144, 204n22; protests over beef imports from, 150, 151–52; student protests against, 110, 151, 204n23; and Vietnam War, 148, 206n11
Uprising Rally to Defeat the April 13 Decision and to End Dictatorship, 131
Urban Industrial Mission (UIM), 68–69, 71–72, 77
Uri Party, 185
U.S. Cultural Center protest, 110

value change, intergenerational, 168–69, 172, 173
Vietnam War, 148, 206n11
vocational education: and compulsory service, 104–5; development of, 33, 89–90, 92–95, 96–97, 176; and Great Workers' Struggle, 106; in high schools, 94–95, 96, 103–4, 105, 106, 118; in-plant, 96–97, 103, 105; as stabilizing to authoritarian regime, 8–9, 89–90, 100–106, 176. *See also* worker activism and labor movement
vocational education as destabilizing to authoritarian regime: and development of worker activism, 2, 10–11, 90–91, 105–6, 119; and failure to maintain programs, 13, 91, 105–6, 119, 176. *See also* worker activism and labor movement

Vocational Training Act, 93
Vocational Training Special Measure Act, 97
voter participation: and age, 159; fluctuations in, 200n12; and generational differences in political attitudes, 156–58, 159, 161; in 1985 National Assembly election, 127–28, 142; in Taiwan, 178–79

wages, 17, 35, 41, 60–61
welfare: benefits and authoritarian regime, 30, 38; facilities in industrial complexes, 59
women workers: *gongsuni* term, 36; and housing, 61; labor activism/union formation by, 40, 53; and light industry, 207n15; and propaganda on economy, 36–37
Wonpoong Textiles, 66, 67, 200n17, 203n13
worker activism and labor movement: alliance with student movement, 1, 7, 13, 40, 41, 70–71, 198n3; in China, 22–23; and Christian activists, 41, 68–69, 71–74, 77, 85; and class consciousness, 13, 59, 63–66, 68, 75; colonial period, 39; and concentration of workers, 45–46, 50–54, 55, 58–59, 79–81, 84, 176, 177, 180–82; datasets, 18–19; and democratization of workplace, 41; development of, 2, 10–13, 26–27, 39–42, 180; ecology-dependent strategies, 57, 66–68, 71–74, 75, 78–83, 106, 176; homogeneity of workers, 56, 58–59, 64, 82, 86; interfirm solidarity action and strikes, 40, 57, 66, 74–88, 90, 204n21; political focus of, 40, 78; repression of, 13, 34–36, 67–68, 77; and small group

networks, 13, 56, 65–66, 68, 69, 71–72, 75, 79, 82–83, 85, 88; and social activists, 41, 68–74, 75; students-turned-workers, 22, 70–71, 73–74, 79, 86; and worker identity, 46. *See also* ecology of industrial complexes and labor movement; Great Workers' Struggle; June Democratic Uprising; Kuro Solidarity Strike; vocational education
workweek, duration of, 200n10
World Cup generation: defined, 149, 150; and generational differences in political attitudes, 150, 155, 156, 163, 171, 172

yahak. See night schools
Y.H. Incident/Y.H. Worker Protest, 69, 200n16, 204n24
Y.H. Trading Company, 66, 67, 69, 200n17, 203n13, 204n24
Yi Chaesŏn, 37
Yi Ch'ŏl, 129
Yi Hanyŏl, 198n13
Yi Min U, 209n6
Yi Oksun, 67
Yonsei University, 16, 91, 107, 110, 111, 115, 128
Young Catholic Workers. *See* Jeunesse Ouvrière Chrétienne (JOC)
Young Men's/Young Women's Christian Association, 85
Youth Coalition for Democracy Movement, 128, 141, 142
Yusin generation: defined, 149; and generational differences in political attitudes, 156, 163, 170, 171, 172

Zhao, Dingxin, 56
Ziblatt, Daniel, 15

Printed and bound by CPI Group (UK) Ltd, Croydon, CR0 4YY
31/07/2025

14712021-0002